# SLAPSTICK COMEDY

From Chaplin's tramp to the Bathing Beauties, from madcap chases to sky-scraper perils, slapstick comedy supplied many of the most enduring icons of American cinema in the silent era. This collection of fourteen essays by prominent film scholars challenges longstanding critical dogma and offers new conceptual frameworks for thinking about silent comedy's place in film history and American culture. The contributors discuss a broad range of topics including the contested theatrical or cinematic origins of slapstick; the comic spectacle of crazy technology and trick stunts; the filmmakers who shaped the style of early slapstick; and comedy's implications for theories of film form and spectatorship.

This volume is essential reading for anyone seeking to understand the origins and continued importance of a film genre at the heart of American cinema from its earliest days to today.

**Tom Paulus** is Assistant Professor in Cinema and Theater Studies at the University of Antwerp and the organizer of "(Another) Slapstick Symposium."

**Rob King** is Assistant Professor in Cinema Studies and History at the University of Toronto and the author of *The Fun Factory: The Keystone Film Company and the Emergence of Mass Culture* (2009).

two perspectives is not at all straightforward; it is not, as one might imagine, that one era's comic transgressions become another era's rose-tinted memories. (To judge from exhibitors' reports, for instance, it is clear that the sound-era Columbia comedy shorts – including the Three Stooges – were *from the beginning* appreciated as nostalgic throwbacks to "good old-fashioned" slapstick, long before their television syndication beginning in the 1950s.)[7] Rather, the dichotomy speaks to strictly temporal differences in how audiences have sought to appropriate slapstick's comic anarchy to their cultural presents, whether as a challenge to the dead weight of tradition, a goad to cultural change, or as a retrospective memory of past happiness; a crossroads where the radical project of identifying newness intersects with the conservative comforts of the past. The jubilant alterity of slapstick comedy has thus come to function simultaneously as obsolescence, incapable of signifying a stable kind of novelty. Yet the problem here is not only the entanglement of these two convictions, but also the critical and historiographic pitfalls involved in each. If, at one extreme, a commitment to slapstick's vernacular properties, as in Seldes, has at times shaded into an idealization of comedy's supposedly insubordinate energies – a critique frequently leveled against Bakhtin's discussion of the carnivalesque[8] – then, at the other extreme, the lures of nostalgia have just as frequently produced an overly insulated historicism that fails to rise above empirical issues of credit listings and performer biographies. Any assessment that would position Slapstick against the broader movement of social and cultural history is bracketed off from the outset.

In offering this volume, then, we have been guided by the goal of presenting scholarship that overcomes this polarization, *not* by suppressing one approach in favor of the other, but by a synthesis that combines the achievements of each, both the sensitivity to the rigorous biographical and industrial research often found in the work of non-academic slapstick historians and a theoretical and theorized awareness of the politics of slapstick's difference as a form of film practice. One such possibility for synthesis would be to approach slapstick in terms of what Fredric Jameson has called the *ideology of form*, that is, an attention to the "varied sign systems which coexist in a given artistic process *as well as* in its general social formation."[9] What would be required from this perspective is an approach that reconstitutes the formal qualities of texts or groups of texts in terms of broader cultural discourses and the dialectics of specific social structures; and it is this shared commitment to understanding artistic form *and* social location, and to relating each to the other, that broadly characterizes the spirit of the present collection. To insist on the importance of slapstick, from this perspective, does not entail the fetishization of a dead comic tradition, nor is it straightforwardly to conflate difference with subversion; more productively, it is to propose a vision of American

trademark "thrill comedies," by the contemporary sequence of Keaton's *The Three Ages* (1923), and by the later Laurel and Hardy two-reeler *Liberty* (1929) prompt Jacobs to consider how the modern skyscraper modeled a specific comic structure, an "architecture of attractions," with another encounter, another gag on every storey. Such spatial sequentiality – floor upon floor, gag upon gag – can be read as a vertical analogy to the horizontal trajectory of chase comedy, one of slapstick's most familiar subgenres and the focus of the final chapter in this part, Charles Wolfe's "California Slapstick Revisited." Whereas the concept of a vertical "architecture of attractions" relates slapstick most directly to the skyscraper metropolis of New York or Chicago, the horizontal dispersal of the chase found its natural setting elsewhere, in the topography of Southern California. Elaborating on film historian Jay Leyda's term, "California Slapstick," Wolfe illustrates how urban planning on the West Coast readily accommodated mobile comedy, with de-centered trajectories across rural and urban spaces compressed, extended, and reordered in highly variable ways.[22] As Wolfe shows, such links between cinematic form and material environment make slapstick not only a valuable historical record of that most quintessentially modern of cities, Los Angeles, but an object lesson in how early filmmakers learned to reconfigure that environment into ludic, imaginary worlds.

Full of power-driven pratfalls and elaborate stunts, slapstick comedy provided the means for inscribing the body as a central term of cinematic pleasure. Yet the historiography and theory of cinema have tended to marginalize comedy's carnal spirit, instead emphasizing categories associated with comprehension, cognition, and, more generally, the "senses at a distance" (sight, hearing). The chapters in the final part of this anthology, "Bodies and Performance," seek instead to place the body front and center to their analyses, tracing the varied significance of the corporeal as comic spectacle, from the sheer violence of the slap (Andrin), through the modernist appropriation of Chaplin's pantomime as *cinéplastique* (Sargeant), to the fashion and titillation of the Bathing Beauties (D'Haeyere). They also address vectors of physicality ranging from the performances of individual stars to the accumulated bodies of the Keystone cops.

Broadly speaking, the four chapters here pursue two distinct trajectories, the first historical in nature, elaborating the social and cultural frameworks that shaped the display and reception of slapstick bodies during the silent era; the second more theoretical, establishing the implications of the corporeal for our understanding of slapstick as a cinematic mode. Beginning with history, Amy Sargeant's "Dancing on Fire and Water: Charlot and *L'Esprit nouveau*" discusses the evaluation of American slapstick in the context of 1920s French modernism, examining art critic Elie Faure's writings on Charlie Chaplin in *L'Esprit nouveau*, the journal of the Purist movement. Faure's formal functionalism — famously expressed in his coinage of *cinéplastique*, the conception of cinema as a combination of forms either in movement or repose — moved into the realm of the metaphysical with *Danse sur le feu et l'eau*, his 1920 treatise on history as a moral and aesthetic concept, in which the rhythmic, angular performances embodied by Chaplin were said to inspire "lyrical exaltation … which permits the most elevated morality." Yet what would Faure, who despised the "cult of beauty" and celebrated the gawky, abrupt angularity of Chaplin's body, have made of the focus of the second chapter in this part, Mack Sennett's bathing girls? In "Splashes of Fun and Beauty: Mack Sennett's Bathing Beauties," Hilde D'Haeyere explores the contrast between knockabout comedians whose nicknames, "Fatty," "Slim," "Shorty," or "Baldy," described their grotesque physical appearances, and the Bathing Beauties' show-stopping displays of beautiful, healthy young bodies. Perhaps Faure would have loved Sennett's girls as serially produced commodities, as commercial types and trademarks, for, as D'Haeyere shows, the use of the Bathing Beauties in Sennett's promotional campaigns appealed not only as "cheesecake" for the male gaze, but also as fashion models showing an audience of Jazz Age female fans what to wear on the beach.

Both Sargeant's and D'Haeyere's chapters illustrate how slapstick's appeal to corporeal fantasy was negotiated within discursive frameworks related to the historical context of modernity — whether of artistic modernism in the case of Chaplin's *cinéplastique* or of modern gender ideals in the case of the Bathing Beauties. But they also might be taken as indices of the changing ways of observing or responding to the body itself during this period; on the one hand, a spectatorship like Faure's, attentive to an ineradicable individuality, to the unique physiognomy of the performing body (an "auratic" spectatorship, to return to Benjamin's famous essay), on the other, a commodity-oriented attention, more attentive to the dispersal of symmetric and regularized types (a symptom of mechanical reproduction, or of what another Frankfurt scholar, Siegfried Kracauer, termed the "mass ornament").[23] Indeed, as a number of historians have observed, the experience of the body available within modernity was predicated on just such an inner contradiction. That experience stressed the uniqueness of the performing self — as encompassed in the ideal of what historian Warren Susman long ago described as "personality," the injunction that one be distinctive, follow one's own feelings, stand out from the crowd. Yet the possibilities for individuality were at the same time tempered by the very tools with which it was to be achieved; fashion, obviously, but also photography and cinematic representation, all of which condemned the ideal of unique selfhood to the de-individualizing logic of mass production, mass diffusion, and mass imitation.[24] Modernity's production of subjecthood thus heralded a body in tension, a figuring of the corporeal both as source or "proof" of self *and* as mimicry of others, in which identity could be said to be enacted both from the inside out *and* from the outside in.

It thus makes sense that slapstick – the most "embodied" of early genres – should so explicitly have straddled both sides of that dichotomy, as our two final, more theory-driven chapters show. In "Back to the 'Slap': Slapstick's Hyperbolic Gesture and the Rhetoric of Violence," Muriel Andrin formulates the paradoxes of the slapstick body in what might be called "tropic" terms, studying knockabout as a genre founded on the rhetorical trope of hyperbole. Bodies in slapstick, Andrin argues, are subjected to such exaggerated degrees of violent assault that they are no longer read as "real," but as idealized vehicles of a wish-fulfillment that would see its logical culmination in the entirely unreal characters of later cartoons. An impasse thus ensues: the slapstick body becomes the focus of a materialist fascination whose very intensity renders its object both immaterial and unreal – an imagining of the body that suspends the self or, more accurately, that does not properly constitute a self at all. A related theorization of slapstick bodies is offered by Jennifer Bean in our last chapter, "The Art of Imitation: The Originality of Charlie Chaplin and Other Moving-Image Myths," a study of the phenomenon of Chaplin imitators during the silent era. Investigating popular discourses of "Chaplinitis," Bean argues that what made Chaplin unique was that, paradoxically, he was endlessly imitable, a given emphasized by his own talent for mimicry. As in the volume's opening part, the themes of originality and imitation return as key terms; only here those themes are extended into the question of spectatorship, which Bean analyzes in terms of mimetic affect and the imitative interactions linking comic bodies to their audiences. Through mimesis, she argues, the viewing subject is neither stabilized nor rigidified by means of identification, but instead brought into a kind of ideational mimicry of the comic behaviors depicted onscreen, a suspension of the boundaries of self that produces laughter. "To be *beside* oneself with laughter, to wander away from the self," Bean concludes, "hints at the power of . . . comedy to generate a kind of physical ecstasy" – an observation that speaks to slapstick's promise and pleasure as a cinematic form inscribed in the paradoxes of the modern subject, and that provides, we feel, an appropriate ending to this volume.

15

## notes

1. Gilbert Seldes, "The Keystone the Builders Rejected," in *The 7 Lively Arts* (New York: Sagamore Press, Inc., 1957 [1924]), 14, 15, 16, 20.
2. On these and similar defenses of slapstick in the 1920s, see Lea Jacobs, *The Decline of Sentiment: American Film in the 1920s* (Berkeley: University of California Press, 2008), 1–24.

3. Theodore Dreiser, "The Best Motion Picture Interview Ever Written," *Photoplay*, August (1928): 32–35, 124–129.

4. Wid Gunning, "Slap Stick and the 'High Brows,'" *Wid's Films and Film Folks*, January 6, 1916. Thanks to Alicia Fletcher for bringing this article to our attention.

5. Antonin Artaud, *Theatre and Its Double* (New York: Grove, 1958), 142–144; Mikhail Bakhtin, *Rabelais and His World*, trans. Helene Iswolsky (Bloomington: Indiana University Press, 1984); Jean-Luc Comolli and Jean Narboni, "Cinema/Ideology/Criticism," in Leo Braudy and Marshall Cohen, eds., *Film Theory and Criticism*, 6th edn. (New York: Oxford University Press, 2004), 816.

6. James Agee, *Agee on Film: Criticism and Comment on the Movies* (New York: Modern Library, 2000), 393–394.

7. See Ted Okuda and Edward Watz, *The Columbia Comedy Shorts: Two-Reel Hollywood Film Comedies, 1933–1958* (Jefferson: McFarland & Co., 1986), 14.

8. On this objection to Bakhtin, see Peter Stallybrass and Allon White, *The Poetics and Politics of Transgression* (Ithaca: Cornell University Press, 1986), Introduction.

9. Fredric Jameson, *The Political Unconscious: Narrative as a Socially Symbolic Act* (Ithaca: Cornell University Press, 1981), 98–99 (italics added).

10. Quoted in Eileen Bowser, "Introduction," in Eileen Bowser, ed., *The Slapstick Symposium* (Brussels: Fédération Internationale des Archives du Film, 1988), i.

11. See Tom Gunning, *D. W. Griffith and the Origins of American Narrative Film* (Urbana: University of Illinois Press, 1992).

12. Peter Krämer, "Vitagraph, Slapstick and Early Cinema," *Screen* 29.2 (1988): 100.

13. Donald Crafton, "Pie and Chase: Gag, Spectacle and Narrative in Slapstick Comedy," in Bowser, ed., *The Slapstick Symposium*, 49–59.

14. Eileen Bowser, "Subverting the Conventions: Slapstick as Genre," in Bowser, ed., *The Slapstick Symposium*, 13–17. The shift from comedy to drama at Biograph was also discussed at the Slapstick Symposium by Bowser's colleague at MoMA, Jon Gartenberg, while Patrick Loughney of the Library of Congress Motion Picture Division examined Vitagraph's complex comedy output, consisting of comedy chases, trick films, and sophisticated domestic comedies. Patrick Loughney, "Leave 'em Laughing: The Last Years of the Biograph Company"; Jon Gartenberg, "Vitagraph Comedy Production," in Bowser, ed., *The Slapstick Symposium*, 19–29, 45–49.

15. See, for instance, Peter Brunette, "The Three Stooges and the (Anti-) Narrative of Violence: De(con)structive Comedy," in A. Horton, ed., *Comedy/Cinema/Theory* (Berkeley: University of California Press, 1991), 174–187; Peter Krämer, "Derailing the Honeymoon Express: Comicality and Narrative Closure in Buster Keaton's *The Blacksmith*," *Velvet Light Trap* 23 (Spring 1989): 101–116; Frank Krutnik, "A Spanner in the Works? Genre, Narrative and the Hollywood Comedian," in Kristine Brunovska Karnick and Henry Jenkins, *Classical Hollywood Comedy* (New York: Routledge, 1995), 17–38; Frank Krutnik, *Inventing Jerry Lewis* (Washington: Smithsonian Institution Press, 2000); Steve Neale and Frank Krutnik, *Popular Film and Television Comedy* (London: Routledge, 1990), esp. Chs. 2 and 3; Jerry Palmer, *The Logic of the Absurd* (London: BFI, 1987), esp. Ch. 7.

16. Walter Kerr, "Lloyd Hamilton," in Bowser, ed., *The Slapstick Symposium*, 33.

17. Walter Benjamin, "The Work of Art in the Age of Mechanical Reproduction," in Braudy and Cohen, eds., *Film Theory and Criticism*, 801–802.

18. Epes Winthrop Sargent, "The Photoplaywright," *Moving Picture World*, November 11 (1913): 490.

19. Mack Sennett, with Cameron Shipp, *King of Comedy* (San Jose: toExcel, 2000 [1954]), 151.

20. On the feature film and its impact on slapstick comedy, see Neale and Krutnik, *Popular Film and Television Comedy*, 96–131. Ben Singer has recently offered a revisionist account of the rise of the multiple-reel feature, examining how "variety exhibitors" sustained the market for short films throughout the 1910s. See Ben Singer, "Feature Films, Variety Programs, and the Crisis of the Small Exhibitor," in Charlie Keil and Shelley Stamp, eds., *American Cinema's Transitional Era: Audiences, Institutions, Practices* (Berkeley: University of California Press, 2004), 76–100.

21. Miriam Hansen, "The Mass Production of the Senses: Classical Cinema as Vernacular Modernism," *Modernism/Modernity* 6.2 (1999): 69.

22. Jay Leyda, "California Slapstick: A Definition," in Bowser, ed., *The Slapstick Symposium*, 1–3.

23. Siegfried Kracauer, "The Mass Ornament," in *The Mass Ornament: Weimar Essays*, trans. Thomas Levin (Cambridge, MA: Harvard University Press, 1995), 75–86.

24. Warren Susman, "'Personality' and the Making of Twentieth-Century Culture," in *Culture as History: The Transformation of American Society in the Twentieth Century* (New York: Pantheon Books, 1973), 271–285. On the body's status within modernity, particularly in relation to cinema and photography, see, for instance, Jonathan Auerbach, *Body Shots: Early Cinema's Incarnations* (Berkeley: University of California Press, 2007); Jennifer M. Bean, "Technologies of Early Stardom and the Extraordinary Body," *Camera Obscura* 16.3 (2001): 9–56; Jonathan Crary, *Techniques of the Observer: On Vision and Modernity in the Nineteenth Century* (Cambridge, MA: MIT Press, 1990); and Tom Gunning, "Tracing the Individual Body: Photography, Detectives, and Early Cinema," in Leo Charney and Vanessa R. Schwartz, eds., *Cinema and the Invention of Modern Life* (Berkeley: University of California Press, 1995), 15–45.

# originality
# and
# adaptation

# part one

# the good thieves

on the origins of situation

comedy in the british

music hall

o n e

b r y o n y   d i x o n

A few years ago I took a short sabbatical to look at the British Film Institute's (BFI) holdings of archive film material relating to the British music hall. At the back of my mind even then was a curiosity toward finding a link between British performers, trained up on the halls, and the early days of slapstick comedy emanating from Hollywood. Another year spent working on our Chaplin materials intensified this curiosity and I attempted, like many before me, somewhat clumsily to draw a link between Chaplin's comedy and certain traditions of the music hall in nineteenth-century Britain. I was warned that we should be extremely cautious about assuming cause and effect in cases such as these; that just because one thing precedes another, as pantomime does silent film comedy, it doesn't mean an individual such as Chaplin was influenced by it to any significant degree.

These warnings duly noted, I have recently been trying to find some trace of a link between film slapstick and the British comedy tradition in the film record as it relates to music hall. David Robinson and others have already written about the similarities between Chaplin and the clowning traditions passed down from medieval Italy through the diaspora of the *commedia dell'arte* to the British pantomime Harlequinade.[1] Simon Louvish, who has published studies of many individual comic performers, also makes this leap in his book on Stan Laurel and Oliver Hardy. Discussing an 1896 review in *The Era* of Fred Karno's sketch, "Jail Birds," Louvish notes, "We are looking at the 'missing link' between the grotesque antics of clowns such as Grimaldi and the crazy tricks of the future silent cinema."[2] But we need to add some detail to this. At the Chaplin Conference held by the BFI in 2005 there were conversations with Mike Hammond and Yuri Tsivian about the need to compile a "gag-ography" if we were ever to understand the influences of stage comedy on early film. The sources for such a study are difficult, rare, and usually incidental. Apart from tiny nuggets picked out by dedicated researchers like David Robinson, the only way to bridge the gap in our knowledge might be some kind of "experimental archaeology" in which gags or comedic business could be reproduced in performance by contemporary practitioners. It would also take the efforts of a number of researchers to pin down the ancestry of gags, approaching the challenge from different angles. All I can do is offer what information I have found in the film record in Britain and some preliminary observations.

So how *do* you trace a gag? I was not particularly surprised to find little mention of influences in the writings of British comedians working in early film. Slapstick performers, like other comedians, carefully guarded their comedic business: why would any performer admit that their "unique" selling point, i.e., the means by which they could earn a living, was not entirely original? Of course comedy relies on a common pot of gags and business, but performers went to great lengths to conceal the origins of their routines. Every now and then a particularly secure comedian might own up to an influence, but only if he was very well established or was looking back at his career from a safe distance. (Chaplin, the man least likely to admit that his genius was not *sui generis*, was happy to acknowledge some admiration for the clown Marceline and for Max Linder in his autobiography.) As a result of this inclination for silence there is very little evidence for the ancestry of slapstick gags in the memoirs of comedians; almost nothing was written down.

And lest we imply that our legendary performers were guilty of the comedic equivalent of plagiarism, we should unpack what we mean by gags, jokes, "business," and routines. Is it possible to have an original pratfall? When does imitation or mimicry become copying? A good comedian is by nature a good mimic – it is the core of comedy, humor being essentially about recognition. But when is copying a sincere form of flattery, and when is it cashing in on another's success? The "outing" of joke thieves is today a popular pastime for internet contributors, and a great way for people to show off or to reinforce their allegiance to a particular performer;[3] but the complaints about plagiarism around the time of Chaplin's stellar rise in 1914 had a more serious edge. The costume and gags that comprised an entertainer's "act" were vital to his ability to promote himself – his "brand" if you like – and they relied, to an extent, on an element of novelty. As a stage performer you could get a whole season out of one gag, sketch, or routine as you traveled from one town to another (and more if you took it to another country). Once a comedian's material was translated into films, which were exposed to audiences nationwide more or less simultaneously, that element of the novelty value of a particular piece of material was lost, and with it, its earning power.

In the mid-1910s this issue took a quantum leap, as entertainers who had been part of a centuries-old tradition on the stage were forced to confront the new reality of film versus the stage. Billie Ritchie – a Scots comedian who had played lead roles for Karno before Chaplin – was most vociferous in accusing Chaplin of having copied his tramp persona.[4] It is hard not to feel some sympathy for the losers in these new circumstances, even if Ritchie himself was not above copying a gag or two (for example, two weeks after Chaplin released *Work* – released June 21, 1915 – Ritchie came out with a film titled *The Curse of Work* – released July 4, 1915 – on an entirely similar theme).[5] Chaplin may have acknowledged a debt to Max Linder (albeit only in 1921), but Linder had by this time already been taken to court for plagiarizing Karno's sketch, "A Night in an English Music Hall," the very sketch that made Chaplin a star. Of course it only became a legal issue because Karno felt he was missing out financially. The fact is that Linder's 1907 film, *Au Music Hall*, was successful because he was a great performer, just as Chaplin's "tramp" persona was more appealing than Billie Ritchie's. All artists are thieves; the trick to stealing the work of other comedians, as David Robinson likes to say, is to know that you are stealing the good stuff. Chaplin took from Ritchie during their Karno days, Ritchie took again from Chaplin, as did a host of others. During the course of this lively competition, everybody "upped" their game and great strides were made in the development of film comedy.

There is a tendency, particularly with film historians who haven't been exposed to the study of stage history, to assume that "everything starts with Karno." Certainly his companies developed a particular type of ensemble play, although how much this was due to his talent or to that of individual performers is hard to say. Karno was a good businessman and evidently knew talent when he saw it, but he must have had his influences too. His comedians clearly had considerable training in physical comedy before they worked for him, and he employed writers (Sydney Chaplin for one) to help with scenarios based in particular contained settings (a music hall, a football match, a secret society's clubroom, etc.) within which the comedians could show off their "business."

Surviving manuscripts display a marked similarity with other productions of the music hall and popular theater of nineteenth- and early twentieth-century Britain. The difference between Karno and his contemporaries was one of scale. In the 1910s he had as many as 12 separate companies touring at any one time in the major cities of Europe and the United States and, like the emerging Hollywood studios, he brought in the best talent and developed it into a successful format. Stan Laurel was one of his key performers and good enough to understudy Chaplin. He had performed in this kind of sketch or situation comedy before his time at Karno with his father's shows, and continued to do so on the other side of the Atlantic, eventually moving in (and out) of films made in a similar vein. That this model of situation comedy was well established in American vaudeville by the 1910s is clear from a comparison of solo films made by Laurel and those of his future partner, Oliver Hardy. They are in some cases identical – or at least very close – in conception, as in, for instance, Laurel's 1918 *No Place like Jail* and Hardy's similarly prison-themed 1919 *Jazz and Jail*.[6]

As a starting point for thinking about how much of Hollywood's classic silent comedy can be traced to pre-existing performance traditions, I would like to examine the evidence of the film record. Not the record of Hollywood comedies, but that of Britain, from where a significant number of slapstick practitioners originated. I'm fairly sure that early British film was not a major influence on any of the stage comedians who, like Chaplin, Ritchie, or Laurel, later ended up in Hollywood. The best we can hope for, perhaps, is to trace some common elements and evidence of a comedic tradition in the surviving films made by British comedians in the early period. With this in mind I will be focusing on the origin of generic "business," the importance of props, and situation gags.

One could choose many different types of comic scenario that appear in British music hall and early film. Sketch comedies, such as those of the Karno shows, are particularly relevant, as British practitioners trained on the music hall stage would likely have had such scenarios in their repertoire as comedians. These might include comic scenes arising from situations such as the courtroom, football matches, visits to the dentist, visits from the bailiffs or the decorators, encounters in haunted houses, a music hall show, and so on. The comedic possibilities of such various "everyday" settings have been exploited ever since the ancient Greeks. Early film comedy expanded this incrementally. If you run your eyes down the filmography of any prolific silent film comedian, the titles will reveal the recurrence of these situations, not only from one comedian to another, but also within the work of individual performers who would reuse these situations and their concomitant gags several times. For the purposes of this chapter I will trace one such "situation" – the barbershop – which occurs fairly frequently in pre-cinematic media, stage acts, and film comedy, and I will refer to a number of other examples involving dentists, paperhangers, and living statues.

In 1921 Sydney Chaplin produced a feature-length comedy film for Famous Players–Lasky called *King, Queen, Joker*, a fairly conventional story of the mistaken identity genre set in a mythical Ruritanian-type kingdom. The film itself – like most from this era – has not survived complete, but a significant portion still exists in the Chaplin Out-Takes collection now held at the BFI. One long edited section survives together with several sequences of Syd rehearsing on camera. Among these are several comic scenes set in a barbershop. In one, for example, Syd is castigated by the barber for an accounting error and, as he attempts to rectify the situation, takes out a pencil and proceeds to do the sums on a customer's bald head. A further gag has a very familiar look to those who know his brother's work well. In this scene Syd, as the barber's assistant, is shaving a client. Armed with soap and brush, he flourishes his tools as if conducting an orchestra and applies the lather as if accompanied by energetic music with verses and refrains, suddenly slowing down and speeding up in the different passages.[7] Clearly the intention was to have a very precise musical score to the scene to make the gag work. Two decades later, in *The Great Dictator* (1940), Charlie uses exactly the same gag – this time with the synchronized soundtrack making the process more precise and effective. What are we to make of this? Was Charlie's famous musical barber scene a gag stolen from his own brother?

This is a perfect example of the need for caution when assuming that a chronological relationship is synonymous with a causal relationship. It is true that the *King, Queen, Joker* scene predates *The Great Dictator*, but it doesn't necessarily follow that one was copied from the other. A fairly superficial knowledge of the way that Charlie and Sydney Chaplin worked together will also show that their relationship was so close and their influences were so similar that it is hard to tell where one leaves off and the other begins. Charlie often used material that Sydney had written. His Mutual film, *The Rink* (1916), for example, came from Sydney's sketch "Skating," which he had written with Fred Karno. Moreover, a closer look at some of Charlie's films throws up more barbershop gags. In *Behind the Screen* (1916), for example, Charlie plays an assistant to the stage manager of a movie studio. His job is to basically do all of the work while his boss (Eric Campbell) sits around. This gives Chaplin the opportunity to extract a series of gags out of the props that belong to the "situation" in the time-honored tradition of the stage comedian – particularly those of the music hall and especially of the British and European pantomime tradition. In the most famous of these prop-related gags, Charlie gathers up a dozen or so wooden chairs on his shoulder, creating the effect of a hedgehog or porcupine. The film's barber gag, meanwhile, shows Charlie dressing a drawing-room set with a bearskin rug to which he gives the "finishing touches" with the gestures of a practiced barber. He carefully parts and combs the hair, gives the bear's head a scalp massage, administers the hot towel treatment and deftly flicks away loose hairs. All this is done in the throwaway manner that characterizes Chaplin's work; it is no mean feat to throw a dozen chairs over your shoulder. The barber business is relatively incidental to the plot and, apart from showcasing Chaplin's deft pantomime, functions principally to underline the contrast between Chaplin's pride in his work and the laziness of his boss. The casual treatment of the gag feels as if this type of "business" would be expected of any comedian worth his salt. A further barber gag with Albert Austin was attempted in *Sunnyside* (1919), but was cut from the finished film. The footage also survives in the Chaplin Out-Takes collection.

So, the question now becomes, as we try to make a connection with the music hall, whether it was usual for a comedian to have such business or routines at his disposal and how these were learned or passed on. There are several possibilities: (1) a routine, or "business" could be original; (2) a specific routine could be directly taught or passed down from one comedian to another; (3) the comedian was in an environment where he or she was exposed to a variety of generic gags having to do with professions, situations, etc., and these were absorbed more subliminally as part of general training or observation and then combined with the performer's particular set of skills to produce something novel.

In this particular case, we know that the young Charles Chaplin had once worked as a barber's boy and that, courtesy of his mother's acute observational abilities, he was a natural mimic.[8] So it is possible that his barber "business" is original. Option 2 is less likely, but is impossible to prove in any case; if the gag with the bearskin rug had appeared on stage in another production by a different performer we would be very unlikely to find such a specific act in the records. Option 3 is more probable, but can we find any evidence for this? With this in mind we can turn to other instances of barbershop gags from the early period. Below are some examples from the British film record that might illustrate this prevalence.[9]

The first film does not survive, but there is a good description of this one-minute comedy produced by British film pioneer James Williamson in his catalogue of 1898.

*The Clown Barber* (1898) – Williamson Kinematograph Company    "A Gentleman enters barber's shop, knocks and takes seat. Clown enters, to the evident consternation of customer and proceeds with the shaving using a large bowl and brush. He lathers him and then producing a huge razor commences to shave. The customer becomes alarmed and fidgets causing the Clown to cut his head off. The Clown finishes the operation on the sideboard and then sticks the head back on again. The customer now quite happy pays and departs."

The next one *does* survive in a very nice print made from the large format 68 mm film preferred by the British Mutoscope and Biograph Company.

*The Barber Saw the Joke* (1900) – British Mutoscope and Biograph Company In this single-shot film a man sits reading an "Ally Sloper" comic while a barber cuts his hair.[10] The man starts to laugh and the barber reads the comic over his shoulder and starts to laugh as well. He returns to cutting the hair and accidentally cuts the man's ear. The man is angry, takes a sponge to his ear, and then strikes the barber with the sponge, leaving blood on his cheek.

*Sedgwick's Bioscope Show Front* (1901) – Mitchell and Kenyon    An actuality film commissioned by James Sedgwick from the Mitchell and Kenyon Company shows the elaborately decorated frontage of Sedgwick's Bioscope Show at a fair. Showmen perform a comic sketch to entice the fairground punters inside. Two men are seated on the stage with towels around their necks ready for a shave. The barber soaps up one of the men. He continues until the man's face is covered in lather. The man tries to get away but falls over and causes havoc on the stage. Behind the actors are a number of men standing looking at the camera, including the filmmakers. The audience's heads can be seen in the foreground. Children from the audience are congregated on the stage and on the steps leading downward. They smile and cheer at the camera while pushing and

27

Figure 1.1

A fairground barber sketch in Mitchell and Kenyon's *Sedgwick's Bioscope Show Front* (1901). Courtesy of the British Film Institute

tumbling down the steps. A sign is held up reading "Sedgwick's Exhibitions Tonight Living Pictures Passion Play in 16 acts.... Lantern Views."

*A Harlequinade Let Loose* (1912) – Hepworth Manufacturing Company    This comedy was made by the Hepworth Company for release at Christmas 1912. There is a missing section in the BFI print, but we have the description from a contemporary Hepworth catalogue:

> Two or three days before Christmas, a man who is left in charge of the costumes and properties of a Christmas pantomime celebrates the festive season somewhat too early, and falls asleep in a drunken stupor. He dreams that Harlequin and Columbine suddenly appear and summon to them the Clown, Pantaloon and Policeman [end of missing section]. With Harlequin and Columbine in front leading them on to mischief, Clown and Pantaloon steal sausages from the butchers, upset pastries in the baker's, disturb a bill-poster and steal a baby from a pram, all with the policeman in pursuit. Finally, they enter a barbershop, which is advertising "Boy Wanted." Once inside they whitewash the customers [sic] faces with a huge brush and the Clown wields an oversized cut-throat razor, terrifying the clients. They then run off to a lodging house, which despite being described by a sign as "quiet lodgings" turns out to be haunted with pictures and furniture behaving in a peculiar manner. The culprits eventually take refuge in the baskets from which they emerged.[11]

We can see from these three examples that the barbershop as a setting was prevalent in film comedy and that it derived from stage comedy in the popular theater, fairground shows, and music halls of the period. Specifically, such settings derive from the Harlequinade "street" set, which abounded with these shops and street-types, all of which had collections of props from which comedy could be derived. This is the world of the string of sausages, the red-hot poker, the bucket of wallpaper paste, and the slap round the face with a wet fish. In stage versions these props took on exaggerated proportions, partly so the audience could see them clearly, but also for the humor that the change in scale offered. Often the prop would be used to effect a transformation (examples being the Harlequin's bat or "slapstick," a device used like a magic wand to turn people or objects into something else, make them disappear in a puff of smoke, etc.) or it would take on the attributes of another object (such as a string of sausages used as a climbing aid in a version of the Indian Rope trick).

Such props were, moreover, quickly incorporated into film: the transforming slapstick, for example, can be found in early comedies in which it is used to make people appear and disappear (using the miracle of trick photography), to make an action unfold backwards in time (with film printed in reverse), or to effect various other "magic" transformations.

This use of stage accoutrements and the exaggerated proportions of props can be seen in numerous other early films, many of which are simply filmed versions of stage routines. However, as comic filmmakers began to adapt their work to the specific properties of the medium, they dropped the use of exaggerated props (which didn't sit well with cinema's intrinsic realism) and confined transformation scenes to stories of a generically appropriate fantastic nature (such as children's fairytales and the occasional comic fantasy). However, a quasi-surrealist use of props (whereby they take on the attributes of completely different objects) *does* continue into film comedy, as we have seen in *Behind the Screen* with the chair/hedgehog. This is because one of the advantages that film offers is the ability to take the audience closer to the action. If you think, for instance, of the alarm clock sequence in Chaplin's *The Pawnshop* (1916), where the clock "becomes" a human body under the dubious ministrations of Chaplin as surgeon, it would have been considerably less effective to perform on stage. The gag works because we can clearly see Chaplin's facial expressions as he reduces the alarm clock to its component parts, first opening it with a can opener as if it were a can of sardines and sniffing cautiously, then checking for vital signs as if the clock were a patient. Had Chaplin tried to perform this on stage, the alarm clock would have had to be oversized and his movements and expressions less naturalistic and exaggerated, more in the manner of a circus clown.

It is ironic that the alarm clock gag contains one of the very few occasions where Chaplin tried trick photography. After the internal innards of the clock have been taken apart, the cogs and springs are animated to move around independently. This interlude strikes an odd note, adding little to the scene while detracting from the film's inherent realism. It illustrates an important point about the sophisticated audience's mistrust of trick photography. For us to truly appreciate the performer we must see that his performance is real. We need to know he is as good as we think he is. Contemporary and later critics alike have admired Chaplin's balletic movements and genius for pantomime or Stan Laurel's fabulous hat work. Cheating with the camera — to speed up or slow down the action, to use reverse shooting to enable a comedian to do impossible physical feats such as jump to the top of a building or get up out of the splits in one move — is intolerable and strictly the preserve of juveniles. Chaplin, Keaton, and Lloyd used such tricks sparingly and the films of those comedians who continued to use them into the 1920s such as Lupino Lane, who we will discuss below, have always been seen as less brilliant.

The other feature of stage comedy that carried over to film was the settings themselves. Barbershops, dentists, tailors, bakers' shops, boarding houses, and others all featured as settings with comic potential, as did the various related professions (policemen, firemen, laborers, decorators). Chaplin had played in a famous sketch featuring paperhangers, "Repairs" by Wal Pink, on stage in 1906 and would use decorators as a theme throughout his film career, from *Work* in 1915 to *A King in New York* in 1957. Stan Laurel likewise re-used situations in this way: after his time with Karno, he wrote a stage sketch called "Raffles the Dentist," outlining a comic dentist situation. The theme recurs in several of his films, *White Wings* (1923) and with Oliver Hardy, *Leave 'em Laughing* (1928) and *The Dentist* (1931).

We have seen that Chaplin grew up in an environment in which he was exposed to a range of situation gags, and we know that he drew on these in his films. Through his artistry and quick grasp of the new medium he improved upon them and turned them into some of the most brilliant moments in screen comedy. So was he a good thief or was it his own talent that made his films so popular? Was it the tramp character, allegedly stolen from other performers, that propelled him to stardom? Sydney Chaplin, good as he was, and with much the same background, did not quite manage to get his talent across in the same way. Other performers – Stan Laurel, Billie Ritchie, and others with British music hall training – had greater or lesser success, but none equivalent to Chaplin's. We are fortunate to know a lot about the way Chaplin worked because of the survival of the Chaplin Out-Takes collection, from which we can see how he drove himself constantly to improve on gags through improvisation and practice.[12] For other performers of this period, however, we have to rely on supposition or imagination. Not being a performer myself, I have found it incredibly useful to read fictional recreations of comedians' creative methods. One example is Peter Ackroyd's *Dan Leno and the Limehouse Golem* (1994), in which the author imagines the greatest of British music hall stars rehearsing in secrecy behind closed doors. In the following passage, Leno recruits the young Lizzie to record his movements and patter as he improvises, in much the same way as Chaplin did on film:

> "Our prompter ran off with a slangster comique the other day, and sometimes we need a bit of help from that quarter. Do you understand me? Otherwise we might get ballooned off the stage.... [Y]ou can do a bit of playcopying for us, you see. Now let's have a bit of fun, shall we?" He was wearing an overcoat that almost came down to his ankles, and from one of its many pockets he took out a small exercise book and a pencil

which he handed to me with an elaborately low bow. "Write it down as I spoof it."

He splayed his legs wide on the stage, put his thumbs in the pockets of his waistcoat, and then tweaked an imaginary moustache. "I'll tell you who I am uncle, I'm a recruiting sergeant. The other day I was standing at the corner of the street when I saw you uncle, as is your wont." The uncle stood up very straight, as Dan walked over to him with as much ferocity as if he were eight feet high. "Do you want to be a soldier?"

"I don't – I'm waiting for a bus."

I wrote this all down as quickly as I could; then, at the end, he jumped down from the stage and stood on tiptoe to look over my shoulder. "That's a good girl" he said. "You're as neat as a shipping clerk. Uncle, will you sing a nice patter for Lizzie, just to see how fast she can go?" I understood then that part of my new employment was in writing down what Dan called "extempore vocalisation," so that anything said "off the cuff" could be used in later performances.[13]

Likewise, Neil Brand's BBC TV production, *Stan* (2006), imagines Stan Laurel's working method in a scene developing a gag with Oliver Hardy. The author's background as an actor, as well as his extensive knowledge of silent film comedy, makes these imagined scenes persuasive. Neither Laurel or Hardy wrote in detail about their working methods or influences, so this kind of well-informed speculation is particularly useful. Several scenes in Richard Attenborough's *Chaplin* (1992), choreographed by Dan Kamin, also help the modern audience to visualize the process by which physical comedy might be developed. Still, while contemporary writing by performers about this process is rare, there was one who did leave us some detailed evidence.

Lupino Lane (1892–1959), although not as well known now as Keaton, Chaplin, and Lloyd, was a very popular film comedian of the second rank in the 1920s. His style came very much from his background on the English stage, where he had performed since infancy, in pantomime and musical comedy. He came from a theatrical family that claimed an ancestry with the *commedia dell'arte* players of Italy. The Lupinos specialized in harlequinades, pantomimes, and clowning, and later went into musical comedy. While their Italian roots may not have been *entirely* authentic, the Lupino family certainly went back far enough to have developed their own performance traditions. In fact, this extraordinary dynasty of performers made a virtue of handing down material, and routinely trained their offspring in a range of the comedic arts. Young Lupino Lane describes how his father made him and his brother, Wallace, sit in the splits for half an hour every day. He began performing as a toddler and, at a young age, developed the remarkable acrobatic abilities that he exploited in his films both in England and Hollywood. He also made use of stories, scenarios, and sets from the theater to great effect. In *Sword Points* (1928), for example, he uses several dozen stage trapdoors to set up a chase scene in an old baronial house in which he is pursued through walls, floors, and secret panels. Lane may have lacked the sophistication and genius of the top flight of film comedians, but he was certainly very competent at a certain type of tried-and-tested stage comedy, which he adapted well for the screen. In one of his British films, *Tripps and Tribunals* (1918), from a series called *The Blunders of Mr. Butterbun*, we see examples of all of these traits – the use of varying situations with a regular central character, excellent physical comedy in Lane's characterization of an inebriate, the use of a pantomime device (a magic ring which activates when rubbed, like Aladdin's lamp), as well as film tricks.

What is most valuable for our purpose here though is that Lupino Lane, by his very lack of originality, provides us with a definite link with British stage traditions – more so than Chaplin or Laurel, in fact, since his comedy derived quite directly from gags learned in the theater. For example, in his 1928 film, *Roaming Romeo*[14] (more humorously known in Britain as *Bending Her*, spoofing the epic film *Ben Hur* (1925)), Lupino plays a galley slave who escapes the ship with a companion (his brother, Wallace Lupino, who joined him in the early 1920s) and ends up in a Roman palace. Here, he plays through all the gags associated with a Roman setting (gladiators, vestal virgins, etc.), culminating in a much-loved pantomime favorite – the living statue gag. This involved "whiting up" and imitating the poses of classical statuary while trying not to be observed by a pursuer. Attempting to abscond, the characters are caught in a series of increasingly comical frozen poses every time the pursuers turn round. The living statue gags are too much a tradition of comedy for this to be called copying. One example illustrating this direct connection to the British music hall has recently been unearthed by David Robinson, involving the famous clown Marceline, who worked in the British and later American music halls and who had been such an influence on Chaplin.[15] The clown seems to have been a performer in the Grimaldi mold. In his article, Robinson includes illustrations of a routine of Marceline's in which he is whited-up and impersonates a classical statue to deceive a pursuer.

Not only can we see Lupino's indebtedness to music hall traditions in his British and American films, but he also (bless him) wrote it all down. In his 1945 handbook, *How to Become a Comedian*, Lane details the elements of his training, which included: ballet, tap, juggling, acrobatics, fencing,

Figure 1.2

The "living statue" routine from Lupino Lane's *Roaming Romeo* (1928)

boxing, costume design, music composition, mime, singing, producing plays, Shakespearean acting, lighting, elocution, building scenery, as well as all sorts of falls and slapstick play.[16] The book even has diagrams of classic pratfalls (including, incidentally, the full "108," which apocryphally was Mabel Normand's benchmark for a good slapstick performer, which got Chaplin the job with Mack Sennett and was Ben Turpin's trademark pratfall).[17] Another element of the British comedian's basic training, cited by Lupino, is a good knowledge of the popular melodramas of the nineteenth-century theater, such as *The Corsican Brothers*, *Robert Macaire* (a splendid roguish character adopted by nineteenth-century caricaturist Honoré Daumier, arguably a precursor to Ally Sloper), *Jack Sheppard*, and so on. Such well-honed works, which had appeared in multiple versions and many different media, were perfect for developing a character in different situations, just as the pantomime harlequinades had done before them. The book even has a chapter entitled "How to Use Old Gags."

What can we deduce from looking at British films and stage traditions about the origins of film comedy? First, we can infer that there was a collective memory of situations and gags which could be learned, copied, or derived from sketch comedy, the pantomime, and the harlequinade. Second, that ensemble comedy troupes were well developed on the British stage and in American vaudeville, and that there was an impressive amount of traffic between the two. One might go further, if space

33

permitted, to enable a discussion of European comedians who were well integrated into this international theatrical interchange. British comedians would certainly have felt very much at home in the stock companies of film studios such as Keystone or Essanay, and continued to use gags and business inherited directly from music hall traditions. The development of comedic personas such as Chaplin's "tramp" or Lupino Lane's "Nipper" can be traced quite directly to British stage tradition.[18] Performers would often adapt costume and make-up from music hall acts or personalities from printed comics like Ally Sloper, but this changed quite quickly in film as it became obvious that "fixed expression" make-up did not work on screen. The development of a star system in Hollywood, in which individuals were recognized by their faces, combined with the medium's inherent realism, led comedians to drop their "mask-like" appearance.

With the establishment of specialist production studios in Hollywood, film comedy quickly began to differentiate itself from stage comedy by seeking out every advantage that the medium offered, principally realism. Healthy profits meant higher production values, better sets, better performers, and better gags. In British films this did not happen. The most popular pre-World War I comedian, Fred Evans, retained his clown make-up for his "Pimple" character longer than his equivalents in the United States and, as a result, his comedies feel as if they belong to a previous era. Although a superficial glance down the 200-plus titles in his filmography might indicate that Evans was working in much the same way as Chaplin or Stan Laurel, with a well-defined persona in a great variety of comic situations, production values were considerably lower and had not significantly improved by the end of the war when he made his final films. The British industry simply failed to reach the same critical mass of demand, profit, improvement, and inventiveness that characterized the American film comedy business.

By the time a comedian like Lupino Lane left London in 1921 to further his film career under contract to William Fox, there was no question that if he wanted to make comedy films he would have to go to Hollywood to do it. Once there, he could make good use of his British stage background like many before him, and after. Some British comedy traditions would be sustained – the gags, the physical moves, the stories and settings – while others were overtaken by developments specific to film comedy. Out went the trappings of the nineteenth-century theater and music halls, the exaggerated props, fantastical settings, magical devices, clown make-up and costumes, and the language of the harlequinade, so much so that nearly a century later we can hardly understand them. Of course caricature continued on into the 1920s – comedy policemen were still stupid and burglars still occasionally wore stripy jumpers – but generally the characters and the situations of film comedy were changed for something more contemporary and realistic that would not only connect with the audience, but also play to the strengths of the medium of film. Real cars and buildings, real landscapes and trains, gave added scope to the next generation of film comedians.

## notes

1. David Robinson, *Chaplin: His Life and Art* (London: Penguin, 2001), 31.
2. Simon Louvish, *Stan and Ollie: The Roots of Comedy* (London: Faber & Faber, 2001), 54.
3. For example, see http://en.wikipedia.org/wiki/Joke_thievery.
4. From a paper given by Jon Burrows, "Near Broke but No Tramp: Billie Ritchie, Charlie Chaplin and 'That Costume,'" Chaplin Conference, London, 2005.
5. Charles J. Maland, *Chaplin and American Culture* (Princeton: Princeton University Press, 1991), 11.
6. Rob Stone, *Laurel or Hardy: The Solo Films of Stan Laurel and Oliver "Babe" Hardy* (Manchester, NH: Split Reel, 1996).
7. This was first revealed by Frank Scheide in various presentations at the National Film Theatre and the British Silent Cinema Festival, 1998 to 2002.
8. Robinson, *Chaplin*, 41.
9. For more examples of music hall-related films, see Bryony Dixon, "Chaplin in Context: A Catalogue of Music Hall Related Films held by the BFI National Archive, 1895 to 1930," on the BFI Chaplin website at http://chaplin.bfi.org.uk/resources/bfi/in-context.html.
10. *Ally Sloper's Half Holiday* was a popular weekly penny comic. The character of Ally Sloper was extremely pervasive at the turn of the century and penetrated the music hall, early films, lantern slides and merchandising, as well as printed media. The strips themselves frequently set up the same kinds of situation (including of course the barbershop) that later characterized sketch comedy of the Karno type and early film comedy. The character was certainly an influence on film comedians such as Chaplin, and bears a strong physical resemblance to W. C. Fields in his Micawber role from *David Copperfield* (1935). See Roger Sabin, "Ally Sloper: The First Comics Superstar?" (October 2003) online at www.imageandnarrative.be/graphicnovel/rogersabin.htm.
11. For more on traditions of the harlequinade, see Bryony Dixon, "Chaplin and the Harlequinade" (2005) on the BFI Chaplin website at http://chaplin.bfi.org/programme/essays/harlequinade.html, and David Mayer, *Harlequin in his Element* (Cambridge, MA: Harvard University Press, 1969).
12. See Kevin Brownlow and David Gill's documentary, *Unknown Chaplin* (Thames TV, 1983).
13. Peter Ackroyd, *Dan Leno and the Limehouse Golem* (London: Minerva, 1995), 75–76.
14. The film was directed by future RKO director, Mark Sandrich.
15. David Robinson in Frank Scheide and Hooman Mehran, eds., *Chaplin's "Limelight" and the Music Hall Tradition* (Jefferson: McFarland, 2006). For Chaplin's own reminiscence, see Charles Chaplin, *My Autobiography* (London: Penguin Books, 1964), 45–46.
16. Lupino Lane, *How to Become a Comedian* (London: F. Muller, 1945).

17. Mack Sennett with Cameron Shipp, *King of Comedy* (Garden City, NY: Doubleday, 1954), 54.

18. Frank Scheide, "The History of Low Comedy and Nineteenth and Early Twentieth Century English Music Hall as Basis for Examining the 1914–1917 Films of Charles Spencer Chaplin" (PhD dissertation, University of Wisconsin-Madison, 1990).

bryony dixon

# d. w. griffith shapes

# slapstick

two

barry salt

D. W. Griffith had a strong, and unrecognized, influence on the form of American film slapstick. He was a man lacking a real comic touch, but as everyone knows, Mack Sennett came out of his troupe at Biograph to set up the Keystone Film Company, and all those years of being in D. W. Griffith's films had an effect on what Sennett subsequently did.

But before Griffith made films, there were Pathé films, and Griffith saw them before he started directing at Biograph. Amongst Pathé's biggest hits of 1907–1908, was *Le Cheval emballé*. I have written about this film before, but it is worth reminding you of the use of comings and goings on the Pathé staircase in it, and in other Pathé films.[1] A delivery man goes up the staircase and into a room and back onto the staircase, while his horse is shown in a cross-cut sequence eating the contents of a bag of oats outside a grain shop on the street level. These scenes inside the house are all shot from the same frontal direction. *Le Cheval emballé* was so successful a film that it would have been difficult for film people to avoid seeing it in 1908 in New York, but in any case, Griffith made a version of it, at the urging of Mack Sennett and Billy Bitzer, under the title of *The Curtain Pole*, later in the year. At that point Griffith had not developed the idea of using side-by-side spaces shot from the same frontal direction. Ben Brewster has identified *An Awful Moment*, made about a month after *The Curtain Pole*, as the first use of the device, and the next example I know of is *A Wreath in Time*, made another month later, with Mack Sennett in the lead. After that, this layout became more and more frequent in Griffith's scenography. I have illustrated Griffith's way of shooting scenes in adjoining spaces in *Film Style and Technology*, with an example from *The Battle*, but here is another example from *The Sunbeam* (1912).[2] In shots 1 and 2, the little girl leaves her sick mother in their tenement room, and sets off downstairs looking for someone to play with (Figures 2.1a–2.1b). In shots 3 and 4, she reaches the ground floor and accosts a middle-aged spinster in the hallway (Figures 2.1c–2.1d). The spinster rejects her. After more interaction with the spinster, the little girl approaches a man in the hall, and is rejected again (Figures 2.1e–2.1f). He goes into his room, shuts the door, and looks angrily back toward it.

When Sennett, Dell Henderson, George Nichols, and other Griffith actors were allowed to direct at Biograph, it is not particularly surprising that they took up his use of room-to-room movement in side-by-side spaces filmed from the front. The only thing surprising about this is that no-one has remarked on it. In Sennett's case, he began directing comedies for Griffith in 1911, and the side-by-side room staging can be seen in films like *A Convenient Burglar* and *Too Many Burglars*. And so it became the usual way at Keystone of filming scenes taking place in a house with more than one room. A good example from 1913 is *A Healthy Neighborhood*, which Sennett personally directed.

In this film, the comically incompetent Dr. Noodles, played by Ford Sterling, has to give emergency treatment to a girl that his own medicine has made ill. She is in the dining room of her father's house, and then her father rushes out to the right into the adjoining kitchen to get water (Figures 2.2a–2.2b). As the scene continues, Dr. Noodles rushes into the sitting room on the other side of the dining room to secretly consult his medical textbook for advice (Figures 2.2c–2.2d). This latter move is neither necessary nor advantageous from a comedy point of view. It would be more amusing if he was in the same room, and had to resort to various extra comic stratagems to get a look at the textbook without being seen by the others present. Indeed, this would be the way such a scene would have been done on the stage, from whence the situation comes.

Besides this rushing backwards and forwards several times through these three side-by-side rooms near the climax of the film, there are earlier scenes in Dr. Noodles' surgery, with the action going backwards and forwards from his consulting room to his waiting room, and vice versa, which are also side by side, and also shot from the same frontal direction. Sennett also throws in a little weak cross-cutting between

(a)

(b)

(c)

(d)

(e)

(f)

Figure 2.1

Frame enlargements and camera set-up plan from *The Sunbeam* (1912)

(a)

(b)

(c)

(d)

(e)

(f)

Shots 4, 6

Shots 1, 3, 5

Shot 2

Figure 2.2

Frame enlargements and camera plan from *A Healthy Neighborhood* (1913)

parallel actions in this and some of his other films, but this is never particularly effective because it is not related to the drive of the plot.

Dr. Noodles' surgery on the left, and his waiting room on the right, are the location for more movement between adjoining spaces filmed from the "front" (Figures 2.3a–2.3b). Dr. Noodles is engaged in a classic stethoscope routine with his pretty patient, but between them, Mack Sennett and Ford Sterling completely destroy the comedy in this by going through the moves so fast that the rationale for them is completely unrecognizable. Also, having put a dentist's chair in the doctor's surgery, they also fail to exploit it with some of the standard stage gags involving dentists' chairs.

The most obvious feature of *A Healthy Neighborhood* and *The Riot*, the only Sennett-directed films I have seen from the first two years of the company's existence, is the way they are relentlessly crammed with action and continual movement, so that the detail of the narrative is difficult to follow. It is a matter of "Why the hell is he doing that?" most of the time, to a degree that I have never seen anywhere else in a film. As I have indicated with one instance above, this represents a consistent failure by Sennett to develop and milk a number of viable comedy situations. It is just as well he left most of the directing to others at Keystone.

The Pathé comedies were not the only model available to Mack Sennett through the years from 1908 to 1912, before he developed his own sort of slapstick. The Gaumont Company in France also had slapstick units making films from 1906 onwards, but its productions did not feature the use of side-by-side spaces, or indeed any other specific features that are to be found in the first few years of Keystone production. The Gaumont "Calino" films are mostly constructed from a discontinuous series of scenes each exploiting one basic gag, without the use of any moves or gestures that can be seen taken over into Keystone films. Both Pathé and Gaumont comedies use undercranking (accelerated motion) to speed up their action at times, from 1909 onwards, but there is no

(a)                                    (b)

Figure 2.3

The doctor's surgery and waiting room in *A Healthy Neighborhood* (1913) accelerated motion used in the early Keystone period. The total destruction of interior sets, combined with acrobatic tumbling, that is so characteristic of the well-known Gaumont "Onésime" comedy series from 1912 onwards, likewise does not appear in Keystone films, where the violence is focused on people rather than things.

When Charlie Chaplin came to Keystone at the beginning of 1914, he gradually moved toward a slower style of comedy, against resistance from Sennett. This was a matter of leaving space between the gags to give time for the characters' reactions, and hence their thought processes, to be savored by the film audience – not to mention giving the audience time to appreciate the cleverness of the gags, and also the idiosyncrasies of Chaplin's movement, which goes on in the spaces between gags. I think Chaplin's success also made it possible for Fatty Arbuckle to develop his own slower style of comedy. One can see Arbuckle trying to do things differently even in his first days at Keystone in 1913, when he was still one of the mob in films like *The Riot*. In this, while everybody else is throwing bombs and bricks in the usual frenetic Keystone way during the climax of the action, Arbuckle is using his own special sort of slowed-down graceful pitches to launch his missiles.

When Chaplin started directing, he took up the use of side-by-side spaces shot from the front that was standard at Keystone, and he took this style with him when he moved to Essanay in 1915, and on to Mutual in 1916. *His New Job* (1915) provides a good example of this. In this film, the row of side-by-side spaces are areas of the main stage of a large film studio, though some are separated by either the walls of sets, or actual walls. The sequence of events at this point in the film is that Charlie, after a misdemeanor in his new job at the film studio, is sent by the director (Figure 2.4a) to help the studio carpenter (Figure 2.4b). His attempt to saw a plank of wood flips it at the carpenter, knocking him through the door into the property room (Figure 2.4c). The carpenter retaliates by kicking him in the behind after he has picked up the plank (Figure 2.4d), which sends him flying at high speed right through the shooting area, and then another intermediate space, before knocking down an actor in front of the dressing rooms (Figure 2.4g). Charlie then ambles back along his tracks and eventually into the property room, where he is startled by a life-sized female statue (Figure 2.4k). He tips his hat to her (Figure 2.4l), before his next misadventure begins. The gag is the repercussions of Charlie's stupidity in handling wood, with the initial knocking over of the carpenter, topped by the exaggerated distance traveled by Charlie with the plank, culminating in the knocking over of another uninvolved person. The basic elements of this can be seen in my earlier examples (and of course hundreds of other films), but the new element is Charlie's leisurely and unconcerned walk back through the stages of his flight, embellished by funny gestures along the way. In Figure 2.4h he does a silly

(a)

(b)

(c)

(d)

(e)

(f)

(g)

(h)

43

Figure 2.4

Frame enlargements and camera set-up plan from *His New Job* (1915)

*continued*

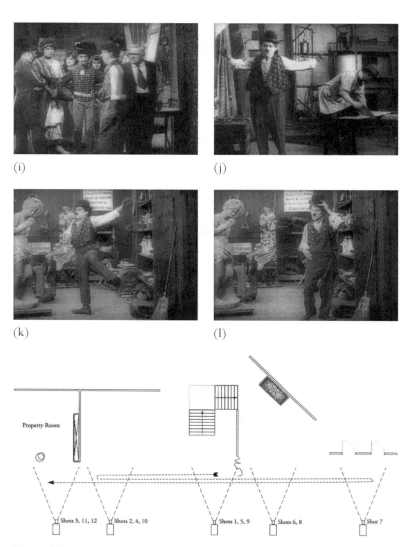

(i)  (j)  (k)  (l)

Figure 2.4

Continued

high lift of his leg, kicking himself in the behind, and in Figure 2.4j he pauses to stretch as a relief from his exertions, before moving into the prop room and acting as though the statue was a real woman (Figures 2.4k and 2.4l). The major traditional theories about humor are obviously relevant in this sequence. That is, Charlie's stupid actions give rise to feelings of superiority in the audience, and the incongruity theory applies to his reaction to the statue, and also to his other unnatural gestures.

## all the right moves

Chaplin's characteristic gestures of arm and leg had not appeared in other earlier film comedians' performances, though I wouldn't be surprised if they were acquired from other stage comedians. The main point is that he filled up so much screen time with them, in a way that other earlier film comedians did not. And there was more time available, because he was making two-reel films, rather than the one-reelers or split reels of earlier film comedies.

In *A Healthy Neighborhood*, Ford Sterling uses a number of funny movements, but some of them are to be found in earlier films. He does a number of agitated runs in exterior scenes, and for these he runs with his legs turned out – with his knees rising to the sides rather than in front as in a normal run. Sometimes in the middle of these runs he does a jump rather than a step from one foot to the other, again with his legs turned out. The same jump can be seen interpolated in the runs of the gendarme in *Le Cheval emballé* (Figure 2.5). The general point about this is that running and jumping with your legs turned out is intrinsically funny, because it is unnatural. This is the incongruity theory of comedy in action again.

Amongst all Sterling's frenetic movement in his surgery, I notice a pose with a momentary position of his hands that later became one of Oliver Hardy's frequent characteristic gestures (Figure 2.6). There is plenty more analysis to be done in this area.

As Chaplin and others developed their comedy, the actual slapstick action became more and more subordinate to other elements. Besides separating the slapstick gags with characteristic perambulations, Chaplin put in more consistent plotting, with dramatic sentiment and love interest, and so did the others, adding real character to the personality of the leading comedians. Only Sennett kept this relentless kind of slapstick going.

Figure 2.5

Ford Sterling doing a funny turned-out jump in *A Healthy Neighborhood* (left), and a gendarme doing likewise in *Le Cheval emballé* (1907)

Figure 2.6

Ford Sterling in *A Healthy Neighborhood* (left), and Oliver Hardy in *Babes in Toyland* (1934)

The square-on stagings also went with the other escapees from the Keystone factory, and in particular Roscoe "Fatty" Arbuckle. However, the Arbuckle Comique films do not make an especially big feature of movement from one adjoining space to the next, although it sometimes appears with distinction, as in *The Cook* (1918). Buster Keaton was brought into films by Arbuckle as an accomplice, rather than a stooge, for his Comique pictures, and in turn went into his own solo series of two-reelers in 1920. Keaton's films are in general made up of a string of separate gags, in which he wrestles with a recalcitrant world, and sometimes wins, sometimes loses, and sometimes draws, as in the example illustrated from *One Week* (1920), the first film he released. The camera is square-on to the room, in the Griffith-Keystone tradition, and his solo action takes place around the center of the room, which is much more particular to Keaton. In this scene, he is laying a carpet in the prefabricated house he is building, but inadvertently nails down his jacket under the center of the carpet. When he realizes this, his solution is to cut a square out of the center of the carpet. The resulting hole he covers with a mat, then replaces the mat with the square of carpet. He writes "WELCOME" on the new mat, and puts it in place in the hall, which is the "topper" to this whole gag sequence (Figure 2.7). It's a weak topper, I dare to say, but any topper is better than no topper. In any case, there are much better gags coming along later in this film. If you want to study the truth of my assertion about this characteristic way in which Keaton's gags are staged, get DVDs of his short films, and run them at eight times normal speed.

The science of mechanics is at the heart of Keaton's comedy, as has been remarked before, but the soul of the science of mechanics is found in geometry, and this is visually manifest in Keaton's films as in no others. The first film he made, though not the first film he released, was *The High Sign* from early 1920. The plot of this film involves Buster being mistakenly taken to be a crack shot by the leader of a gang of criminals, and so recruited into the band. He has to qualify for membership by

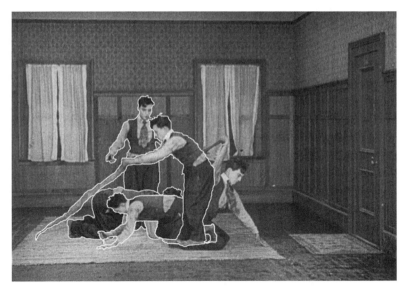

Figure 2.7
Central staging in a routine from Buster Keaton's *One Week* (1920)

killing a rich man, who has refused to be shaken down by the gang, but when Buster finds out what he has to do, he changes allegiance, and tries to fool the gang into believing he has killed their victim. The rich man has equipped his house with numerous concealed doors and traps to save himself from the criminals, and Buster uses these to defeat the gang members when they invade the house, having realized that they have been cheated. An incident that begins the climax of the film is Buster escaping through an upstairs window and grabbing the drainpipe outside. The drainpipe breaks, and he swings down on it describing a circular arc, to dive through the downstairs window. The drainpipe swings back up, which knocks out his criminal pursuer, who is looking through the window after him (Figures 2.8a–2.8b). Both the criminal and Buster shoot straight across the upper and lower rooms, tumbling as they go (Figure 2.8c). Then the remaining gang members chase Buster through the four rooms of the house, which are simultaneously visible on the screen in a unit set shown in cross-section. Buster's path traces a rectangle inside the rectangles of the set (Figure 2.8d). This is the apotheosis of the room-to-room movement constructions of Griffith and Chaplin, taken to a degree that they never achieved or contemplated.

(a)

(b)

(c)

(d)

Figure 2.8

Geometrical paths in a chase sequence from Buster Keaton's *The High Sign* (1921)

From time to time, the essence of Buster Keaton's concerns was summed up in a single frame, like this one from *One Week*.

Figure 2.9

Frame enlargement from *One Week*

**notes**

1. Barry Salt, *Moving into Pictures*. (London: Starword, 2006), 398.
2. Barry Salt, *Film Style and Technology: History and Analysis*, 3rd edn. (London: Starword, 2009), 107.

# genre parody and

# comedic burlesque

keystone's meta-cinematic

satires

three

simon joyce

With all of its attention to first instances (of cinematic techniques, as well
as comparable innovations in distribution and exhibition), it is sometimes
difficult for early film studies to attend to the echoing effects of borrow-
ing and parody. These processes were crucial to the success of Mack
Sennett at Keystone, and yet their functions are obscured by the overrid-
ing desire to identify a distinctive studio style; in many ways, it is only
against such a defined signature that film historians, echoing the practice
of the time in trade journals and fan magazines, are able to consider the
complex questions of influence and imitation that represent one central
strand of the current volume. In this chapter, though, I want to shift the
terms of this discussion in two related ways. As part of a historical argument about the organization of the film industry in the 1910s, I insist on
the importance of Keystone's status as one film brand among many
owned and operated by Adam Kessel and Charles Baumann's New York
Motion Picture Corporation (NYMP), which otherwise specialized in a
very different kind of production, emphasizing westerns, action films, and
historical dramas. As part of a formal argument about film aesthetics,

I underscore the importance for Sennett of his collegial relationship with two celebrated producers of the period, one of whom, Thomas H. Ince, was mainly responsible for the output of those other NYMP productions, under brand names that included Bison, Bison-101, Broncho, Kay-Bee, and Domino. The other was D. W. Griffith, under whose tutelage at Biograph Sennett claimed to have learned the art of filmmaking.

The three men were publicly linked in 1915 by the ill-fated Triangle Film Corporation, when Kessel and Baumann combined the assets of the NYMP — many of the brand names listed above, but most especially the services of Sennett and Ince — with those of Harry Aitken, who ran the Mutual distribution and Majestic production companies (and, in doing so, held the contract for the services of Griffith).[1] From its inception, there was a fatal asymmetry in the conception of the Triangle program, which yoked five-reel features produced under the supervision of Griffith and Ince to a supply of Keystone shorts; both the implied status imbalance and the accompanying financial arrangements would chafe at Sennett, who consistently sought to re-negotiate the terms of his contracts. In many ways, though, the internal struggles behind the scenes at Triangle continued a more public war that Sennett and slapstick had been fighting against highbrow dramas like those produced by Griffith and Ince. In this sense, it is possible to take at near face-value the attitude toward his colleagues that is reported in Gene Fowler's 1934 "as-told-to" biography of Sennett, *Father Goose*, which describes the threesome as "combatants with weapons." Griffith, the passage elaborates, "performed with a rapier, Ince with a saber and Sennett with a bed-slat."[2] What is telling is the blunt force contained in the image of the dueling bed-slat, which seeks to deflate the high-class connotations of rapiers and swords by subjecting to ridicule the implied rules that would govern a fair fight. In filmic terms, Sennett's weapon was a precise and sustained parodying of the work of his colleagues and rivals in a manner that suggests we need to rethink customary notions of a simple, unitary signature. To the extent that a Keystone house style is recognizable, it is so only as a mediated reprocessing of formal elements and narrative traits associated with melodrama, the western, or the historical epic, each of which Sennett sought to neutralize as readily as the bed-slat might blunt the delicacy and precision of the rapier.

50

## a "natural tendency to burlesque": sennett and griffith

It is well known that Sennett, first hired as an actor at Biograph in 1908, sought ways to learn how to direct from Griffith. The story comes to us first from Griffith's wife, Linda Arvidson, whose 1925 memoir, *When the Movies Were Young*, recounts these filmmaking tutorials. "When work was over," she recalled, "Sennett would hang around the studio watching for the opportune moment when his director would leave," and then engineer an "accidental" meeting en route:

> Then for twenty-three blocks he would have the boss all to himself and wholly at his mercy. Twenty-three blocks of uninterrupted conversation. "Well now, what do you really think about these moving pictures? What do you think is in them? Do you think they are going to last? What's in them for an actor? What do you think of my chances?"[3]

As recounted by Arvidson, the anecdote has more to do with Sennett's professional ambitions than with film technique, but Sennett's own version, as presented in his 1954 autobiography, *The King of Comedy*, places greater emphasis on his learning of cinematic form, suggesting that "So far as any knowledge of motion-picture technique goes, I learned all I ever learned by standing around, watching people who knew how, by pumping Griffith and thinking it over."

While representing "the boss" as a Socratic master-teacher, Sennett suggests a decisive point of departure, noting that where Griffith saw the potential for complex storytelling in the now-familiar set of technical innovations that emerged out of his work at Biograph, his eager pupil instead "saw in his great ideas a new way to show the people being funny."[4] That different generic emphasis explains a defensive tone in Arvidson's memories of Sennett, whom she recalls as having "never approved whole-heartedly of anything we did, nor how we did it, nor who did it."[5] What emerges from these accounts, I would argue, is something more than simple emulation, or the redirecting of Griffith's techniques towards comedic ends. In writing about Griffith's farcical chase film *The Curtain Pole* (1909) – in which Sennett stars as a drunken Frenchman who wreaks havoc through a series of elaborately staged sets with a domestic object a little like a bed-slat – Tom Gunning suggests just this kind of comedic adaptation, arguing that the film "seems to predict the future of American film comedy … [by] prophetically announcing the blend of Griffith's editing tempo with comic anarchy that Sennett concocted later at Keystone."[6] In my reading, however, this notion of blending misses the critical edge that Arvidson recalled in Sennett, and which operated in the latter's early filmmaking as the indivisible flipside of imitation.

In a substantial subgenre of meta-cinematic productions, in which the nature of filmmaking itself was the implicit subject of the film, Sennett insistently parodied Griffith, and to a lesser extent Ince, in ways that clarify the adversarial language in Fowler's account of Triangle. Ironically, as we shall see, the critical edge of Sennett's parodies had been substantially blunted by this time of the Triangle experiment, for reasons

51

that have much to do with the re-negotiated budgetary basis of Keystone and its elevated status as the most successful of the three brands. Nevertheless, Sennett himself would continue to insist, however playfully, on an antagonistic relationship with his fellow producers, recalling in the pages of the exhibitors' journal, *The Triangle*, how "[h]e early fell under the influence of David W. Griffith, now with Thomas H. Ince, his associate in the production of Triangle plays. His natural tendency to burlesque every serious thing that Griffith did was the turning point of his career."[7]

It is worth pausing to consider Sennett's use of the term "burlesque," and what it suggests about the nature and intent of his imitations. In a study of pastiche and related generic terms, Richard Dyer identifies burlesque with a juxtaposition of high and low thematic content and forms, reserving the term for cases in which either "high subject matter [is] dealt with in a low manner" (travesty) or a "low subject in a high manner" (the mock epic). Sennett's burlesques take both forms, but Dyer extends his discussion of these formal terms to assess a distinction between parody and pastiche that he sees as more fundamental. Recalling Fredric Jameson's use of the same pairing to highlight a central difference between modernist and postmodernist art – in which the latter famously operates on the basis of pastiche or "blank parody" – Dyer's taxonomy aligns parody with burlesque, travesty, or the mock epic as "evaluatively predetermined" forms, functioning as the vehicles of an overtly critical attitude towards the original. Pastiche, by way of contrast, is evaluatively open, thereby retaining Jameson's sense of a "neutral practice" that fails to register a clearly critical attitude or intent.[8] In a crucial respect, Dyer suggests, pastiche speaks with a doubled voice: on the one hand, it will say, "this is what this sort of thing is like and ... get close enough to convey, or remind us of, the flavour of it"; on the other hand, it declares that "this work is not this sort of thing," but only a mock-up.[9] In the process, pastiche highlights the conventionality or artifice of the original, but for no discernible reason – it lacks, in Jameson's terms, the "ulterior motive" of parody.[10]

I will offer examples below of Sennett films that represent each of these categories, but first I want to consider what is at stake in the more overtly antagonistic impulse to parody. I propose to read the early years of American cinema as a time when a submerged contest occurred between generic forms, central among them comedy and melodrama, each of which laid claim to predominance in the new medium of film. The historical moment is strikingly reminiscent of one that Mikhail Bakhtin proposes for the rise of the novel, when the emergence of a new literary form precipitated a jostling for position and a realignment of the cultural landscape. The novel's hegemony, he suggests, was secured by its ability to parody other genres, and ultimately itself: the novel "exposes the conventionality of their forms and their language," he argues, and thus "squeezes out some genres and incorporates others into its own peculiar structure, re-formulating and re-accentuating them."[11] In the process, it undercuts their reason for existing, offering epic novels that expose the dead-weight conventionality of epic poems while giving readers whatever pleasures they might still have gotten from them.

Film might be seen as standing in a parallel relationship to other art forms (both textual and visual) in the early years of the century. Like the novel, it was inherently connected to the present moment (as opposed to ossified forms like the epic poem or the tragic drama), made use of contemporary technology, was inherently international in its appeal, and sought high- and low-class audiences alike. It was also commonly represented as an amalgamation of theater, literature, music, dance, and so on. Thomas Ince, for one, would make this argument in an unpublished essay from 1921 called "History and Development of the Motion Picture Industry," claiming a unique status for film on the basis that "it is a combination of art and industry and subdivided again, a combination of all the fine arts, and mechanical arts as well." In addition, what distinguished film was its extraordinarily rapid ascension, Ince believed, and he speculated that

> never before in the history of the world has there been
> an industry which has had the phenomenal growth
> and development in the short length of time as the
> Motion Picture Industry. Nor is there an industry that
> holds the promise of a greater and more far-reaching
> future than this newest of all the arts.[12]

If this might be taken as a measure of film's modernity, so too might its internalization of the Bakhtinian contest of forms, which shifted rapidly from an external struggle with other media to an intra-generic rivalry among emerging categories of films.

Such a rivalry is implicit, at least, in Sennett's statements and his parodies of Griffithian melodrama. Perhaps most interesting is the case of *The Lonely Villa* (1909), which (as Linda Arvidson recalled) was "the brain child of Mack Sennett, gleaned from a newspaper — good old-fashioned melodrama."[13] The film features a wife and mother besieged at home by burglars and frantically hoping for rescue from her husband, who is at work. Among other things, the film has become famous for its use of cross-cutting to boost suspense, triangulating between the three locations of the wife, husband, and burglars, as well as for its use of the archetypal trope of modernity, the telephone, as a device to link the first two (until the connection is severed by the third). As Gunning has suggested, parallel editing here "becomes a narrative structure, a way of shaping the relations of space and time" that Griffith would subsequently adapt for various other dramatic situations.[14] As such, Griffithian technique has come to embody the very essence of cinematic melodrama, indicative of how suspense and release can be generated largely on the basis of a film's editing pattern.

This, we might argue, is precisely the kind of lesson that Sennett could have learned from Griffith, and the two became linked through their shared emphasis on editing, representing in the words of *Wid's Films and Film Folk*, "the two greatest living 'tempo builders' in the business today."[15] It is telling that Sennett returned to the basic premise of *The Lonely Villa* at least twice, reworking his own original story idea for comedic effect. The first of these was *Help! Help!*, made in 1912 when Sennett was with Biograph. His parodic intent is immediately signaled by the opening intertitle, telling us that "Mrs. Suburbanite Reads of Burglars Operating in the Neighborhood." The film's interest in middle-class paranoia extends to the shadowy presence of men in cloth caps outside the house to whom we cross-cut. Returning to the lonely wife, we see her glance back to her newspaper and then notice a twitching curtain at the extreme left of the frame – at which point she calls her husband at the office. In the end, the twitching curtain is shown to be caused not by the men outside, who soon disappear from the film, but by that most suburban and non-threatening of accessories, a poodle. In between, Sennett faithfully follows Griffith's model of editing by cutting back and forth between husband and wife, and yet in doing so takes their enforced separation to ridiculous lengths. In *The Lonely Villa*, inconvenient repair work on his car means that the husband is forced to commandeer a nearby gypsy cart, but Sennett extends this into the logic of a comedic nightmare: Mr. Suburbanite's car breaks down twice and finally explodes, after which he takes a farmer's cart, but then has to flog the horse to get it moving, and is ultimately chased on foot by the farmer. Meanwhile, his wife goes to equally absurd extremes in her efforts to avoid capture, which, in the film's melodramatic counterpart, had involved locking and boarding up first one and then a second door; in Sennett's version, she gets to her knees and then climbs into a chest (gets out, and back in again) before finally being rescued.

Sennett makes two significant alterations to the Griffith prototype, which he otherwise follows with a precise mimicry. First, as we have seen, he effectively jettisons the narrative logic of the melodramatic rescue, one which Linda Williams has argued "offers a potential three-way alternation between the endangered person, the entrapper (or pursuer), and the rescuer."[16] In its place, *Help! Help!* insists that supposedly external dangers function as part of a bourgeois imaginary, needing to be conjured by the news media if they are not simply inherent to the suburban mindset itself. Second, following on from this, Sennett develops a formal pattern of alternation that seemingly can be extended indefinitely because he is no longer reliant on a logic of actual danger. Since the obstacles placed in the path of the husband are no longer functional plot devices – in the sense that, by delaying his progress, they elevate an actual and growing threat against which they can be measured – they become the motors of the narrative itself, just as parallel editing comes to drive Griffith's film.[17]

Sennett's second re-make of *The Lonely Villa*, 1913's *The Bangville Police*, transplants this suburban cautionary tale into the countryside. Our heroine – played, as in *Help! Help!*, by Mabel Normand – this time is scared by two silhouetted men glimpsed in the barn, but ends up bolting the door and her closet to shut out her parents, as well as the police. While a nominal menace is conjured by her father wielding a pistol through a crack in the door, the comedy is again ultimately one of mistaken identity; it ends with a double reunion of parents with daughter and the family with the police, all of whom celebrate the birth of a new calf, as longed for by the daughter in the opening title of the film. This transposition of suburban angst into rural wish fulfillment suggests a form of rustic utopia in which the police are ultimately unnecessary; or perhaps it is simply the impossibility of the transposition itself that is being signaled, with sensational melodrama implicitly figured as an urban genre and slapstick as impervious to its clumsily manufactured sense of threat. As with the earlier Biograph film, the principle of parallel editing and the tempo of cutting are placed instead in the service of a new logic and aesthetic rooted in chaos, misunderstanding, and digression.

## meta-cinematic parody and pastiche

Despite its associations with cheap theaters frequented by the lower-class audiences in the United States, melodrama was ideally suited to rearticulation to endorse an agenda of bourgeois uplift, first by theatrical directors like Dion Boucicault and David Belasco, and later by filmmakers like Griffith. Crucial to this project was the projection of an individualist ethos that could resonate with Republican values and the trope of the middle-class home as a privileged space under attack; yet the same sensationalist narrative of menace, rescue, and closure also appears in Sennett's slapstick parodies, which thereby manage to do what Bakhtin argued for the nineteenth-century novel in being able to *provide* and at the same time *satirize* the codified effects of Griffith's melodramas. Indeed, such a desire to have its sensation and parody it too was often foregrounded in Keystone's publicity, which, as Douglas Riblet has pointed out, used seeming oxymorons like "thrilling burlesque melodrama" in advertising the company's films.[18] The other component of a hegemonic cultural form, according to Bakhtin, is a readiness to indulge in reflexive critique and self-parody. Here we might consider the incredible rapidity with which early film came to mock its own founding myths. Already by 1901, for instance, Robert Paul's short film "The Countryman and the Cinematograph" was mimicking the celebrated – if perhaps apocryphal – response to the screening of Lumières' *Arrival of a train at La Ciotat* six years earlier, in a way that amplified the original story while shifting its terms of reference. Crucially, in Paul's version it is the rube, and not the urban sophisticates of the Parisian Grand Café, who has trouble separating material reality from filmic fiction.[19]

Sennett himself would play such a character repeatedly, and it is worth thinking about how such a rural figure might have functioned in relation to Keystone's predominantly city-based, working-class – and also heavily immigrant – audience. In one example, *Mabel's Dramatic Career* (1913), he plays a rube designated in company publicity as "Zeke,"[20] whose momentary infatuation with an urban sophisticate causes his real love, Mabel, to head to the city – and ultimately to a successful career in Keystone comedies. So far, this meta-cinematic story feels formulaic, rehearsing a narrative of accelerated stardom that was becoming increasingly familiar from fan magazines and studio publicity. Predictably, Zeke himself shows up in the city and sees a movie theater poster advertising Keystone's *At Twelve O'Clock* with a picture of Mabel. That 1913 film is now lost, and is seemingly not the film we see played on-screen in *Mabel's Dramatic Career*; it was, however, the first of the company's mock melodramas, a parody of Griffith's *The Fatal Hour* (1908), another film in which parallel editing generates the suspense of an attempted rescue, this time as the

Figure 3.1

Production still from *Mabel's Dramatic Career* (1913). Courtesy of the Academy of Motion Picture Arts and Sciences

hands of a clock count down.[21] In Sennett's reworking, Zeke recognizes his old love in the film and, short-circuiting the suspense, tries to shoot at the melodramatic villain on-screen; then – in an oddly truncated coda – he finds the actor at home, living in domestic bliss with Mabel and their children, and fires at him.

Although it purports to represent life behind the scenes, it is unclear from the film-within-a-film whether we should view Mabel as a comedienne or a dramatic heroine. We see her audition by making broadly dramatic arm gestures, but also doing pratfalls, so that it is unclear whether the film that Zeke watches is supposed to be taken as melodrama or (as the poster outside might indicate) as mock-melodrama. Either way, Sennett economically reworks his own film to fashion a dual critique of the genre, both for its contrived plot situations and for its audience response. Zeke's absurd reactions not only take to extremes the emotional investment that melodrama actively encouraged, they also imply a critique of the sensational narratives designed to elicit such response in the first place. If that is the case, then the urban audience for slapstick comedy could feel doubly superior, enjoying the displacement of the terms by which it was customarily ridiculed: for its gullibility concerning the codes of visual literacy, its over-investment in narrative, and its relishing of spectacle. In this sense, parody articulates an attitude of superiority and knowingness (in particular about forms of generic coding) that is the exact opposite of the dumb ignorance of which the slapstick audience was often accused, while the supposedly more sophisticated clientele that Griffith and others sought to attract through melodrama is ridiculed in its place.

We can understand the compensatory functions of these parodies better if we return to my starting point, the launch just two years later of the Triangle Film Corporation. The amalgamated company had originally been proposed under the name of "S.I.G.," combining the surname initials of its three celebrated producers (Sennett–Ince–Griffith), and advance advertising indicated the extent to which it would trade upon their reputations. The name was changed to Triangle, a guiding metaphor that still implied the mutual interdependence of three forces, though these might equally have been Kessel, Baumann, and Aitken, or Triangle's ambitious effort at vertically integrating production, distribution, and exhibition. The first announcement of the long-rumored new company in *Motography* appeared under the headline "BIG THREE FORM TRIANGLE FILM," with the accompanying text – announcing first that "D. W. Griffith, Thomas Ince and Mack Sennett are to be producing directors as well as officers of the company," and mentioning Aitken, Kessel, and Baumann only in a subsequent paragraph – implying a continuing prioritization of the role of the producers.[22] Five months later, as rumors were already circulating that Griffith had failed to hold up his part of the bargain, *Photoplay* reported that "Mr. Sennett and Mr. Ince, probably very busy men, have time to direct their own pictures. Why cannot Mr. Griffith do the same?" Explicitly reading the company name as shorthand for the three star directors, the article proceeded to ask, "Why call a thing a triangle when for all practical purposes it has only two sides?"[23]

Within the block booking structure envisaged by Aitken, Kessel, and Baumann, and in spite of efforts by Sennett to negotiate a position of parity, the Keystone comedies were still considered junior partners to the feature films. The opening program, premiering at New York's prestigious Knickerbocker Theater in September 1915, is a useful case in point. As first announced in the pages of *Motography* in late August, the opening – featuring "Douglas Fairbanks, Raymond Hitchcock and Frank Keenan, each in an original play of an hour's length or more," supervised by Griffith, Sennett, and Ince, respectively – was designed to initiate a model of "triple stellar bills" that would become "the rule of the new enterprise."[24] While the Ince contribution would eventually change, both it and Griffith's were consistently billed as five-reel features; by contrast, there was an ongoing uncertainty about Sennett's *My Valet*, which was advertised ambiguously as simply "a Keystone" two weeks later, then a four-reeler the following week, and a "three-reel farce" on the week of the opening.[25] An article cleared up the confusion, but in doing so indicated how Sennett's ambitions conflicted with the Triangle masterplan. It explained:

> On account of the contracts that the corporation is making with exhibitors throughout the country it has been decided to present four plays the first week as well as in the succeeding weeks. That was the original plan, but the desire of Messrs. Sennett and Hitchcock to run "My Valet" as a four-reeler allowed only three plays.

As a result, a "somewhat abbreviated" version would be screened, along with a Keystone "costume burlesque."[26]

We can see Sennett's work being downgraded here, and his directorial ambitions held in check, as his films are assigned the role of comedic support. And indeed, it is hard to see how they could have functioned otherwise, given the high-art pretensions of Triangle's founders. Aitken, for instance, grandly proclaimed his creed in the first issue of *The Triangle*, announcing his belief

> that motion pictures are a wonderful civilizing influence; that first class motion pictures break down hard-shelled prejudices, make for the elimination of sectional differences, and promote better understanding between artificially created classes of people. Good art makes better men, and good pictures should illustrate good art and good morals, fine motives, high ideals.[27]

The impulse to parody is one effective weapon for puncturing such pretensions, as we have seen, since one of its immediate consequences is to level the playing field by subjecting to scrutiny these reflexive judgments about the "good," "fine," and "high." If that leaves as the only operating criteria the successful, then Sennett would score the last laugh, as Triangle exhibitors routinely demanded more Keystones in order to break even, eventually forcing those films to be made available on the open market. As Rob King notes, this is precisely the message its founders did not want to hear: that "for all its highbrow credentials, the Triangle Film Corporation had ironically been kept afloat by Sennett's slapstick comedies."[28] This success would be trumpeted in the opening issue of the new *Mack Sennett Weekly* in January 1917, in which Sennett crowed that the open market policy signaled "the gratifying growth of our film plays. The demand for these comedies has now become so great that, from a business standpoint, it is no longer practicable to market them in connection with any other picture service."[29]

At the same time, however, extant Keystone pictures from the Triangle period display little of the parodic force that was visible in earlier films like *The Bangville Police* or *Mabel's Dramatic Career*, and instead resemble the pastiches that both Richard Dyer and Fredric Jameson identify with a more neutral form of imitation. Perhaps the most sophisticated of these pastiches is *A Movie Star* (1916), featuring Mack Swain as a western actor who is shown watching his own film, *Big-Hearted Jack* from "Thrill'Em Pictures," in the company of adoring fans. The theater looks like a slightly upgraded version of the one in *Dramatic Career*, and the film-within-a-film that we see — projected first on the movie screen through double exposure, and then full screen — similarly improves upon the earlier film's mock-melodrama. To begin with, as production files make clear, it is not a recycled Keystone release, and great effort has gone into producing a believable imitation western, right down to the design of appropriate lettering for the "Thrill'Em" title-cards. We also see substantially more: over ten minutes of *Big-Hearted Jack* appears within the roughly 24 minutes of *A Movie Star*, whereas we see only two-and-a-half minutes of the inset film in *Mabel's Dramatic Career*.

Like many of the westerns that were a staple of NYMP's early Bison and Broncho imprints, *Big-Hearted Jack* offers a horseback chase, a threatening band of Indians, a shoot-out, an endangered heroine, and an ineffective rival for her affections. Most likely, the film was made using the same props and settings as those sincere westerns, following a model of economic recycling that the NYMP had encouraged ever since moving production out to California.[30] Unlike the earlier parody melodramas, the inset western is not particularly funny, and presumably is not intended to be; its only real joke is to cast the overweight Mack Swain in the central role of hero and have him perform all the feats expected of the western star. As a pastiche, it has no interest in diminishing the original form that it is imitating; indeed, in many ways it *shares* the values of the western, most notably its investment in the persona of the hero. The humor is almost all driven by the meta-cinematic frame, in which the pompous "Jack" combines the roles played by Normand and Sennett in *Mabel's Dramatic Career*. His viewing pleasure is repeatedly disrupted by requests for speeches to the star-struck audience, but in between he gets to guide them in their responses to the film; led by its star, most audience members are able to cry, clap, and marvel in all of the appropriate places. The only hold-outs are a jealous boyfriend, who maintains a deliberate non-engagement with the film as a protest against Jack's flirtatiousness, and a morally superior Shakespearean actor (described as "an old legit" in the film's printed synopsis), who is probably also jealous of the audience's enthusiasm for low cinema – even if a close-up of his business card, telling us he specializes in "Leads and Heavies," suggests that his work might be closer to Jack's than he lets on. It is crucial to note, moreover, that the

Figure 3.2

Production still from *A Movie Star* (1913). Courtesy of the Academy of Motion Picture Arts and Sciences

responses incited by Jack are not inappropriate, as is the case with *Mabel's Dramatic Career*. Indeed, *A Movie Star* makes clear, in part through the snobbish disdain of the Shakespearean actor, that the audience's cinematic pleasure is genuine, even if it has to be coaxed. In that sense, where "Zeke" was too actively involved with the melodrama unfolding on-screen, the viewers for *Big-Hearted Jack* are too passively in awe of the star's presence, but nonetheless capable of performing "proper" spectatorship.

For a studio that famously had problems dealing with stars — to the extent that its managing director would ruefully describe a pattern in which actors would "start with Sennett and get rich somewhere else" — the joke of the film is a complicated one. As Ambrose, Swain had been heavily promoted as a Keystone star and recurring character around the time the studio had its short-lived success with Chaplin and was looking for his successor. Inevitably, though, "Big-Hearted Jack" has to be taken down, in what feels a little like a *pro forma* slapstick ending: his aggressive wife sees him flirting with his female admirers and beats him with an umbrella all the way home. By displacing the critical mockery away from its audience and onto its own promotional and exhibition practices, Keystone would seem to be fulfilling Bakhtin's key requirement that a hegemonic form be prepared to ridicule itself as well as other genres, but what slips beyond the horizon of ridicule is the form of the western itself. The humor is even less visible in the earlier *Hogan Out West* (1915), featuring another recurring Keystone character played by Charlie Murray. Murray's wiry frame lends an air of comic incongruity similar to that of Swain's comic girth, and he too can successfully perform the role of the western hero, ultimately saving the girl from a shack loaded with dynamite like the one in *Big-Hearted Jack*. The oddest moment in *Hogan Out West* is its finale, as the shack explodes and the protagonist is propelled into the air, to land first on a church steeple and then a city street, replete with a hat and umbrella. What is awkwardly being attempted here, I think, is what Jack's hectoring wife performs at the end of *A Movie Star*: the reintegration of Keystone into the urban world of slapstick after its brief sojourn in the landscape of the western. The transition seems especially grating, though, because we have so fully absorbed the conventions and values of the other genre, in a manner that feels very different from the earlier parody melodramas.

61

## conclusion: "why good films are costly"

As Dyer argues, a pastiche is easier to mistake for what it imitates than a parody, in part because it inevitably "facilitates an experience" of the other work, and the more complicated aim of its author is something like that which Dyer ascribes to Proust in replicating the prose style of the Goncourt brothers: "It demonstrates that Proust could write like the

Goncourts if he wanted," even as his "easy, unmocking ability to repro-
duce the form and style" of the latter insists that he does not want them
"knocked down or reacted against."[31] Sennett also wants us to recognize
his ability to stage a western in miniature, just as effectively (and presumably more efficiently) than Tom Ince could, and in doing so he gives the
genre a tacit approval that he had earlier withheld from melodrama.
Returning to the terms set out by Bakhtin, we might say that pastiche
separates the twinned strategic intentions behind parody, offering an imitation (and thus, the pleasures of the original) but not an attendant critique (with the implication that such pleasures are at the same time
unworthy or inauthentic); indeed, as the comparison of *A Movie Star* and
*Mabel's Dramatic Career* suggests, there is an underlying calculus here, with
the critical impulse inevitably dissipating to the extent that the accuracy
of the imitation increases.

This is not to argue that pastiche represents a simple withdrawal from
the contest of forms that was Bakhtin's central focus. In the case of
Sennett, indeed, we might consider his western pastiches as the continua-
tion of the "bed-slat" battle by other means, offering an implicit argument for parity with Ince that, in the larger context of Triangle, had as
much to do with the distribution of resources as it did with prestige. It is
no coincidence that research into Triangle's complicated financial
arrangements, first by Kalton Lahue and more recently by Rob King, has
revealed a substantial increase in the financing of Keystone products in
this period. Precise figures are impossible to calculate, but King's estimate
that the cost of producing a two-reeler rose from around $7,000 to $20,000
gives a useful indication of the trajectory, as does his assessment that
much of the additional expense was made visible in the filmic *mise-en-scène*.
Increasingly, King notes, Keystone traded the representation of working-
class culture for "depictions of luxury and consumer pleasures," staged in
"opulent, upper-middle class settings."[32] We might point to another
installment of the Hogan series, *Hogan's Aristocratic Dream* (1915), made
shortly before the Triangle launch, to illustrate this. Essentially the same
protagonist (though in reality a bum) opens the film by dreaming an
elaborate and costly fantasy of life at a royal court, rife with a familiar set
of courtly intrigues and culminating in the kind of elaborate sword fights
that were a hallmark of the historical genre. What we get here, and also
in *Ye Olden Grafter* (1915), is the transposition of slapstick violence into a
different social register; both are pastiches that produce no polemical
effect beyond the obvious burlesque of being Keystone comedies set in
jarring historical and social contexts.

Where I depart from both Lahue and King is in their supposition that
the impulse for greater spending originated outside of Sennett and Keystone itself. For Lahue, "cost consciousness became less of a concern than
it ever had before" for those in "the New York office," whom he claims

"begged Sennett to spend more money on his comedies," while King similarly suggests that Harry Aitken "consistently encouraged his three producers to spend more money than was required to bring costs up to the standard he considered desirable."[33] There is some evidence for these claims, most notably in the disastrous hiring policy that Triangle heads imposed on Sennett by offering inflated salaries to Broadway and big-time vaudeville stars who invariably failed to make the transition to film. But there is also evidence that Sennett was seeking to upgrade the look of the Keystone comedies, and was happy to spend additional production revenues, in part because it allowed him something closer to parity with Ince and Griffith. The most telling evidence for this can be found in an interview that Sennett gave to *Moving Picture World* in August 1914, at least nine months prior to the formation of Triangle, and at a time when he and Ince were hoping to force contract re-negotiations with Kessel and Baumann. Sennett's principal bargaining chip during those negotiations was the recently completed *Tillie's Punctured Romance*, an unprecedented six-reel comedy starring Chaplin, Normand, and Broadway star Marie Dressler (who had been hired by Sennett himself). In the interview he praised the film's lavish budget: "We have spared no necessary expense," he boasted,

> As an illustration of this, we wanted a real snow scene. A company was sent up into the mountains, twelve or fourteen thousand feet above sea level. The party camped out in the snow, and was gone a week. Some fine stuff was obtained, but we used just one hundred feet. That was what we wanted.

This leads Sennett to consider in more general terms the future of filmmaking, and comedy specifically: "We intend to try to steadily improve our productions and also from time to time to change the character of the work," he claims, having

> near[ed] the stage where we want to advance the scope of our subjects — not that the public shows any indications of being tired of Keystone stuff, but we desire to anticipate the wishes of the public, to keep ahead of the times.

As Sennett looks ahead, he previews the managerial language of the Triangle heads in his stated desire to spend more on productions: "It is our view," he opines, "that to be stingy in making pictures is to pursue a policy that is penny wise and pound foolish. A poor way to make money is to try to save it out of the film."[34] We can compare such statements with those made by Aitken on the launch of Triangle, or the editorial statement in the first issue of *The Triangle*, which insisted that "Sometimes lavish expenditure is the surest economy," or even Sennett's own comments in *Mack Sennett Weekly*, such as his editorial comment from January 1917 explaining "Why Good Films are Costly": in every case, there is the same insistence that the quality of a film flows directly from its initial production cost.[35]

As I have tried to argue, the revised budgetary basis of Sennett's films from around 1914 onwards coincides with – and may even drive – a content shift from parody to pastiche. The films from 1912 to 1913, like *Help! Help!*, *The Bangville Police*, and *Mabel's Dramatic Career*, function as travesties of the high-blown moral pretensions of Griffithian melodrama, showing how inappropriate its sentiments could be when transposed into other locales or generic forms. By contrast, the values of the western survive relatively unscathed to the extent that they supply dramatic underpinning for later comedic pastiches like *A Movie Star* or *Hogan Out West*, although it would no doubt be reductive to see in such a shift an endorsement of the latter genre where the former is subject to critique – indeed, the western emerges from these pastiches *as* a form of melodrama in many respects. The difference is attributable more, I would argue, to a changing conception of the place of film in the social order of the mid-1910s, and to a greater commitment – on the part of Sennett, as well as his immediate superiors – to producing a high-quality product in which "lavish expenditure" (if necessary) would be rendered visible on-screen. These two phases of Sennett's filmic output, characterized in turn by parody and pastiche, were not, then, working in opposition to each other, but instead were complementary battles in a larger war for recognition and respect, with each of his moves dictated to a remarkable degree by those of his triangulated combatants, D. W. Griffith and Thomas Ince.

### notes

1. For background on the history of Triangle, see Kalton C. Lahue, *Dreams For Sale: The Rise and Fall of the Triangle Film Corporation* (South Brunswick: A. S. Barnes, 1971); and Rob King, " 'Made for the Masses with an Appeal to the Classes': The Triangle Film Corporation and the Failure of Highbrow Film Culture," *Cinema Journal* 44.2 (2005): 3–33.
2. Gene Fowler, *Father Goose* (New York: Avon Books, 1974), 48.
3. Mrs. D. W. Griffith (Linda Arvidson), *When the Movies Were Young* (New York: E. P. Dutton, 1925), 77–78.
4. Mack Sennett, *The King of Comedy* (Garden City: Doubleday, 1954), 55.
5. Arvidson, *When the Movies*, 77.
6. Tom Gunning, *D. W. Griffith and the Origins of American Narrative Film: The Early Years at Biograph* (Urbana: University of Illinois Press, 1991), 132.
7. See "Sennett Has Big Army at Laugh Factory," *The Triangle*, March 11 (1916): 3.
8. Richard Dyer, *Pastiche* (London: Routledge, 2007), 24. Jameson's famous description of pastiche as "blank parody" can be found in his *Postmodernism, or the Cultural Logic of Late Capitalism* (Durham: Duke University Press, 1992), 17.
9. Dyer, *Pastiche*, 89.

10. Jameson, *Postmodernism*, 17.

11. M. M. Bakhtin, *The Dialogic Imagination: Four Essays*, trans. Caryl Emerson and Michael Holquist (Austin: University of Texas Press, 1981), 5.

12. See Thomas Ince, "History and Development of the Motion Picture Industry," unpublished manuscript, Arts Library Special Collections, UCLA.

13. Arvidson, *When the Movies*, 100. As Gunning argues, however, the film bears striking resemblance to a French play from 1901, *Au Télephone*, and to a Pathé reworking of the same material, *Terrible Angoisse*, which was released in the United States in 1908 as *A Narrow Escape* (D. W. Griffith, 195–196).

14. Gunning, *D. W. Griffith*, 204.

15. "Tempo – The Value Of It," from *Wid's Films and Film Folk*, October 7 (1915), cited in Douglas Riblet, "The Keystone Company and the Historiography of Early Slapstick," in Kristine Brunovska Karnick and Henry Jenkins, eds., *Classical Hollywood Comedy* (London: Routledge, 1995), 178.

16. Linda Williams, *Playing the Race Card: Melodramas of Black and White from Uncle Tom to O. J. Simpson* (Princeton: Princeton University Press, 2002), 131.

17. In terms first proposed by Roland Barthes, we might say that melodrama's emphasis on the hermeneutic code, through which mystery is "suggested, formulated, held in suspense, and finally disclosed," is displaced here by one of its constituent tropes, delay. See Barthes, *S/Z*, trans. Richard Miller (New York: Noonday, 1974), 19, 75.

18. Riblet, "The Keystone Company," 180.

19. This is one of the reasons, Tom Gunning has suggested, why the Lumière story has continued to circulate; hearing or seeing it, we can't help but measure our own distance from that other audience, whether separated in time (as the novices of film's prehistory) or space (as our own country cousins). See Gunning, "An Aesthetic of Astonishment: Early Film and the (In)Credulous Spectator," reprinted in Linda Williams, ed., *Viewing Positions: Ways of Seeing Film* (New Brunswick: Rutgers University Press, 1995), 114–133.

20. See the advertisement in *Moving Picture World*, September 20 (1913): 1245.

21. As Kalton Lahue and Terry Brewer describe the plot of *At Twelve O'Clock*, "The rejected lover bound lovely Mabel tightly in front of an old grandfather's clock, which had been timed to fire a bullet at the stroke of twelve." See Kalton C. Lahue and Terry Brewer, *Kops and Custard: The Legend of Keystone Films* (Norman: University of Oklahoma Press, 1968), 45.

22. *Motography*, July 28 (1915): 204.

23. *Photoplay*, December (1915), cited in Anthony Slide, *The Kindergarten of the Movies: A History of the Fine Arts Company* (Metuchen: Scarecrow Press, 1980), 8.

24. "Opening Bill of Triangle: Three Big Features," *Motography*, August 21 (1915): 339.

25. See Triangle advertisements in *Motography*, September 4 (1915): 13; September 11 (1915): 13; and September 25 (1915): 21.

26. "Triangle Bill Changed: Second Keystone Comedy Scheduled," *Motography*, September 25 (1915): 627. The original plan had been made clear, both in the trade press and in Sennett's own contract with Triangle from July 30, 1915, in which Keystone agreed to furnish two films per week, of 1,800–2,300 feet. This, as well as the re-negotiated contract from September 1916, are in the Mack Sennett collection at the Margaret Herrick Library, Academy of Motion Picture Arts and Sciences.

27. Aitken, "The Great Triangle Idea – Its Full Scope and Purpose," *The Triangle*, October 23 (1915): 7.

28. King, " 'Made for the Masses,' " 19.

29. "Sennett Tells of New Plans: Releases are Unrestricted," *Mack Sennett Weekly*, January 1 (1917): 1.

30. In *Father Goose*, for instance, Gene Fowler notes that

> Whenever Ince had a big picture in progress, he would telephone the news to Mack … [who] who "would concoct a story suitable to the background of the Ince super-special, take his comedians to Santa Monica, stop the dramatic director and shoot scenes with his clowns in front of the Ince actors. These "spectacles" enhanced Sennett's reputation. His competitors could not afford such grand-scale efforts.
>
> (148)

31. Dyer, *Pastiche*, 60, 62.

32. King, " 'Made for the Masses,' " 24.

33. See Lahue, *Dreams for Sale*, 133; King, " 'Made for the Masses,' " 9.

34. "Mack Sennett Talks About his Work," *Moving Picture World*, August 15 (1914): 968.

35. See editorial in *The Triangle*, 23 October (1915): 2; editorial in *Mack Sennett Weekly*, 15 January (1917): 1.

# both sides of the

# camera*

roscoe "fatty" arbuckle's

evolution at keystone

f o u r

j o a n n a   e .   r a p f

In the second decade of the twentieth century, during cinema's adolescence, Roscoe "Fatty" Arbuckle, a cherub-faced innocent with a very large body, created comedy on the silent screen that, for a time, rivaled Charlie Chaplin's in popularity. Both men wet their film feet, literally and figuratively, at Keystone and became skilled behind the camera as well as in front, with their own studios and full artistic control of their films. But unlike Chaplin, Arbuckle is largely forgotten, remembered today, if he is remembered at all, for the infamous scandal that destroyed his career.

Remarkably, there are no major critical studies of his work.[1] His neglect is due to a number of factors, including the notorious scandal that effectively ended his stardom, helped to erase him from the annals of comic film history, and to dump him into the garbage heap of Hollywood's sordid past. But other reasons include the fact that, until some recent DVD releases, his films have been hard to see; unlike Keaton, he had no Raymond Rohauer to "rediscover" him, nor did he have the inclination or foresight of a Lloyd or Chaplin to preserve his work. It has also

Figure 4.1

Arbuckle at work behind the camera. Courtesy of the British Film Institute

been said that he never developed a distinct persona, such as Chaplin, Keaton, or Lloyd, a "failing" that is also occasionally applied to Harry Langdon, who has suffered similar critical neglect. Langdon and Arbuckle share some other interesting similarities, notably that their personae often embody a disturbing combination of childish behavior and adult drives. Arbuckle, like Langdon, could be an innocent country rube, a flirt, or a hen-pecked husband with a wandering eye. He could be a drunk, a bum, a swell-about-town, or a young lady in drag. His characters cover a range of social classes, unified only by the fact that they are played by a very fat man. This has led some to suggest that another reason we have almost erased him from our critical and cultural memory is that even his "[m]ultiple characters suggest how much like us he was, constantly testifying to a commonly shared nature or sameness."[2] Except for his size, he was not unique enough, and his size was usually not the center of his gags; he became "too much an undifferentiated type."[3] Yet that "sameness" was something for which he aimed in his work. In an interview with Robert F. Moore in *Motion Picture Classic*, he explained that he preferred comedy to drama because "it is a study of human nature":

> You put a character in a certain farcical situation, and then figure out what he will do. *What he does must be typical.* For the audience laughs not only at the screen comedy, but also, in some degree, because the same sort of incident has happened to them.[4]

To Moore he suggests that the "incident" or gag – which he defines as "a piece of by-play which has no direct connection with plot" – should be "burlesque rather than slapstick, for burlesque is the highest type of the dramatic art, and all comedians should strive for it."[5] It is not at all clear what he means by "burlesque." As quoted by his wife, Minta, Arbuckle used the word in a disparaging sense when he said he did not initially like doing movies: "This kind of work is like dropping from grand opera to burlesque."[6] If burlesque is beneath opera, then slapstick would seem to be an even lower form, a type of fast-paced comedy with minimal plot where, as Arbuckle observed, the gags are unconnected to any kind of narrative progression.[7] But as Arbuckle evolved as a director, he obviously became more and more interested in narrative, presumably relating gags to what he called "burlesque" rather than slapstick, in the service of "dramatic art."

As a performer, however, he was also unconventional, defying the stereotype of the large comic by being remarkably agile. In a *Photoplay* article discussing the Arbuckle unit's later work at Fort Lee, New Jersey, Randolph Bartlett writes, "A, in addition to standing for Arbuckle, stands for acrobatic, agile, athletic, ablebodied [sic], alert, active, animated, alive, astir, and so on."[8] As Sam Stoloff notes, his comic effects "were frequently a result of this sense of incongruity between his girth and his agility."[9] For Stoloff, Arbuckle had "a baby's body grown to monstrous proportions" so that he was simultaneously asexual and "voraciously hypersexual."[10] In the light of the scandal that later destroyed his career, this uneasy hybridity perhaps explains why James Agee ignored him in the 1949 breakthrough *Life* essay, "Comedy's Greatest Era," that helped return Chaplin, Keaton, and Lloyd to public acclaim, and why Walter Kerr barely mentions him in his landmark work, *The Silent Clowns*, where he describes

Sennett's Keystone comedies as "primitive," and compares their raucous playfulness to the behavior of chimpanzees.[11]

The perspective on film comedy that dismissed early slapstick as "primitive" is, fortunately, no longer in favor. A revival of interest in the early work of Roscoe Arbuckle has contributed to the recognition of the sophistication of much early cinema. In a review in the *Village Voice* of the 2004 film series at the American Museum of the Moving Image in New York, "Fatty Arbuckle and Friends," Jim Hoberman singled out Arbuckle for praise: "Agile and buoyant, Arbuckle bobs and weaves among the gross stereotypes of Sennett's Keystone comedies, floating slightly above the ruckus of that expulsive, brutish world like a rogue helium balloon."[12] More recently, the Museum of Modern Art (MoMA) presented a program in 2006, "Rediscovering Roscoe: The Careers of 'Fatty' Arbuckle." The plural in the title is significant, for Arbuckle cannot be pigeonholed in one career alone; he was an actor, director, producer, and mentor to other performers. The program note by Steve Massa begins:

> A fresh look at the films of Roscoe "Fatty" Arbuckle has been long overdue. For more than eighty years, in the wake of the famous scandal and trials that buried his reputation in the 1920s, it has been impossible to separate the legend surrounding Arbuckle from his work as a filmmaker and comedian. With the exception of his shorts with Buster Keaton, Arbuckle was routinely dismissed as "primitive," "vulgar," or "not funny in himself," and until recently the films were rarely revived. The time has come to give the man, who for a number of years was second only to Chaplin in popularity, his due. A large number of his films survive revealing an immensely likeable clown, an innovative comedy creator and a sophisticated director.[13]

Arbuckle's work at Keystone between 1913 and 1915 substantiates Massa's claim in the last sentence, including the fact that he was not just a clown, but also a "sophisticated director." He joined Mack Sennett's fledgling company in April 1913. While there, he appeared in over 100 one- and two-reelers, and like many on the Sennett lot, including Mabel Normand, went from being simply a performer and then a star in front of the camera, to becoming a director behind it. K. Owen in *Photoplay* for August of 1915 told his readers: "In addition to being an athlete and comedian, Roscoe is also one of the premier comedy directors in the movies. He directs all his own plays and has turned out more comedies than any man in the business."[14] Beginning with *Barnyard Flirtations* in March of 1914, he directed all his own films for Keystone, Triangle/Keystone, and Comique up until 1920, "with the exception of a few comedies directed by Charles Chaplin (*The Masquerader*, 1914, *The Rounders*, 1914), Mack Sennett (*The Little Teacher*, 1915), and co-directed by Ferris Hartman (*The Waiters' Ball*, 1916)."[15]

When Arbuckle came to Keystone, the resident "fat" comic was Fred Mace. Originally trained as a dentist, Mace had quit that profession for a career in musical comedy and became one of the founding members of Keystone. (An advertisement for the new Keystone label in November 1912 even lists Mace's name first in the company's talent roster, citing the leading players as Fred Mace, Mabel Normand, Mack Sennett, and Ford Sterling, starring in "High Class Comedy and Dramatic Subjects."[16]) Almost forgotten now, Mace rapidly became a major player in film comedy. A *Photoplay* report from December 1912 testifies to his remarkable popularity:

> Fred Mace (Keystone) is known from coast to coast as a comedian without a peer. His funny antics on stage have kept audiences in a constant roar whenever he has appeared, and now that he has been coaxed from the musical comedy stage to the broader field which films afford, he has well nigh doubled his previous popularity, for he is now playing to thousands nightly where before he could only play to hundreds at one time. If you want a hearty laugh just hunt up the nearest theater showing a Keystone and we'll guarantee you'll chuckle.[17]

There is no evidence that Arbuckle was hired as a "replacement" for Mace, although this is often mentioned. In an interview with George A. Posner in *Motion Pictures*, September 14, 1914, Arbuckle himself says he had been at Keystone for four weeks before Mace left in May of 1913 to make comedies for Harry E. Aitken's Majestic Motion Picture Company.[18] It is sometimes said that Mace and Arbuckle both appeared in *The Bangville Police* (d. Henry Lehrman, April 1913), but a close look at this hayseed collection of country-clad cops does not show Arbuckle. Mace is the bespectacled chief of police, with a long goatee that Mabel Normand playfully pulls at the end, and Charles Avery rides with him in the malfunctioning #13 car, but the other four cops seen running across the hillsides to rescue Mabel from supposed burglars do not include Arbuckle. *The Foreman of the Jury* (d. Mack Sennett, May 22) is also commonly listed as an early Keystone pairing of Mace and Arbuckle, but again there is no evidence for this since the film is lost.[19] However, *The Gangsters* (d. Henry Lehrman), with Mace and Arbuckle, released on May 29, is extant and in the collection at MoMA. This may be Arbuckle's first film for Keystone and he plays a prominent role as a cop dealing with a group of gangsters headed by Mace.[20] Nicknamed "Spike," Mace's character has a background in boxing, a sport that had always been of great interest to the comic. In fact, between 1912 and 1914 he played a boxer named "One Round O'Brien" in a series of films, first for Sennett and than at Majestic. He also spent some time in the spring of 1915 in Havana "where he and H. H. Frazer cooked up a scenario to be built around the Johnson–Willard fight there on the fourth of April."[21] In *The Gangsters*, there is a fight over Spike's girl, in which Roscoe is hit with a boxing glove and, in response, does his famous push-with-his-belly at Mace. The gangsters then pull off Roscoe's pants (a comical embarrassment that would occur in a number of subsequent Keystones) and Arbuckle returns to the police station *sans* trousers. After a title card, "War is Declared," we see a number of the cops similarly losing their pants to Spike's gang. Cinematically, there is nothing particularly subtle about this short. Shot with a stationary camera, there is one memorable moment where a threatening Mace walks toward the camera into a close-up, much like the villains in D. W. Griffith's *The Musketeers of Pig Alley* (1912), and there is an eloquent long shot at the end of the film as the cops are rescued from the water and hauled on ropes up a bridge. There is little narrative; typical of the early Keystones, the scenario is basically an excuse for a string of fast-paced gags. Stoloff describes the slapstick format:

> Violent, gag-based short comedies which escalated in tempo until they concluded with a crescendo of acrobatic chase and combat. These climactic battles usually included thrown projectiles (often but not necessarily pies), kicks in the rear, somersaults, belly flops, and frequently concluded with all participants doused in some convenient body of water.[22]

This is certainly true of *The Gangsters*; but as a director rather than as a performer, Arbuckle soon moved beyond the simple formula.

His jolly, youthful appearance belied his intelligence. An article in the *New York Telegraph* for October 31, 1915 commented on the fact that

> Roscoe Arbuckle has attained such a high pedestal in laugh filmology by reason of his brain as well as his weight-ridden physique. Roscoe may act foolish before the camera, but he is one of the most sensible young men in pictures. He is ... the right hand man of Mr. Sennett and is responsible for the success of many of the films in which he does not appear at all ... but has directed.[23]

Arbuckle came to understand that film offered possibilities not available on the stage, where he had begun his career, including not only the tricks and pacing of editing (for which Sennett was known), but also the eloquence of reactive performance during long durational takes, the subtlety of small details, the emotion behind the quotidian, and the use of depth of field. It is commonplace to see what is sometimes called a "maturing" of his comic style when Keystone merged with Triangle in 1915 and there was an attempt, as Rob King has shown, to appeal to a more refined audience.[24] Playful comedies that delighted in calling attention to their own artifice gave way to a more classical and sentimental narrative form, as can certainly be seen in Arbuckle's first film for Keystone/Triangle, *Fatty and Mabel Adrift* (January 1916).

Figure 4.2

A sentimental moment from *Fatty and Mabel Adrift* (1916). Roscoe accepts Mabel's rock-hard biscuits – with the help of his brilliant dog, Luke. Courtesy of the Academy of Motion Picture Arts and Sciences

In Arbuckle's work before 1916 there may be nothing as sentimental or touching as Roscoe gently accepting Mabel's rock-hard biscuits – with the help of his brilliant dog, Luke – or that glorious shadow kiss of his new bride, about which his neighbor, Hobart Bosworth, wrote in February 1916:

> You manage to infuse these things with a genuine and very pure sentiment that leavens all the mass of farcical action, and I don't know how you do it. I lay much of it to your own personality which is wholesome and decent. Your touch is so sure, and right in the midst of some uproarious situation, you give a touch that is as full of poetry and sentiment as anything I ever saw. Many times since I saw "Adrift" I have said that the business of the shadowy good-night kiss was the most touchingly poetic thing I have ever seen in a motion picture.[25]

But there is a good deal that is gentle, subtle, and touching before 1916. In *I, Fatty: A Novel*, author Jerry Stahl has Arbuckle say about the shorts he directed while working at Educational in the 1920s and 1930s, after the scandal: "I was trying to capture a feeling, not just set up a gag."[26] Like others at Keystone, he was masterful at setting up gags, but as a director he quickly learned how "to capture a feeling" through his use of reaction shots, detail, and long durational takes. He was also a perfectionist, a director with a penchant for a high shooting ratio, a characteristic we commonly assign to Chaplin. Kalton Lahue notes that he spent a whole day shooting the pancake-flipping sequence in *Fatty's Tintype Tangle* (July 1915), which lasts only a few seconds on screen.[27] Arbuckle's perfectionism initially irritated Mack Sennett, who shot fast and tried to use everything he captured with the camera. But Arbuckle's films made money, so Sennett allowed him free rein.

In a number of interviews throughout his early career, Arbuckle talks about the development of his techniques. Randolph Bartlett has Arbuckle describe how he figures out gags ahead of time on paper: "Naturally, I figure pretty carefully, because I don't want to roll off a roof more than seven or eight times just for a foot or two of film."[28] In *Motion Picture* for March 1918, Arbuckle wrote, "I really build the scenarios as I work on a picture, tho naturally it is essential to have some sort of skeleton to follow.... So much goes into a comedy that is not apparent in the finished product."[29] More specifically, a publicity release from Paramount Pictures by Charles E. Meyer, dated June 1917, quotes Arbuckle on directing a scene:

> All you have to do in comedy is to count one, two three, four, five [sic]. This is just the simplest kind of human situation, but it must be spaced before the

camera. In comedy only one person can get a laugh at a time. When two people try to get it the situation is spoiled.... There is a rhythm to comedy just as surely as there is to a symphony or a sonata. You must be able to count the beats in the action on the screen or it is not done properly. There is nothing strange or remarkable about that. It is one of the fundamentals of good comedy.[30]

Sennett often had his whole crew striving for laughs. Arbuckle shaped his films differently. He was known to be generous with his actors, allowing them to shine in individual comic routines. "An actor doesn't lose anything by effacing himself once in a while," he said in an interview with Elizabeth Seas in 1916.[31]

The public's taste for comedy seems to have evolved between 1913 when Arbuckle joined Keystone and 1916 when he went east to shoot for Sennett at the Triangle/Keystone studios in Fort Lee, New Jersey. This is evident from a series of *Photoplay* pieces covering Charlie Chaplin's career from his start at Keystone in 1914 to his work at Essanay in 1915. Chaplin is described in June 1915 as "an orgy in a pantry; a thin show salesman in Roscoe Arbuckle's pants; a lunch counter in an earthquake park adjoining an asylum."[32] In that same issue, in a call for short comedies, *Photoplay* cautions: "Remember, that it is the situation that makes for real comedy and not foolish, childish acting, such as has been indulged in so freely in the past and of which the public has now become tired and disgusted."[33] In July, Harry C. Carr began a four-part story on Chaplin, who was then called "the most popular comedian that the motion picture industry has yet produced."[34] This issue includes a picture of Chaplin, "Champion of Laughmakers" and Arbuckle "the Giggle Dreadnought" at the San Francisco Fair.[35] They are good friends. The August article on Chaplin discusses his time at Keystone, suggesting he did not fit into the Sennett style of work. After Sennett let him do his own direction,

> Chaplin introduced a new note into moving pictures. Theretofore most of the comedy effects had been riotous boisterousness. Chaplin, like many foreign pantomimists got his effects in a more subtle way and with less action.... By making the most of the little subtle effects, Chaplin enlarged the field of all motion picture comedies.[36]

75

The third part of this series in September compares Ford Sterling's speed with Chaplin's comedy, which is described as "slow and deliberate," making "a great deal out of little things – little subtleties."[37] The conclusion, in October, simply states: "It is plain to the careful observer that

Chaplin is *working toward something entirely new in pictures*. In a general way, his idea is that comedy should be more subtle and have more real story."[38] Since both Chaplin and Arbuckle worked together at Keystone and were friends, they no doubt influenced each other as directors. In 1916, discussing Sennett's decision to send him east to direct, Arbuckle sounds very much like Chaplin in his recognition that comedy has changed: "Mr. Sennett trusted me to come to New York.... He knows my ideas are along the newer lines of screen comedy." Asked if the public wants the kind of comedy that gets "its laughs mixed up with its thoughts," he replied: "I'm banking on it." He goes on to state confidently: "I believe in comedy that makes you think, and I believe that the time has come to put it on – and that's what I am going to do."[39] (It is worth noting that Mabel Normand, who also directed, was similarly aware that comedy was changing. In an article by James R. Quirk in 1915 she said, "The comedy of four or five years ago was a very different affair from those made today."[40])

Arbuckle's sensitivity and subtlety are most obvious in the films he did with Normand, especially the so-called "Fatty and Mabel" series. Those he did with his wife, Minta Durfee, and other actresses, tended to be more gag-oriented, anti-sentimental, and in their own way, subversive. *Fatty Joins the Force* (November 1913) was directed by George Nichols, who had been an actor with Sennett at Biograph, working under the direction of D. W. Griffith. Nichols' first credit as a director was also at Biograph in 1911, and he would rejoin Sennett early in Keystone's career. *Fatty Joins the Force* seems a typical Sennett product, involving a park location, scenes in the water, the Keystone Kops, and even a pie in the face (put on Arbuckle by a young Jack White, who would grow up to be a top comedy producer for Educational Films in the 1920s and who employed Arbuckle as William Goodrich after the scandal). Its loose narrative makes fun of the traditional happy endings of comedies, and spoofs the idea of a faithful romance. Pushed in the water by Minta, Roscoe rescues the police commissioner's child, is rewarded by a position on the force, becomes a victim of some youngsters' pranks, loses his clothes, and runs around the streets as a "wild man" while the cops think he has drowned. Recovered, Roscoe does not get the girl, but ends up in jail for being the victim of a prank while the girl flirts with another man. This "plot," as in many other Keystones, reinforces an idea explored by such scholars as Peter Krämer that it is possible to read cultural critique (even if not intended) behind "slapstick's violent subversion of the social order."[41] But basically, the narrative is an excuse for a series of gags, none of which is particularly ingenious. The falls show off Arbuckle's remarkable acrobatic agility; the crosscutting between the cops searching the pond while others chase their "wild" and undressed comrade through the park creates a certain amount of fast-paced tension (how will it end?); but almost everything is in medium shot, with a stationary camera. For example, at the end, when

76

Roscoe, wet and bedraggled, is hauled into the police station, the scene is all in medium shot, as if the characters were acting on stage to the camera in third row center of the audience. After Roscoe is carried off to jail, there is a cut to a famous close-up of his face behind bars (famous because of the later scandal), another cut to the same medium shot as before as Minta flirts with the police chief, and finally, a closing close-up of Arbuckle's face, seeming to react in anger to both his jailing and the flirtation.

*A Bath House Beauty* (April 1914) again features Minta, but this time Arbuckle is directing and the cinematic quality of the film is notably superior to the earlier Nichols film. The narrative, however, is still relatively undeveloped, simply providing a spine that allows for a series of fast-moving gags and a brief, unsentimental conclusion. It starts with Fatty and his prudish wife and bratty son at the beach. Fatty sees an alluring Minta in her bathing costume and sneaks away from his family to spend time with her. They go dancing, which allows Arbuckle to show off his considerable grace and agility, reflecting Louise Brooks' sensual observation: "He was a wonderful dancer. It was like floating in the arms of a huge doughnut."[42] Minta's boyfriend (Edgar Kennedy) spots them of course and this sets off a conflict (allowing Roscoe again to do his belly bump) and a chase. He runs into the ladies' dressing room and emerges "disguised" as a large woman in a garishly striped bathing costume. As a girl, he can fool everyone but his son, who recognizes his father and tells the mother. Darting back into the ladies' dressing room (he tries to go into the men's room, but is not allowed by an attendant), Roscoe horrifies Minta who is in there changing and recognizes that he is a man when he loses his wig. She calls the Keystone Kops. This expands the chase through the seaside amusement park, with not only the rival after Fatty, but also the cops and the family. Cutting between long shots and close reaction shots of Fatty's face, Arbuckle uses this setting to create dramatic moving action, putting his camera on a roller coaster with the cops in one car and Fatty in another. As audience members, we share the ride with Fatty, looking directly at his terrified face as his car rolls up and down the sinuous tracks. Lauren Rabinovitz, in an essay about Coney Island comedies, has written that one of the pleasures of early cinema was its "visceral engagement and *jouissance*," the audience's thrill in actually experiencing physical sensation rather than being a passive observer.[43] *A Bath House Beauty* is a perfect example of this, predating Arbuckle's later Comique film with Buster Keaton, *Fatty at Coney Island* (1917), which Rabinovitz discusses. With quick cutting between long shots and close-ups as the chase builds, we also experience Fatty on a merry-go-round and a whirl-a-ding, a contraption whose use is thoughtfully anticipated in the background of the film's very first shot. It all ends, like so many Keystone films, with a motorboat and a dock and everyone falling into the water, including Fatty, who is pushed in by his wife.

In June of the same year, Chaplin and Arbuckle appeared together in *The Knockout*, along with Minta. This boxing comedy is noteworthy for a number of reasons, besides the fact that it once again ends, like *A Bath House Beauty*, with everyone falling off a pier into the water. The boxing scenes certainly seem to have influenced Chaplin, who would include similar moments in *The Champion* (1915), *The Kid* (1921), and *City Lights* (1931). Besides the elaborate fight choreography, it also has a sophisticated self-reflexive camera movement similar to what Arbuckle will later use in *That Little Band of Gold* (March 1915); some subtle comic detail, including a bit of hand/paw confusion with Arbuckle's dog, Luke, who unfortunately drops out of the second half of the picture; and superb reaction shots. The director of *The Knockout* is unclear. If Yallop is correct, and by March 1914 Arbuckle was directing all his own films (with the exceptions he mentions), then he directed this one, but Yallop does not list a director for *The Knockout*. Charles Avery is sometimes credited as the director, but there is no reliable evidence for this.[44] Avery came with Sennett from Biograph as an actor, and was one of the seven original Keystone Kops. By 1914 he was assisting as director on a number of shorts, but he seems to have worked primarily with Charles Parrott (later famous as Charlie Chase). Steve Massa suspects that both men may have had a hand in *The Knockout*, but the skillful direction suggests Arbuckle's innovative work.[45]

In the first shot of the film, Arbuckle, who plays a character called "Pug," emerges from a store eating an ice-cream sandwich and holding Luke. He sees Minta. She sees him, and calls him over. It is here, in medium shot, that there is the confusion over whether she is patting Luke's paw or Pug's hand, a subtle detail not characteristic of Keystone chaos. But there is plenty of such chaos in the film. Pug gets mad when he sees a member of a gang flirting with Minta and, in a shot almost identical to Lehrman's of Mace in *The Gangsters*, he walks into a menacing close-up. There are a number of expressive reaction shots of Minta's face as she watches a fight between Pug, the flirt, and the rest of his gang, from which Pug emerges victorious, suggesting he could be a successful boxer. The heart of this film is built around boxing, as Pug prepares to fight Cyclone Flynn (Edgar Kennedy), who has been impersonated by two hungry bums. The two, overhearing Pug lifting 500 lbs in the training room, get scared about fighting him and send off a note suggesting they go "halves" rather than try to kill each other in the ring, a plot device Chaplin will later use in *City Lights*. When the real Flynn comes into town, the bums are discovered and Pug ends up in the ring with a powerful opponent.

There are two especially noteworthy moments as Pug prepares for the fight. The first is a delightfully self-conscious scene where Pug, embarrassed to change into fighting clothes in front of Minta, goes off to the side and starts to remove his pants. But then he looks directly at the camera with the realization that it is looking at him. He gives a little embarrassed aside, then gestures for the camera to rise up until he can no longer be seen below the waist. When he has put on his shorts, he then acknowledges that the camera can move back down to reveal him full-figure. He turns and gives a little wave good-bye as if to let viewers know they can again become absorbed in the narrative. Sennett's Keystones were often self-conscious, but not as subtly as this. Arbuckle will do something similar in *That Little Band of Gold*, discussed below, and also in *Fatty at Coney Island*. The second noteworthy moment is back in the training room, as Pug is lifting the 500 lb weight. Here we see three men in the background throwing a medicine ball back and forth. Arbuckle was learning to make use of the back of the frame as well as the foreground for dramatic purposes. These three men soon stop their exercise to come forward to react to Pug's strength.

The fight itself is a masterpiece of choreography in the ring, with cutting back and forth between three locations: (1) the boxing match between Pug and Flynn, with Charlie Chaplin as the referee; (2) the audience's reactions (Minta attends the fight dressed as a man); and (3) Mack Swain, who has appeared as a threatening gambler who tells Pug he will kill him if he doesn't win the fight. The activity in the ring belongs to Chaplin, a time to show off his unique balletic skills, and if Arbuckle is the director, he generously lets his friend steal this part of the show. Chaplin slides along the ropes, and at one point, having been knocked down, gives himself the ten count. Chaplin will duplicate the masterful intermingling of referee and fighters with far more elaborate camerawork in *City Lights*. By 1916 Arbuckle would know better than to allow more than one person to be the comic center, but here there are two – maybe three – and the sequence goes by so fast it is hard to appreciate all the action. Within just a couple of years, his sense of pacing would be much surer, although he always maintained his generosity toward other performers.

With the exception of its concluding sequences, *The Knockout* is shot with a largely stationary camera. But in the classic Keystone chase that ends the film, the camera is mounted on a truck or car as it follows Pug, firing two pistols, running over rooftops after Flynn, with the cops in pursuit. Rooftop chases were popular in these early films, and the influence of Arbuckle's staging is possibly seen in Chaplin's *The Kid* and Buster Keaton's *Sherlock, Jr.* (1924), which Arbuckle is rumored to have co-directed. Even Luke gets into a rooftop chase in *Fatty's Faithful Fido* (March 1915), another unsentimental film with Minta that has essentially no story, displays Arbuckle's dancing skills, and ends again in water, this time with Fatty and Luke in a washtub in a Chinese laundry.

Minta is not in *When Love Took Wings* (April 1915), but like so many of her films with Arbuckle, it has an ironic view of romance, albeit with more sophisticated technique than the earlier work in 1914. The plot is basic: three men want to marry the same girl (played by an unidentified actress who is not a regular Keystone player). Joe Bordeaux has the initial engagement, Roscoe, describing himself in a note as "Reckless Fatty," seems to be the successful suitor, but the girl's father favors neighbor Al St. John. As director, Arbuckle initially sets up three locations of action: outside the house, the parlor, and the kitchen. At various times there is a suitor in each location and Arbuckle cuts between them to set up reactions in a skillful use of off-screen space. There's a clever visual pun when Joe Bordeaux, who is in the kitchen, accidentally sits on the stove while Al and Roscoe are in the other rooms pursuing their desire to marry the girl: he's on "the hot seat." But the most elegant shooting is in an extreme long shot of Bordeaux and Roscoe fighting each other on a hill while the girl in question watches off-screen. Not only is this an effective juxtaposition of an extreme long shot with a close-up, it is also simply visual poetry. The climax is an even more elaborate chase than in *A Bath House Beauty*, cross-cutting between four lines of action. The first involves Roscoe and the girl in an airplane, with long shots of an actual plane skillfully cut with medium close-ups of the couple done in a mock-up cockpit in the studio. The second is rival Joe Bordeaux racing after them on a bicycle in a medium shot. The third is Al St. John and the father (Frank Hayes), who we see in a long shot racing along in a car. And fourth, the ever-ineffectual cops are also in a car, but our perspective on them is mostly from a high-angle long shot. This is a visually impressive variety of shots, and Arbuckle skillfully cuts between them. After Roscoe drops a bomb on the cops and they fall out of their car, they cease to have any function in the film. It's often been noted that the cops frequently just make token appearances in these later films, a reminder of the Keystone hallmark. The ending, ironically played in front of a wall hanging saying "God Bless Our Home," reveals that the much-desired girl has been wearing a wig and has no hair. Her grotesque appearance causes her to be rejected by Roscoe and Al, but poor Joe is stuck with her. The dramatic chases after romance are undercut; it has not been worth it.

There is nothing sentimental about these four films: *Fatty Joins the Force*, *A Bath House Beauty*, *The Knockout*, and *When Love Took Wings*. They are, in a way, anti-comedies, using comedy to spoof comedy. The films Arbuckle directed with Mabel Normand, on the other hand, have a lot more feeling in them and seem to embody what both Arbuckle and Normand later commented on as the trend of "new comedy." The "Fatty and Mabel" series began in January 1915. The scenarios tend to involve a greater sense of narrative, peppered with cute moments and intimate details, concluding with the happy ending expected of classical comedy, and directed with a good deal more technical sophistication than the earlier films. *Fatty and Mabel's Simple Life* (January 1915), for example, begins with rural happiness. Fatty and Mabel are clearly in love and flirt with each other around the barnyard. Both play affectionately with calves, and at one point, after Mabel gives Fatty a quick kiss, he playfully pretends to wipe it off his lips. Title cards tell us "She was happy" and he was "poor but honest." Such pastoral innocence belies the sexually suggestive sequence that follows as Fatty sticks his finger through a hole in the fence between them. A reverse angle close-up shows us the hole and wiggling finger from Mabel's point of view, and she then squirts milk at the finger from the udder of a cow she is milking. She pulls on the udders on her side of the fence while Fatty withdraws his finger on his. He looks through the hole with one eye, and another reverse angle close-up shows us his eye looking through the hole; again Mabel squirts milk in that direction. The sequence also has a hose shooting water through the hole, Mabel's father getting hit at different times with both water and milk through that hole, and a mix-up with a farm hand (Joe Bordeaux) who is initially accused of the water assault.[46] It is doubtful Arbuckle had read Freud's *Three Essays on the Theory of Sexuality* (1905) or *Jokes and Their Relation to the Unconscious* (1905), but since Freud was discussing human behavior, the undercurrent of sexual tension in the barnyard is a natural, albeit probably unconscious, expression of his ideas.

James L. Neibaur rightly comments about Arbuckle and his evolution as a performer and director: "There was a definite human element to his character, even early on, and he added greater nuance as he refined his directorial vision and presented more subtle touches of cleverness to his slapstick Keystone comedies."[47] A fine example of these subtle touches comes in *Simple Life*'s climactic chase. Arbuckle anticipates the beautiful extreme long shot in *When Love Took Wings* as the couple is being chased in a misbehaving car by the Squire's son, who Mabel is supposed to marry in order to pay off the mortgage, and by Mabel's father, along with the Keystone Kops on bicycles. Arbuckle discussed the car sequence in the *Photoplay* interview with Randolph Bartlett in order to explain the reality of his stunts:

> Of course, now and then we do a trick film, but everyone knows it is a trick when they see it – there is no bunk about it. In fact, it was in one of these trick pictures that I took the longest chance of all. This was the picture called "Fatty and Mabel's Simple Life." In one scene I was backed against a tree by a runaway Ford. We had a man crouching down on the floor of the machine working it from the pedals. All he had to guide him was a line on the ground. He would run the machine up to this line, at which time it pressed close against me; then he would back up a few feet, and then

run into me again. It gave the impression that the car
was doing this without some sort of control, so it was a
trick picture and yet it wasn't. But if that man ever had
gone past that line I surely would have had an attack of
indigestion.[48]

As Fatty tries to get control of the misbehaving car, he approaches it gin-
gerly, and gives it a gentle pat as if to calm it down. This is the kind of
subtle gesture that Keaton would learn from him a few years later.

The pacing in this film, compared to *The Knockout*, is much better. It
begins slowly in the barnyard with some of the gags described above and
builds to the classic Keystone chase. In cutting between scenes, Arbuckle
allows his performers their own time on screen, especially Mabel
Normand, with her expressive face, as she is locked in her room by her
father and reacts to Fatty, who is outside trying to rescue her by climbing
a ladder. The climax of the chase has Mabel shot up to a tree limb by an
explosion from the miscreant car, and with a few quick cuts, Arbuckle
seems to show her flying up out of the frame and then hanging from the
branch. In trying to rescue her again, Fatty falls down a well, and we see
him in a medium close-up hanging upside down. As everyone in the
chase comes to the rescue at the end, there is a beautifully executed and
complex gag where the cops are pulling each other up and down on a
rope from the tree to the well, all ending up in the water, in typical Keystone fashion. But, unlike the Minta films, this comedy ends with a completed romance. Roscoe and Mabel find the minister who is coming to
marry her to the Squire's son, and he marries them instead; a happy
ending as both Fatty and Mabel look at the camera (the audience) and, in
direct address, mouth what has just happened.

Arbuckle allows Mabel Normand even more solo screen time with
expressive reaction shots in the following month's *Mabel and Fatty's Married
Life* (February 1915). In this film he carefully follows the advice quoted
above:

> In comedy only one person can get a laugh at a time.
> When two people try to get it the situation is spoiled....
> There is a rhythm to comedy just as surely as there is
> to a symphony or a sonata.

Unlike the early action-oriented Keystones, *Married Life* is a kind of psychological comedy with Mabel, as Fatty's wife, presented as a young girl
with an overly active imagination. This is cleverly set up in the opening
scene in a park, where an affluent, well-dressed, and attentive Fatty sits on
a bench with his wife who is reading. The first title card says, "She reads
exciting books." We are introduced to an organ grinder with his monkey,
and after the monkey interrupts the couple and Fatty and the organ

grinder fight (there is a fine, menacing close-up of the organ grinder's face), it looks as if the scene is over as the couple leaves. But what Arbuckle has done, in terms of narrative, is set up the organ grinder and the monkey as significant players in the rest of the film. It's a simple story, but with a real plot, where Mabel, left home alone, reads in a newspaper about "Bold Daylight Robberies," and initially thinks her husband, who has returned home to get some papers, is a robber.[49] From another room, she fires a gun at him, while he hides in a closet, thinking *she* is a robber. It's a double misperception. His reaction of fear is shot in medium close-up. When he comes out of the closet with his hands up and discovers his wife, the medium two-shot is one of joy, relief, and affection that will anticipate the film's conclusion.

Alone again, Mabel next peeks through the window and notices the organ grinder and another man, who, she assumes, are daylight robbers scouting out her house. In fact, they are only looking for the monkey, but we, as the audience, do not know this yet, nor does Mabel. The curtain next to her starts moving, and here Arbuckle, as director, allows her a long, durational (23-second) reaction shot during which she expresses her fear in various ways. Her hat rises up and down, and in an intimate detail that reveals her thinking, she twirls her finger at her head as if to say, "Am I crazy?" When the organ grinder knocks at her front door, Arbuckle gives us a beautifully framed two-shot of Mabel's head on the left of the frame, the organ grinder's on the right, and the side of the open door between them as one struggles to enter and the other to keep him out. The climactic chase, with the Keystone Kops trying to come to the rescue, followed by Fatty and a pal, is also shot creatively, not just in the cross-cutting between Mabel, her intruders, and the rescuers, but also in the high-angle long shots Arbuckle uses to show the cops speeding down a road that runs along some trolley tracks, followed by Fatty and his pal, who abruptly turns and runs the other way as Fatty continues on. The "rescue," of course, turns out to be unnecessary as the misperceptions are resolved and the organ grinder gets his monkey back from behind the curtain. The ending of this film, like *Simple Life*, is a happy one, but more expressive. Arbuckle shows the couple together again in a medium shot. His face shows total exasperation with his impressionable wife, but the expression gently transforms to love, and they kiss.

It is Ford Sterling to whom Arbuckle gives some lengthy reaction shots in *That Little Band of Gold*, released in March. Kalton Lahue calls this film the "best" of the Fatty and Mabel series, although his pre-VHS and DVD memory of the film's structure is inaccurate and he wrongly describes its pace as rapid.[50] The narrative is circular, beginning with what is, essentially, a prologue of Mabel and Fatty marrying at a courthouse. A title card then tells us, "And now she waits for him," and the film jumps forward to a point some time after the marriage, showing an unhappy

Mabel crying in front of a mirror because of her philandering husband. The conclusion has the couple remarrying at the same courthouse with which the film began in another of the happy endings characteristic of this series. In between, however, Fatty's flirtations lead to divorce proceedings. There is some typical Sennett violence, but no chases. The heart of the comedy is in a variety of reaction shots, what Lahue calls "the profuse, yet subtle expressions of the cast."[51]

For example, when Fatty, who has married into a wealthy family, takes his annoying mother-in-law and Mabel to the opera, he sees his friend, played by Ford Sterling, in another box with two women. They acknowledge each other, and what follows is a series of lengthy reaction shots. Initially, director Arbuckle gives Sterling a long, 18-second shot during which he reacts to the two women he has brought to the opera. Sterling smells one of them, makes faces, and rolls his eyes. There is a leisurely pan across the balcony and a tilt up, as a moving camera takes us from one side of the opera house, where Fatty sits in a box with his two women, to the other side where Sterling sits with his. Arbuckle is the subtler actor as they both mime about leaving. Commentators have often noted how natural Arbuckle appears before the camera, and it is obvious in juxtaposition to Sterling. This is a remarkably long sequence composed of nothing but the two characters reacting to each other and their women. The women, too, react to scenes from the opera that are, in turn, intercut with general reactions from the audience as a whole. The sequence ends with both men leaving their boxes, and this sets up a subtle use of depth of field in front of the ticket booth. As Sterling and his two women exit, we see in the rear of the frame a man in the booth answering the telephone. As director, Arbuckle never calls attention to this bit of business, but it is noticeable, and it happens for a reason, because later in the film Sterling will call the box office to have the man tell Roscoe's wife that he is flirting with another woman at a café. Arbuckle has skillfully and unobtrusively used depth of field and a seemingly inconsequential action to set up a dramatic moment later in the film. Another fine use of depth of field occurs earlier, when Fatty, in a bedroom seen in the back of the frame, is about to take his pants off to dress to go to the opera. His valet is behind him, even reflected in a mirror, getting out Fatty's dress clothes while Fatty in the center of the frame takes a drink. As he is nonchalantly unbuttoning his pants, the valet motions out of the bedroom door towards the camera to remind him that he is being watched – by the camera. Roscoe signals "oops," and closes the door. There is a lot of direct address to the camera in the Keystone films, but not many moments like these where the gag involves breaking the diegesis so that the audience is not only made aware of itself watching the film, but also of the mediating presence of the camera. It is similar to the moment from *The Knockout* described above, except that, in *That Little Band of Gold*, Arbuckle is using a long durational take with depth of field – the important action takes place in the back of the frame. As director, he is giving us a lot of visual information that makes the *mise-en-scène* a lot more interesting than in the earlier – possibly Avery-directed – film.

As a performer, Arbuckle shows his range throughout these films, playing an innocent country boy in *Fatty and Mabel's Simple Life*, a middle-class businessman in *Fatty and Mabel's Married Life*, and a wealthy, philandering husband in *The Little Band of Gold*. He did not have a consistent persona, but there is something consistently endearing about him in all these roles. Matt Zoller Seitz quite rightly sees the Fatty and Mabel shorts as a dry run for *The Honeymooners*, not just because Jackie Gleason and Roscoe Arbuckle both play big men involved with smaller and often smarter women, with whom they are reconciled at the end of each comic drama, but also because they both "found ways to laugh at life's unremitting harshness."[52] In *Photoplay* in 1919 someone wrote of Arbuckle that he is "the defiance that we humans must hurl at woe," and that "he typified the happy, serious spirit of the American: the ability to see the funny side of anything, however seemingly tragic," which could also be said of Gleason.[53] According to Buster Keaton, Arbuckle "had no meanness, malice, or jealousy in him. Everything seemed to amuse and delight him."[54] Arbuckle himself once said that although humorists are often thought to be melancholy, that mood would not apply to him. "But I am sometimes pretty serious – generally when I'm thinking of something funny."[55]

Clearly, his ability to think up funny situations and put them on screen evolved rapidly from the time he first came to Keystone in 1913 to when he left to shoot for Triangle/Keystone on the east coast in December of 1915. He learned the importance of pacing and when to slow down, to exploit the eloquence of reactive performance, especially in long durational takes, to utilize small, often subtle details to bring out feeling, and to create a *mise-en-scène* that allowed him to play with depth of field. Like his friend, Charlie Chaplin, he was truly "working towards something entirely new in pictures." But as his technical skills evolved, he never entirely abandoned the subversive social critiques that can easily be read in the unsentimental early Keystones, such as those he did with his wife, Minta Durfee. Although the popular "Fatty and Mabel" series may be warm and charming, there is an undercurrent of an ironic perspective on cultural rituals. As their director, Arbuckle "still managed to include sly digs and satiric observations on marriage and male–female relationships."[56] Most of these comedies involve complex domestic entanglements, jealousies, misunderstandings, and misperceptions. Arbuckle knew that the awkwardness and confusion of romance and marriage are great comic sources, a study in the gap between the ideal and the real, and that wedded bliss often ends unhappily. But, as he said himself, he was not a melancholy man. He loved laughter, and his embrace of cherished moments of joy is obvious in his work. Patient and good-natured, Roscoe Arbuckle was a creative and ingenious filmmaker and a pioneer of comic cinema.

joanna e. rapf

## notes

\* For invaluable assistance with this chapter, I would like to thank Rob King, Steve Massa at the Billy Rose Theatre Division of the New York Public Library of the Performing Arts, and Ron Magliozzi and Charles Silver at the Museum of Modern Art who set up screenings of Arbuckle films not available elsewhere.

1. David Yallop's *The Day the Laughter Stopped* (New York: St. Martin's Press, 1976), as the title indicates, deals mostly with Arbuckle in the context of his trial, as does Andy Edmonds' *Frame-Up!* (New York: William Morrow and Co., Inc., 1991). However, the filmography in Yallop by Samuel A. Gill is still invaluable. Stuart Oderman's biography, *Roscoe "Fatty" Arbuckle* (Jefferson: McFarland, 1994), is just that, a biography and not a critical study, while Robert (Bob) Young's *Roscoe "Fatty" Arbuckle: A Bio-Bibliography* (Westport: Greenwood Press, 1994) is primarily useful as a research tool, although it contains fascinating new material based on personal interviews with Arbuckle's first wife, Minta Durfee. In some ways, the most interesting study of Arbuckle to date is Jerry Stahl's novel, *I, Fatty* (New York: Bloomsbury Publishing, 2004). More recently, James L. Neibaur has focused on Arbuckle's collaborations with Buster Keaton in *Arbuckle and Keaton* (Jefferson: McFarland, 2007).

2. J. P. Tellotte, "Arbuckle Escapes: The Pattern of Fatty Arbuckle's Comedy," *Journal of Popular Film & Television* 15.4 (1988): 178.

3. Ibid.:172.

4. Robert F. Moore, "Feeding with Fatty Arbuckle," *Motion Picture Classic*, n.d.: 46, in the Arbuckle clippings file, Billy Rose Theatre Division, New York Public Library (hereafter, BRTD). (My emphasis.)

5. Ibid.: 46.

6. Robert (Bob) Young, "Roscoe 'Fatty' Arbuckle," *American Classic Screen*, November/December, 1977: 39.

7. See Donald Crafton, who elaborates on this subject in "Pie and Chase: Gag, Spectacle, and Narrative in Slapstick Comedy," in Kristine Brunovska Karnick and Henry Jenkins, eds., *Classical Hollywood Comedy* (New York: Routledge, 1995), 106–119.

8. Randolph Bartlett, "Why Aren't We Killed? A Keystone Confession Which Must Not Be Read by Insurance Agents," *Photoplay*, April (1916): 82, Arbuckle clippings file, BRTD.

9. Sam Stoloff, "Normalizing Stars: Roscoe 'Fatty' Arbuckle and Hollywood Consolidation," in Gregg Bachman and Thomas J. Slater, eds., *American Silent Film: Discovering Marginalized Voices* (Carbondale: Southern Illinois University Press, 2002), 158.

10. Ibid.

11. Walter Kerr, *The Silent Clowns* (New York: Alfred A. Knopf, 1979), 62–63. See also James Agee, "Comedy's Greatest Era," in *Agee on Film: Criticism and Comment on the Movies* (New York: Beacon Press, 1958), 2–19.

12. Jim Hoberman, "Fatty Arbuckle and Friends," *Village Voice*, September 13 (1994): 59.

13. Steve Massa, Program Note, "Rediscovering Roscoe: The Careers of 'Fatty' Arbuckle," Museum of Modern Art (April 20–May 15, 2006).

14. K. Owen, "Heavyweight Athletics: Some Advice from One of Our Leading Stout Boys – Roscoe Arbuckle," *Photoplay*, August (1915): 36.

15. Yallop, *The Day the Laughter Stopped*, 309.

16. *Photoplay*, November (1912): 143.

17. *Photoplay*, December (1912): 111.

18. Arbuckle clippings file, BRTD. In this same interview he also comments that *The Gangsters* is among his "worst" films. Mace returned briefly to Keystone in July of 1915, as reported in *Reel Life* on July 17: "Fred Mace, one of the four original players in Keystone comedies has returned to the Edendale studios" (Mace clippings file, BRTD). He appeared in only seven Triangle/Keystone comedies, before announcing once again his intention to start his own company. He was found dead in a New York hotel in December of 1917.

19. See, for example, the imdb.com data on the film, accessed January 17, 2009.

20. A commentary on imdb.com wrongly identifies the gang leader as Nick Cogley.

21. Untitled note in *Photoplay*, June (1915): 136.

22. Stoloff, "Normalizing Stars," 152.

23. Arbuckle clippings file, BRTD.

24. Rob King, " 'Made for the Masses with an Appeal to the Classes': The Triangle Film Corporation and the Failure of Highbrow Cinema," *Cinema Journal* 44.2 (2005): 3–33.

25. Quoted in Oderman, *Roscoe "Fatty" Arbuckle*, 92.

26. Stahl, *I, Fatty*, 270.

27. Kalton C. Lahue, *Mack Sennett's Keystone: The Man, the Myth, and the Comedies* (South Brunswick and New York: A. S. Barnes & Company, 1971), 83.

28. Bartlett, "Why Aren't We Killed?" 84.

29. Roscoe Arbuckle, "The Cost of a Laugh," *Motion Picture*, March (1918): 69–70.

30. Arbuckle clippings file, BRTD.

31. Quoted in Robert (Bob) Young, *A Bio-Bibliography*, 126.

32. Julian Johnson, "Impressions," *Photoplay*, June (1915): 49.

33. "Short Comedies Wanted," *Photoplay*, June (1915): 131.

34. Harry C. Carr, "Charlie Chaplin's Story, Part I," *Photoplay*, July (1915): 26.

35. Photograph in *Photoplay*, July (1915): 139.

36. Harry C. Carr, "Charlie Chaplin's Story, Part II," *Photoplay*, August (1915): 46.

37. Harry C. Carr, "Charlie Chaplin's Story, Part III," *Photoplay*, September (1915): 107.

38. Harry C. Carr, "Charlie Chaplin's Story, Part IV," *Photoplay*, October (1915): 98–99. (My emphasis.)

39. Quoted in Robert (Bob) Young, *A Bio-Bibliography*, 126.

40. James R. Quirk, "Mabel Normand," *Photoplay*, August (1915): 41.

41. Peter Krämer, " 'Clean, Dependable Slapstick': Comic Violence and the Emergence of Classical Hollywood Cinema," in J. David Slocum, ed., *Violence and American Cinema* (New York: Routledge, 2001), 104.

42. Quoted in Elliot Stein, review of "Rediscovering Roscoe" at the Museum of Modern Art, *Village Voice*, April 19 (2006): 60.

43. Lauren Rabinovitz, "The Coney Island Comedies: Bodies and Slapstick at the Amusement Park and the Movies," in Charlie Keil and Shelley Stamp, eds., *American Cinema's Transitional Era: Audiences, Institutions, Practices* (Berkeley: University of California Press, 2004), 173.

44. See, for example, the imdb.com data on Avery, accessed January 17, 2009, where *The Knockout* is the only Arbuckle film listed on Avery's filmography.

45. Massa's comment about *The Knockout* is in an e-mail to the author, February 13, 2008.

46. Arbuckle will use the same hole and a similar gag in *Fatty's Plucky Pup* (June 1915).

47. Neibaur, *Arbuckle and Keaton*, 9.

48. Bartlett, "Why Aren't We Killed?" 84.

49. Rob King, in a note to the author, has commented that the plot situation in *Mabel and Fatty's Married Life* replays an earlier Sennett Biograph, *Help! Help!* (1912), also featuring Normand, who again acts the paranoid wife, with Fred Mace as the husband.

50. Kalton Lahue, *World of Laughter* (Norman, OK: University of Oklahoma Press, 1972), 81.

51. Ibid.

52. Matt Zoller Seitz, "You're the One for Me Fatty," *New York Press*, April 19–25 (2006): 21.

53. Quoted in Simon Louvish, *Keystone: The Life and Clowns of Mack Sennett* (New York: Faber & Faber, 2003), 86.

54. Quoted in Robert (Bob) Young, "Roscoe 'Fatty' Arbuckle," 41.

55. *Philadelphia Ledger*, March 20 (1921), Arbuckle clippings file, BRTD.

56. Massa, "Rediscovering Roscoe."

# mud pies and tears

## little mary's funny side

f i v e

a n k e   b r o u w e r s

This chapter seeks to reclaim Mary Pickford as one of the comic minds who, from the second half of the 1910s onward, created successful mainstream comedy features that included both sophisticated and slapstick elements. I will argue that Pickford, fully exploiting the creative freedom offered to her by a protected environment under the Artcraft banner, as well as an ideal working situation with a creative team of like-minded collaborators, made a reformative move similar to the one Charlie Chaplin made around 1915, but in reverse. At the time, Chaplin actively sought to clean up his short comedy, which was considered as unsophisticated and vulgar by middle-class and conservative tastes. (He started this reformation by including romance elements in *The Tramp* in 1915, then moved on to the socially conscious *The Immigrant* in 1916 and beyond; though he maintained his burlesque on both uplifters and the bourgeoisie.[1]) As part of this new style, he alternated gags with pathos and sentiment. The more sophisticated part of the mix, qualities associated with nineteenth-century Victorianism, would commend the Chaplin comedies to respectable middle and upper classes. Pickford, on the other hand, inversely added more comedy to her predominantly dramatic or melodramatic repertoire. Although praised for her versatility during her long career, Pickford has been discussed only sparingly as a comic actress, most likely because her iconographic child roles in sentimental films have dominated perception and shaped memory ever since her retirement from the screen in 1934. Paradoxically, however, we will see that it was her "sentimental," if rather impish, child persona that became the vehicle for moments of pure slapstick in otherwise inoffensive features.[2]

The typical Pickford film provides a perfect balance between comedy and pathos. Throughout her long career she kept refining the mix, trying to come up with the perfect recipe that would satisfy both the demands made by the increasing standardization of feature film production (narrative coherence, psychological characters that propel a causal and logical plot) and her own artistic ideal of an emotional experience that provided occasion for both tears and laughter.[3] I hope to show the irony of Pickford's inclusion of outright slapstick comedy within a chiefly sentimental framework, considering that reform and uplift movements, arguably sentimentalism's main legacy, had been partly responsible for slapstick's temporary demise in the early 1910s.[4] I will also look at one of Pickford's key collaborators, screenwriter Frances Marion, whose scripts abound with detailed descriptions of funny business, as well as humorous intertitles and slangy dialogue titles. These intertitles often played on mild class/ethnic/racial stereotypes and emphasized the naughty-but-nice quality of the Pickford films, which were designed to be recognizable to all audiences but offensive to none. Pickford and Marion's early reliance on the comic (as well as pathetic) potential of intertitles would soon be perfected by the Hal Roach productions of the late 1910s and early 1920s, notably in the Harold Lloyd features. Thus, I will argue, Mary Pickford's comedies of the 1910s constitute a noteworthy chapter in the history of the transformation of slapstick for the era of the feature film.

The turn to comedy to spice up and modernize a repertoire that boasted the grave or melodramatic narratives of *Hearts Adrift* (Porter, 1914), *Tess of the Storm Country* (Porter, 1914), and *The Dawn of a Tomorrow* (Kirkwood, 1915), was not such a radical shift for either Pickford or her audience, for she had always been comfortable in either mode. A taste for balancing moods was probably developed from two major influences early in her career: her formative years at the theater (most importantly her stint in a number of David Belasco's productions) and her three years at Biograph, where she developed her skills as a motion pictures actress. At Biograph she was cast in a variety of roles, among which were numerous comic ones that had her frequently co-starring with Mack Sennett and Billy Quirk in frivolous yet harmless stories involving misunderstandings, backfiring schemes, romantic shenanigans, and, on occasion, even cross-dressing. Kemp R. Niver, who published a rare book devoted to Pickford's comic films made between 1909 and 1912, noted that although Pickford has been praised as a dramatic actress, "rarely has her talent as a comedienne been given the attention it warrants."[5] Her contributions as comedienne have indeed been overlooked or underrated. At Biograph she learned to switch moods at the drop of a hat, acting in a serious drama on one day and starting in a comedy the next.[6]

During her years with Belasco, Pickford had enjoyed a similar regime of drama and comedy. Barry Salt notes how the rules for appropriate and successful dramatic construction of feature-length motion pictures were, to a large extent, extrapolated from theatrical practice (and from normative theatrical advice manuals). Among the many guidelines listed, a central, recurring concern was the need to balance out narrative development in terms of moods (humor and pathos) – in other words, to add variety and contrast. A good play, and by extension a good photoplay, needed to strike different emotional chords to satisfy the audience.[7] The desirability of the alternation of comedy and pathos was noted by a critic for New York's *Dramatic Mirror*, reviewing a David Belasco–Henry DeMille production from 1889: "There is ... just enough pathos to evoke feminine tears, and just enough humor to keep the masculine portion of the audience from falling asleep."[8] Variation was just the thing to keep the new mixed audiences interested, and as an established practice of a legitimate stage, it became accepted as a main convention for good dramatic construction on film. The trickling over of theatrical conventions of dramatic construction into feature film production was no historical accident, since most scenarios based on existing material were adapted from either an original play or a play from a book, and Pickford often relied on pre-tested materials to guarantee success.

According to Barry Salt, Pickford "got it right" – i.e., successfully mixing comedy and pathos – from *Rebecca of Sunnybrook Farm* (Neilan, 1917) onwards.[9] Significantly, *Rebecca* is one of the earliest features with both Frances Marion as scenario and title writer and Marshall Neilan, who had co-starred with Pickford in earlier James Kirkwood features, as director. Neither Marion nor Neilan ever wrote or directed a script totally devoid of funny business. In the same year that *Rebecca* was released, Marion, by then already an esteemed screenwriter, had tried her hand at straight-out slapstick, writing a feature for Marie Dressler's Film Corporation. *Tillie Wakes Up* (Davenport, 1917) sees Dressler as the titular character being manhandled and ridiculed by technologies of modern entertainment at Coney Island, her heavy body displayed in a variety of unappealing and unflattering positions, a fairground attraction in itself. Most of the film, especially the happy end in which two estranged married couples reconcile after driving their car into the ocean, is reminiscent of numerous Keystone endings. While under contract at MGM, Marion even managed to include several laughs in her script for the Lillian Gish prestige picture,

*The Scarlet Letter* (Seastrom, 1926), which contains a literal slapstick scene: one of the members of the Puritan congregation is slapped with a big stick for being unable to control his "wanton nose," i.e., for sneezing. From the few surviving Neilan features that didn't star Pickford we can deduce that even his dramas contained some light and funny episodes. (One wonders what Neilan made of his adaptation of *Tess of the d'Urbervilles*, a lost film produced in 1924 with Blanche Sweet; it's likely that he found some jokes in the bleak tale of a seduced peasant girl.) The director with the happy-go-lucky lifestyle ended his crippled career the same way he had begun it: directing slapstick two-reelers.

When features came to hold sway in Hollywood, comedy did not follow suit and the short-film format remained the norm. Bar a few exceptions, it wasn't until the late 1910s that star comedians made the switch to features. Richard Koszarski takes Douglas Fairbanks as a notable exception to this trend, producing comedy features from his debut, *The Lamb*, with the Triangle Film Corporation from 1915 onward.[10] Initially, Fairbanks relied on adaptations of successful Broadway comedies, but soon he developed original scripts with the writing team of Anita Loos and John Emerson, based on his energetic juvenile screen persona. The Fairbanks team constructed his comedy around more or less realistic (if still somewhat stereotypical) characters and situations, adding romantic plots and athletic gags displaying the incredible feats of the star's body. Laughter was generated not only from Fairbanks' amazing stunts, but also largely from situation comedy satirizing contemporary American society at large (its "aristocracy," its national obsessions and fads), aided enormously by Loos' clever intertitles. The vogue of the "literary" title, as Lewis Jacobs termed it, was kick started by Loos and became immensely popular in comedy, especially in slapstick.[11]

Koszarski does not consider Pickford as another notable exception to the scarcity of feature comedy producers in the early days of the full-length film, although her films were quite similar in conception to Fairbanks'. In fact, several Pickford productions of the late 1910s were sold as comedies, albeit mixed with a sentimental ethos and "tender pathos," and even her most outwardly dramatic features contain numerous gags and moments of pure Chaplinesque comedy. Admittedly, she made some very serious films (*Madame Butterfly, Pride of the Clan, Stella Maris, The Little American*) and lots of melodramas (*In The Bishop's Carriage, Hearts Adrift, Tess of the Storm Country, The Dawn of a Tomorrow, Fanchon the Cricket*), but a significant amount of her most popular productions of the 1910s were comedies (*Caprice, Such a Little Queen, Rags, M'Liss, Rebecca of Sunnybrook Farm, Amarilly of Clothes-Line Alley, Johanna Enlists, The Hoodlum*). In his chapter on Pickford from *Movies in the Age of Innocence*, Edward Wagenknecht had no qualms comparing Little Mary's "high jinks" to those of "the slapstick artists who did nothing else."[12] Wagenknecht did not stand alone with this comparison: luminaries such as Iris Barry and James Card also recognized in Pickford touches of what they termed the "Chaplinesque" — mostly in her ability to solicit sympathy for disheveled and dogged characters "failing to keep their place."[13] Wagenknecht notes that some of Pickford's gags perceived as Chaplinesque were actually done before Chaplin did his, suggesting a mutual indebtedness during their long careers. Likewise, her never-ending war with simple machinery and objects of everyday use both looks back to early gag films and ahead both to Chaplin's struggle with (and transformation and mimicry of) objects and to Keaton's dramaturgy of mechanics: in *Pollyanna* (Powell, 1920), Pickford tries hard not to get her aunt's squeaky clean floors dirty with the mud on her shoes, but in the effort gets caught in her aunt's knitting, which she innocently unravels as she carefully tiptoes through the house in a typical slapstick moment. *Rebecca of Sunnybrook Farm* features another slapstick bit reminiscent of Mutual-era Chaplin revolving around a divided door — after closing a Dutch door behind her, Rebecca finds the upper sash still open. On closing this part she accidentally bumps open the lower sash. Peeping from under the upper part, she crouches to close the lower part, bumping her head as a finish.

The Pickford–Chaplin–Fairbanks connection would be formalized through the foundation of United Artists in 1919 and in the marriage of Pickford and Fairbanks the following year. Yet the connection established itself much sooner on a creative level, with Pickford and Chaplin exploring similar comic–pathetic possibilities, Chaplin and Fairbanks giving acrobatic clowning a ballet-like elegance and suppleness, and Pickford and Fairbanks working from solid scenarios (establishing their respective personas of "American Aristocrat" and "America's Sweetheart") with clever intertitles.

The rise to fame of the United Artists, America's first megastars, can to a large extent be attributed to their blending of both dramatic and comedic elements appealing to *all* members of the new cross-class audience targeted by the movie industry. By the time Pickford, Fairbanks, and Chaplin were making their first comedy features, the attacks on physical, gag-oriented comedy films first made by uplifters, reformers, and women's and church groups in 1908, were continued with only moderately less fervor and rhetorical flourish in the pages of the movie industry's own trade press, most notably by *Moving Picture World* critic Epes Winthrop Sargent.[14] As Henry Jenkins has extensively documented, the debate over two seemingly antagonistic strands of comedy — the Old Comedy of Victorianism versus the New Comedy of the Modern Age — that had occupied critics in the nineteenth century, when society had attempted to formulate and designate an acceptable function and role for comedy, was still cause for reflection in the first decades of the twentieth century. In line both with the overall sense of propriety promoted by the age and with sentimental and Arnoldian norms regarding valuable cultural production, Victorian arbiters of taste had generally decided "that comedy should serve a serious purpose; laughter be subordinated to didacticism and restrained through a strong-felt sense of morality, propriety and ethics."[15] Proponents of a more restrained and "thoughtful" type of comedy that required at least moderate intellectual or cognitive activity had been vehemently opposed to the crude and vulgar shocks of vaudeville and burlesque later adopted by slapstick. Tenets of Old Comedy still shone through in Sargent's attempts to convince movie audiences that they could do with less "low" comedy (the chases, the pie or water throwing, the rumbling, tumbling, and stumbling down) and were actually craving more intelligent entertainment. Contrary to earlier attempts to abolish slapstick and replace it with middle-class situation comedy, Sargent's own severe attitude toward slapstick, echoed by women's committees and church groups, merely implied that he wanted the genre *contained* by principles of classical narrative structure enabling a more refined response.[16] For Sargent the key to better comedy was in the writing, which he found sadly lacking. The need for better scenarios and better intertitles was a general concern for the still-young movie industry of the mid-1910s, resounding in a wide variety of scenario manuals, critical reviews and interviews given by leaders of the industry.[17] In the chapter devoted to comedy of her manual, *How To Write for the "Movies"* (1915), Louella Parsons emphasized that

> [t]he comedy must have at least a semblance of a plot.
> The comedy that is a series of chases, with the colored
> woman and the big fat policeman bringing up the rear,
> is by no means all the motive power you need.... A
> funny incident with no plot is not comedy screen
> material, for along with it you need a plot.[18]

With this clear dismissal of typical slapstick routines, she then approvingly quotes Lew Fields (of Weber and Fields): "Comedy must have a plot. The so-called slapsticks, with just a lot of horse play and no connecting link are stupid. Every comedy I put on has a bit of heart interest and a real motive."[19]

Although her films are never mentioned by Sargent — he urged his readers mainly to look at the Sidney Drew films for more sophisticated, story-based comedy — Pickford seems like a case in point for both his and Parson's aesthetic: in her comedy features from the mid-1910s onwards she embraced carefully constructed narratives with clearly motivated psychological characters in which comic situations were distilled from the plot and from realistic situations. She had been one of the pioneers of restrained, natural acting, and most of her stories were familiar, human and wholesome, ideally suited for the whole family. Moreover, in line with the ideals of refined comedy, her films often provided a didactic moral lesson.

What set Pickford (and Chaplin and Fairbanks – and later Lloyd and the other Roach comedians) apart from Sidney Drew and the Vitagraph comedians was that while she did try to move slapstick more in line with middle-class taste, she did not sanitize or "contain" it to the extent that Sargent had in mind; Pickford's comedy was accessible and harmless but never completely "nice" or "clean" or "polite," let alone "refined." As a producer and studio head, Pickford was well aware of market conditions, and she refused to throw out anything that could appeal to any segment of her now broader than ever audience, even if it wasn't the classiest material. (Similarly, when her audience indicated quite late in her career that they still preferred her as a little girl, she tried her best to comply, playing a 12-year old in *Little Annie Rooney* (Beaudine, 1925) when she was 33.) Pickford was a businesswoman first, and if she thought that traditional slapstick could still do business, she would never excise it from her product just because the critics told her to. Consequently, apart from the constant alternation of tears and laughter, there is a stunning amount of unmitigated slapstick in almost all of her features. If not entirely "contained," these slapstick moments are of course still functional in that they are tied to the development of Pickford's persona, used to illustrate both the jaunty and fiery, as well as the innocent, nature of her most beloved creation, "Little Mary." The child character gave Pickford more leeway to explore the less sophisticated aspects of comedy because, as a child, she enjoyed fewer restrictions and was not yet expected to follow all the rules of propriety and decency.[20] Fairbanks made full use of the same liberties in his incarnation as "America's juvenile." To illustrate, let's turn to the example of the Hector Turnbull-scripted *Less than the Dust* (Emerson, 1917), a Victorian role-reversal drama in which Pickford plays Radha, an Indian girl and "waif of the Bazaars," who eventually learns of her true English origins and transforms from Indian waif to English wife. In alternation with the drama of inheritance and parentage, *Less than the Dust* also features an old-style accumulative chase sequence. Here, not only youth but ethnicity as well gives occasion to rough things up without offense. When Radha is negotiating the price of a fabric for a new sari and runs off with more than she paid for, she is chased through the streets of the bazaar by the market vendor. During her flight, Radha plunges into a sacred pool – "profanation!" – which causes an enraged mass of worshipers to join in the chase. In the end, Pickford runs for protection from the mob to her English beau, with some politically incorrect business of blaming the village Mohammedan. The chase is minimally tied to the plot, but provides us with some character background and local color.[21] Most importantly, it stresses the devil-may-care attitude typical of the young that is such an important part of the Pickford persona.

There are more examples of slapstick chases — together with water throwing, the target most mentioned in Sargent's attacks — in other features: *Daddy-Long-Legs* (Neilan, 1919) has Pickford chased by Victorian charity donators; *Little Lord Fauntleroy* (Green and Jack Pickford, 1921) sees her pursued by a bully and an angered mob of casual bystanders; and *The Hoodlum* (Franklin, 1919) features Pickford on the run, Chaplin-style, from a police officer whom she skillfully dodges and outwits, only to be outdone by mice in the cellar where she attempts to hide. Again, all sequences have narrative motivation — the former two cases give proof of the characters' fundamental goodness, the chases resulting from a misunderstood attempt at benevolence or the desire to defend the family honor. In *The Hoodlum* the trouble with the law illustrates Pickford's complete assimilation to her (undercover) role as street urchin. However, the main motivation is less narrative causality or even character development, more a sense of mischievous fun. The chase was not the only slapstick routine that Pickford included with some frequency. *Suds* (Dillon, 1920) has a delightful sight gag (a "switch image," in Noël Carroll's terminology)[22] neatly making fun of Pickford's most recognizable and bankable feature, her famous golden locks. After an intertitle has informed us we are about to witness "the boudoir secrets of a duchess," an iris slowly opens on a close shot of curly blonde hair carefully being brushed. Contrary to what we would expect, these are not Mary's pretty curls, but the

Figure 5.1

The funny side of Little Mary. Mary Pickford in *Johanna Enlists* (1918). Courtesy of the Mary Pickford Library

mane of the male "lead," the horse Lavender. Meta-references or jokes regarding Pickford's most famous attribute (like Chaplin's mustache and cane or Lloyd's glasses) also pop up in *Rebecca of Sunnybrook Farm*, *M'Liss* (Neilan, 1918), and *Tess of the Storm Country* (Robertson, 1923), where a great fuss is made over Pickford washing her uncouth hair. The result — the well-known coiffure in full splendor — is extra pleasing.

If slapstick is to a large extent about the instant gratification of seeing people skip, fall, and tumble, there is also quite a lot of that in most Pickford films. In *Johanna Enlists* (Taylor, 1918), a light comedy with a patriotic agenda, the titular heroine is a temperamental, dreamy, and clumsy girl, whose unladylike postures reach new heights when she falls off the porch while peeling potatoes. Next, she accumulates bodily harm while cooking dinner. First, she burns herself at the stove, which causes her to drop something on her foot; angered, she kicks the object that caused her harm, which of course only brings about new pain. As she tries to calm herself, she leans against the stove ... and burns herself anew. These short bits can be classified as part of character exposition, but surely they are easy, deliberate laugh-getters as well. Self-inflicted pain due to temper tantrums, clumsiness, and anger at annoying objects is a recurring routine that became part of the Pickford persona (like Keaton's deadpan, Lloyd's clumsiness, and Chaplin's walk). In both *M'Liss* and *The Hoodlum*, Mary's "piggies" are hurt from kicking an object in a "hissy fit." The latter film also includes a scene in the pouring rain when Pickford, 25 cents short of an umbrella, attempts to stay dry by "shadow walking" behind a man with an umbrella, a funny bit typical of Chaplin and Keaton (see, for instance, *Sherlock Jr.* (1924)). Also like Chaplin in his later *A Dog's Life* (1918), we find that Molly O. of *The Foundling* (O'Brien, 1916) in many ways resembles the little outcast dog she befriends, a comparison made explicit when Pickford is caught in the nets of an overzealous dogcatcher. The shared hard lot of orphan and stray — "You and me is orphants," Molly says — produces incidents both comic and touching: after Molly discovers that her little friend has given birth to a litter of puppies (as in the switch-image ending of *A Dog's Life*) she innocently acts surprised at finding her dog "married."

Perhaps the best example of Pickford's insertion of slapstick bits in a predominantly sentimental storyline we find at a point halfway through Maurice Tourneur's 1917 *The Poor Little Rich Girl*. A gang of naughty street boys sneaks into the garden of a luxurious city home to retrieve their baseball, but they are discovered by rich girl Gwendolyn, who, by way of parental punishment, happens to be dressed in a tomboy's get-up. She pompously tells them her name and that she is, in fact, a boy. The ruse is taken to the next level when the leader of the gang calls her a "sissy," and a mud fight — the next best thing to a pie fight — ensues. Gwendolyn proves to be an excellent mud thrower, and close-ups inform us of the delicious mess the children are making of each other and themselves. Finally, the family's gardener intervenes in the muddy spectacle by squirting the boys with his hose à la Lumières' famous mischief gag film. Covered by layers of mud and dirt, in a boy's get-up and with her golden curls tucked under a cap, Gwendolyn suffers the same treatment. When this small instance of mistaken identity (and gender) has been solved, she sinks to her heels and starts to whimper. Not, as we may expect, because she is all wet and dirty, but because, as she tells the gardener in the clincher title, "You just spoiled the best fight I ever had!"

In her autobiography Frances Marion writes that she and Pickford thought up the mud-fight scene on the spot, "carried away by [their] own brand of humor," much to the annoyance of their director, artsy Frenchman Maurice Tourneur. The two friends, in Marion's words, "ganged up on poor serious Mr. Tourneur and either sweet-talked or fast-talked him into letting us include some wild comedy scene."[23] The exact reason for Tourneur's reluctance to include scenes that were neither in the original play nor in the continuity script is not given; perhaps he feared that all that mud would clot the narrative or at least mess up the production schedule. It wasn't that Tourneur couldn't take a joke – as Kevin Brownlow points out, labeling Tourneur as adverse to comedy is unfair and untrue as most of his films contain humorous instances.[24] (In *A Girl's Folly* from the same year, co-scripted by Tourneur and Marion, a comedy scene involving a mouse and four petrified girls has very little to do with the plot but is very funny in its own right.) The point Marion was making – "ganging up on poor serious Mr. Tourneur" – is that *they*, the Pickford outfit, were all for letting one slip in, just like the rambunctious, slightly rebellious little rascals Mary played in most of her comedies. Moreover, the introduction of an unscripted comic bit in a sentimental story dealing with child neglect and promoting Victorian family values, a most radical change of tone in a largely pathetic context, fitted the ideal of variation discussed above.[25] High-contrast, radical shifts of tone and mixing the modern and the sentimental, was probably what Marion meant by "[their] own brand of humor."[26]

Contrary to what this anecdote would imply, most of the comedy *was* scripted – or it was at least indicated when some comic "business" was desirable in the shooting script. This example from the *Johanna Enlists* shooting script illustrates this detailed comic intentionality:

> Int. Kitchen – Ransallar home – CLOSE UP
> Johanna at stove taking some loaves of bread out of the oven. She burns her hand on the pan, drops it on her foot – kicks the stove – almost breaks her foot – hopping on one foot – stumbles against the hot stove – FADE OUT.

Int. Kitchen – Ransallar home – CLOSE UP
Johanna at sink – an enormous stock of dishes piled up
– she turns the faucet on – the water comes with such
force that it splashes all over her – FADE OUT.
Ext. Veranda – Ransallar home.
Johanna on sweeping – the twins on making a kite –
the porch is littered up with paste, papers, etc. Johanna
sweeps a great gust of dirt over the twins – and ends by
sweeping the twins right off the porch – FADE OUT.[27]

By way of a conclusion, I want now to take a closer look at the intertitles
– both dialogue and expository titles – that are such a crucial part of the
way the jokes are set up or "clinched" in the Pickford–Marion comedies.
Although for silent filmmakers intertitles were the only means of narration available next to the moving photographic images, they have
remained a largely understudied narrative device for creating or influ-
encing atmosphere, mood, or even genre.[28] For specific genres, comedy in
particular, clever dialogue and exposition became crucial tools, even
defining characteristics. Rightly credited with establishing the standard
for a new, more ambitious kind of intertitle – where the vogue in the
early 1910s was for telling stories with an absolute minimum of words[29] –
is Anita Loos, whose talent for overt, witty narration resulted in a wave of
imitations. Lewis Jacobs mentions how the screen was "deluged" with
Loos-style "literary" intertitles.[30] Puns, alliterations, *double entendres*, and
other *bon mots* in the style of Dorothy Parker and the Algonquin wits
became a staple not just of sophisticated comedy (remember that the
master of the genre, Lubitsch, was known more for being witty with
images alone) but of most slapstick of the 1920s. Hal Roach, in particular,
was quick to realize that by adding not just believable situations and characters, but also wisecracking intertitles, he could differentiate his product
from the Sennett output, which by the mid-1910s was not only under
attack from the moralists but was starting to appear a bit long in the
tooth compared to what Gerald Mast describes as the "American push
and 'git' " of the comedies Loos was writing for Fairbanks.[31]

The narration in Pickford's films appears to adhere to the same principles that guided her ideas on dramatic construction, once again opting
for a combination of varied modes of address, ranging from sentimental
empathic appeal and flowery metaphor to ironic asides or colloquialisms.
Frances Marion provided intertitles that could either be taken straight or
with a wink. Kevin Brownlow points out that Frances Taylor Patterson,
one of the first academic instructors of "photoplay construction,"
detected and appreciated Marion's "bantering humor" in the titles of the
seemingly saccharine *Pollyanna*, thus providing audiences with the choice
of either swallowing the mawkishness or not. In *Pollyanna* Marion lets the

glad girl's habit of happiness veer close to cynicism when she sees the positive in the death of a parent because death is still to be preferred to being a minister in the Ozark Mountains.[32] Other examples illustrate Marion's constant alternation of moods in the titles. In *The Poor Little Rich Girl*, the introductory intertitle, "The Tyrants of Modern Civilization, Servants – By Position. Masters by Disposition," in the satirical mode expected from Marion's pal Anita Loos, is soon followed by the compassionate (yet tonally still somewhat ambiguous), "Empty hearts./Empty lives./Empty homes./Poor little rich girl." Later dialogue titles make the most of Gwen's youthful naiveté, as in this exchange with an annoyingly stuck-up playmate: "My mother says your mother has a social bee in her bonnet," to which Gwen indignantly replies: "She has not. It's a bird." But these jokes (situation and titles are repeated almost verbatim in *Pollyanna*) are later followed again by the rhythmic repetition of pathetic intertitles such as "Poor – Little – Rich – Girl" and "My Poor Little Girl!/ My Poor Little Girl," maneuvering the story back onto its dramatic sentimental track.

In one- or two-reel narratives expository intertitles were useful for compressing time, but also for introducing characters in a pithy and poignant manner. In comedies this provided choice occasion for clever one-liners or conceits. Such vignette introductions remained a staple of Pickford's comedy features, as our example from *The Poor Little Rich Girl* shows. In *Amarilly of Clothes-line Alley* (Neilan, 1918), a rich socialite is introduced: "Among the Four Hundred we find Mrs. David Phillips, who believes in the Fourteenth Commandment – 'Thou shalt not forget thy pose.'" In *Johanna Enlists*, the paterfamilias enters the play as follows: "Johanna's pa claims he is 'jest full of idears.' He proves it – by never letting one of them escape." In true mood-variety style, both *Amarilly* and *Johanna* abandon the wisecracking towards the end of the film when a requisite dramatic turn demands emotional gesturing and emotive close-ups instead of funny lines.

In general, the "literary" gag title could be of two kinds: those that are jokes and are funny on a purely verbal level, such as wisecracks, puns, *double entendres*, or satirical comments, and those that work in relation to the preceding or following image, establishing a relationship of ironic incongruity comparable to the effect of the "switch image." Examples of Loos-like punning abound, as in *Amarilly* when the titular character's mother is introduced as "maid in Ireland," and in *M'Liss* when a title comments on Pickford having cut off the tail feathers of her father's hen to put on her now fashionable hat as "The end of a perfect tale." *Johanna Enlists* provides examples of the "switch title": "Johanna's ma, being ghastly good, has brought up her children on that excellent principle – 'spare the hairbrush and spoil the young one.'" The next shot, of course, shows "Maw" Ransallar giving a good spanking to Johanna's younger brother. When, moments later, Johanna is looking to be given the same treatment, the narrative doubles back again as the audience is discreetly taken aside by a title: "As we have shown you – graphically and geographically – where ma lays on the hairbrush, we'll spare Johanna's blushes and discover her the next morning at 6 AM."

That last aside implies an omniscient narrational presence familiar from Victorian novelists like Thackeray or Dickens, but unusual for American filmmaking in the late 1910s, when rules of invisible storytelling were being standardized and narration was becoming less self-conscious. While overt narration remained acceptable in classical storytelling at the beginning and/or near the end of the film, the explicit intrusion of a narrating voice *throughout* the film was almost exclusively comedy's domain.[33] Like Loos before her,[34] Marion did not limit herself to prologues or codas to assert a narrating voice: two-thirds into *M'Liss* "the plot curdles with the arrival of another stranger," while about midway in *Pollyanna* a title intervenes to casually compress time: "So let us draw the veil and pass on, say three or four months later."

Dialogue titles in the Pickford films were often in a socio- or regiolect, useful for stereotyping or adding local color, but also for exploiting "old comedy" situations based on gender, age, class, and ethnic difference. (DeMille's *Chimmie Fadden* films, about a lower-East-side Irish rascal, extracted humor from the same sources.)[35] Colloquialisms could signal ignorance or lower-class status on the part of the speaking character, but mostly they indicated simplicity, honesty, youth, and rebellious defiance of verbal propriety. In the comedies of the 1910s, Pickford's character is usually young, uneducated, lower class, or ethnic, from the country or the streets, expressing herself mostly in dialect or child language. In the Bret Harte story, *M'Liss*, Pickford's feisty miner's daughter breaches both decorum and the rules of grammar: surprising her handsome teacher with a homemade present she wants to know, "Which is correct – brung or brang?" "Why – bring" "All right – I bringed you a present!" In *Johanna Enlists*, a sick soldier wants to thank Johanna for taking such good care of him by calling her his "Joan of Arc," to which she indignantly replies: "My name ain't Joan Vark – it's Ransallar – Johanna Ransallar!!"

Surely, funny intertitles and playful narration, especially in introducing a scene or a character, are not specific to Pickford and Marion; you'll find Loos-style titles in several quality films from the mid-1910s onwards.[36] As Kristin Thompson notes, the tendency to use cleverly written titles is especially apparent in the comedies Buster Keaton and Harold Lloyd made from about 1920 onwards. Thompson actually refers to the *features* made by Keaton and Lloyd, but "literary" titles are much in evidence in two-reelers from the same period. Title and image are incongruously matched, for instance, both in the early Keaton short, *Neighbors* (1920), and in his feature, *College* (1927). In the former the expository title,

"The Flower of Love could find no more romantic spot in which to blossom than in this poet's Dream Garden," is followed by a shot of Buster and his sweetheart separated by a shabby fence in a tenement neighborhood, while in the latter the locale established by a title, "On the Sunkist slopes of the Pacific, where land and water meet – California," is belied by a shot of Buster and his mother looking miserable in a downpour. Most Lloyd shorts from 1920, written and titled by Roach Studio-assigned wit H. M. "Beanie" Walker, also employ overt narration mainly for preliminary exposition and character introduction, but a narrating voice also intrudes at transitional moments to establish a new locale or time frame ("2 A.M. That wonderful hour when the back fence cat clears his throat and reaches for the high C" from *An Eastern Westerner*), to comment on character or action ("He doesn't know whether the Canary Islands are in Buzzards Bay or the Eerie Canal but he is on his way" from *Captain Kidd's Kids*), or to burlesque the sermonizing title in the flowery "rosy-fingered dawn" style[37] also evoked in our two Keaton examples ("Again – A lone wanderer roams the world facing the drab dawn of a dead tomorrow" from *Number, Please?*).

My point is that, especially in the 1910s, the Pickford films at times not only looked like, but also *read* (or, if you will, *sounded*) like, the slapstick features of the 1920s. I want to stress again that despite receiving scarce scholarly attention as comedies,[38] these must be considered important transitional films that can be categorized as neither straight dramas, situation comedies, or slapsticks, but as a combination of both, a new mix to appeal to a new mixed audience. Like the light comedies scripted by Loos based on situation and character, but at the same time still catering to the audience for physical gag humor, the Pickford films, by constantly shifting tone between pathos and comedy and back again, by mixing elements of "high class" and "low" humor (having realistic characters in believable situations perform the kind of physical bits normally reserved for clowns in baggy pants), showed comedians hesitant about abandoning the short film how the feature could be a workable framework for comedy.

### notes

1. Charles Maland, *Charlie Chaplin and American Culture* (Princeton: Princeton University Press, 1989), 16; Richard Koszarksi, *An Evening's Entertainment* (Berkeley: University of California Press, 1990), 176.
2. Koszarski notes how Harold Lloyd achieved a similar make-over in his switch from the rather vulgar and clownish "Lonesome Luke" character to the more middle-class, well-meaning "Harold." Koszarski, *An Evening's Entertainment*, 176.
3. Kevin Brownlow, *The Parade's Gone By...* (Berkeley: University of California Press, 1968), 134.
4. Eileen Bowser, *The Transformation of Cinema, 1907–1915* (Berkeley: University of California Press, 1990), 183.

5. Kemp R. Niver, *Mary Pickford, Comedienne* (Los Angeles: Locare Research Group, 1969), unnumbered introduction.

6. For instance, after Pickford's dramatic role in *The Lonely Villa* (1909) she was cast as a bystander in *The Peach-Basket Hat*, a chase film. And after wrapping production of the cross-dressing comedy *Getting Even* in September 1909, she immediately started filming *The Broken Locket*, a sentimental temperance drama.

7. This was done most effectively from the feature era onwards, although Barry Salt notes that in some Griffith Biograph shorts there is alternation of this type within a one- or two-reel film. Barry Salt, *Film Style and Technology: History and Analysis* (London: Starword, 1992), 113.

8. Quoted in Sumiko Higashi, *Cecil B. DeMille and American Culture: The Silent Era* (Berkeley: University of California Press, 1994), 49. The DeMille–Belasco production under review was *The Charity Ball*, the play that opened the third regular season of Frohman's new Lyceum Theater.

9. Salt, *Film Style and Technology*, 113

10. Koszarski, *An Evening's Entertainment*, 175.

11. Lewis Jacobs, *The Rise of the American Film: A Critical History* (New York: Teachers College Press, Columbia University, 1968), 221.

12. Edward Wagenknecht, *The Movies in the Age of Innocence* (New York: Limelight Editions, 1997), 159.

13. Wagenknecht, *The Movies in the Age of Innocence*, 160.

14. Bowser, *The Transformation of Cinema*, 179–184; Jenkins, *What Made Pistacchio Nuts?* (New York: Columbia University Press, 1992), 48–58.

15. Henry Jenkins, *What Made Pistacchio Nuts?*, 29. Jenkins notes how James Sully, a leading nineteenth-century child psychologist, attributed to humor a wholesome, refreshing function that could help "perfect" character (30). This Arnoldian conception of art – as a site to strive continuously for the perfection of society – was part of Victorian genteel culture and still influenced representational strategies in art at the beginning the twentieth century. See Sumiko Higashi, *Cecil B. DeMille and American Culture*, 9.

16. Jenkins, *What Made Pistachio Nuts?*, 51.

17. See Bowser, *The Transformation of Cinema*, chapter 9.

18. Louella Parsons, *How to write for the "Movies"* (Chicago: A. C. McClurg & Co., 1915), 99 and 120.

19. Parsons, *How to write for the "Movies,"* 100.

20. Gaylyn Studlar notes, with Sally Mitchell, that Pickford's juvenile characters make the transgressions and breaches of decorum inappropriate to a grown woman acceptable because she is, after all, only a child. See Gaylyn Studlar, " 'Oh Doll Divine' Mary Pickford, Masquerade, and the Paedophilic Gaze," in Jennifer M. Bean and Diane Negra, eds., *A Feminist Reader in Early Cinema* (Durham: Duke University Press, 2002), 356.

21. Hugo Münsterberg noted that the chase sequence was most often used in slapstick, but that it could also "be put into the service of much higher aim" when it was used for plot and character development. Hugo Münsterberg, *The Photoplay: A Psychological Study* (Mineaola: Dover Publications Inc., 1970), 14.

22. Noël Carroll, "Notes on the Sight Gag," in *Theorizing the Moving Image* (Cambridge: Cambridge University Press, 1996), 146–157.

23. Frances Marion, *Off With Their Heads* (New York: Macmillan Co., 1972), 43.

24. Kevin Brownlow, *Mary Pickford Rediscovered* (New York: Harry N. Abrams/Academy of Motion Arts and Sciences, 1999), 128.

25. Prior to the mud-throwing scene, *The Poor Little Rich Girl* features comic scenes involving shenanigans with a plumber and organ grinder and Gwen's quibble with the daughter of her mother's friend; these were (presumably) scripted and taken from the play and/or book.

26. Marion, *Off With Their Heads*, 43.

27. Script in the Paramount Scripts collection at the Margaret Herrick Library, Academy of Motion Picture Arts and Sciences.

28. In his entry on *True Heart Susie* for *The Griffith Project*, Tom Gunning notes that even Griffith's idiosyncratic use of titles has received little scholarly attention. Gunning's remark is true for most critical analyses of silent films. If considered at all, intertitles are usually studied for plot, seldom for style. See: Paolo Cherchi Usai, ed., *The Griffith Project*, vol. 10 (1919–1946) (London, BFI Publishing, 2006), 22.

29. Bowser, *The Transformation of Cinema*, 140.

30. Jacobs, *The Rise of the American Film*, 221.

31. Gerald Mast, *The Comic Mind: Comedy and the Movies* (London: New English Library, 1973), 180.

32. Brownlow, *Mary Pickford Rediscovered*, 169.

33. David Bordwell, *Narration in the Fiction Film* (Madison: University of Wisconsin Press, 1985), 167; Kristin Thompson, "The Formulation of the Classical Narrative," in David Bordwell, Janet Staiger, and Kristin Thompson, eds., *The Classical Hollywood Cinema: Film Style and Mode of Production to 1960* (New York: Columbia University Press, 1985) 186.

34. In *His Picture in the Papers* (Emerson, 1916) the viewer is urged to note a "hygienic" kiss between two characters. At another point in the story a title "begs leave" to introduce a dull character. In *The Social Secretary* (Emerson, 1916) the narrative voice reappears in the story while punning on a character's occupation: "Now here returns to our story Mayme's Portugese count whose lime business has been squeezed by the war."

35. Higashi, *Cecil B. DeMille and American Culture*, 63–71.

36. Kristin Thompson points out that the Loos-style "literary" intertitle became the norm for both comedies and dramas by the 1920s. Bordwell, Staiger, and Thompson, *The Classical Hollywood Cinema*, 187.

37. Ibid.

38. Only Walter Kerr among the major historians of comedy considers Pickford worthy of mention, next to other "non-comedians" like Fairbanks and Gish.

# mechanics and modernity

# part two

# mack sennett vs.

# henry ford

six

eileen bowser

Automobiles and movies arrived in tandem in the 1890s, two life-changing products of the mechanical age and the age of invention. In the following decades Henry Ford brought us affordable cars for the common man and Mack Sennett gave us slapstick comedies that did their best to take apart, deform, and destroy the wonderful new machines. The careers of the two entrepreneurs were parallel in a number of ways, but this chapter refers to Henry Ford and Mack Sennett as symbols rather than specific individuals, that is, as the fathers of, respectively, the mass-produced automobile, and the slapstick comedy of the 1910s and 1920s. I want to show how they signify two opposing strains in American life during that time.

Before the advent of the Model T Ford, the automobile was a toy for the rich, and a sign of success. A moving-picture theater manager in the first decades of cinema boasted of his elite clientele by the number of cars parked outside. A movie star showed his or her success on the screen and in private life by owning and driving an automobile. To drive a car became a symbol of the New Woman's emancipation, and the movie star led the way on and off the screen. Mary Pickford in *A Beast at Bay*, early in 1912, drives her boyfriend to the train station and is forced at gunpoint by an escaped convict to drive in a high-speed chase with a train engine. The automobiles of the upper class were shown off in actuality films of car parades and car races, a favorite topic in slapstick comedies for years to come. Barney Oldfield and other famous racing champions crossed over from actuality films to fiction, playing themselves or fictional characters, or performing as stunt men. In the opening title of *Move Along* in 1925, although the Model T was now widely available, class differences are still pointed: "The wealthy get their bumps in life the same as the poor – only they don't bounce as high in their expensive cars as the poor do in their tin lizzies." Following is one of those opening-shot gags that are specific to the film medium, a shot that sets up a false premise: a wealthy man sits in the back of his chauffeur-driven open car enjoying his cigar, sharing satisfied smiles with Lloyd Hamilton, who is sitting next to him, smoking his own cigar. The car then moves ahead to reveal that Hamilton is actually sitting on the back of a horse-drawn dray cart, which soon bumps him off into a puddle.

The automobile comedy existed before Sennett started making movies or Ford invented the Model T. The British led with films made at the turn of the century: Cecil Hepworth presented several trick film comedies with a Monty Python sensibility, such as *Explosion of a Motor* Car (1900), in which an automobile containing four passengers drives toward the camera and explodes, sending all the pieces into the air. A policeman rushes to the scene and looks up through a telescope as bodies fall to the ground. He records the event in his notebook. The same bystander policeman is still observing and recording the destruction in 1929 when Jimmy Finlayson takes apart Laurel and Hardy's pickup truck in *Big Business*. Hepworth followed *Explosion of a Motor Car* with *How It Feels to Be Run Over* (1900), a little nonsense film showing an accident in which the car comes directly at the camera, followed by black film leader on which has been scratched stars and a title: "Oh, Mother will be pleased." Two years later, Hepworth made *How to Stop a Motor Car* (1902), a trick film about a policeman who tries to stop a car and is run into and literally knocked to pieces, but then reassembles himself. An inspector, stopping by the scene, shows him the correct way: the inspector turns his back on an approaching car and causes it to bounce off his body. These are literal statements of modern man's encounters with the machine, expressed in slapstick comedies as man's collisions with the machine, or Sennett vs. Ford. These comedies generally show man defeated by the machine because he doesn't understand how it works or because he doesn't know how to handle the frightening new power and freedom of movement. Yet he survives after all because he is never really injured, even when the vehicle runs him over or blows him to pieces. But I don't think he is happy about it.

Henry Ford first introduced his Model T in October 1908, and with it achieved his goal of making a cheap automobile. That same year Mack Sennett found employment at the Biograph studio in New York, where he remained until setting up his own company late in 1912. Between 1909 and 1927, when the Model T was discontinued, it was the top-selling car in the world, with a sales record of well over 15 million cars. Henry Ford changed the concept of an automobile as a possession reserved for the wealthy to an everyday necessity for the working man. His efficiency methods and his systems based on the principles of Taylorism were widely admired and highly influential within factory production everywhere, and brought him extraordinary success in the 1910s and 1920s. When Mack Sennett founded Keystone he began to build what would become a kind of efficient factory system for producing slapstick comedies on a regular release schedule. Perhaps the Keystone madhouse may not be closely compared with a factory assembly line, but Sennett kept a similar strong, central control of the several companies with productions going on at the same time. By February 1914, Keystone production had increased to seven companies with seven directors.

In New York City, according to a *New York Times* columnist, pedestrian deaths increased from 232 in 1910, steadily through the 1920s, peaking in 1929 with 952 deaths.[1] After that they began to decrease through the decades up to the present day, with 166 pedestrian deaths in 2006. I think we may have to blame that fatal 1910–1929 surge on the advent of the Model T, which also brought about traffic jams and parking problems. This downside to the advent of the affordable automobile may be seen in comedies in the many scenes of traffic congestion, traffic cops, incompetent garage mechanics, and cars running into or over people, or dragging them along behind. The Keystone Kops were more often dragged behind the paddy wagon than allowed to ride in it. An outstanding example occurs in the chase sequence of *Wandering Willies* (1926): the cops, at first clinging to each other and struggling to stay in the vehicle, are pulled off and swept in a line behind it, dragged through the countryside, wrapped around poles, and otherwise thoroughly mistreated.

Mabel Normand took to the wheel – metaphorically and in actuality – when she directed and starred in *Mabel at the Wheel* in 1914, the year the Ford plant achieved the production rate of a complete chassis every 93 minutes (eventually they got it down to mere seconds). One wonders how many of those cars were destined to be demolished by the Keystone demons of excess and delirium. The production of *Mabel and Fatty's Simple Life* in 1915 was reported in trade periodicals to be extra expensive because the explosions destroyed two automobiles. The anarchist Mikhail Bakunin famously proclaimed back in the nineteenth century, "The passion for destruction is also a creative passion."[2] The destructive slapstick comedies from Sennett and his followers I take to signify the nihilistic strain that existed in American life, the opposite side of the coin of the idealism, optimism, and ambition for success personified by the young Henry Ford and exemplified in the cheerful energetic comedies of Douglas Fairbanks. I envision a cynical Mack Sennett running his studio empire from the bathtub he kept in his office, mocking whatever Americans took seriously. To be sure, the unruly anarchic spirit of the Sennett comedy was contained within an increasingly organized film industry and the growing dominance of the feature film. It was an expression of the absurdity of life within ten minutes or half an hour of the film theater's program.

In the first year of Keystone's existence, Mack Sennett was already using automobiles to add to the speed of comic chases. In *Barney Oldfield's Race for a Life* (1913) Mabel Normand is tied to the railroad tracks while the hero races to the rescue, with Barney Oldfield driving his famous racing car. A week later, Mabel, in *The Speed Queen*, is driving a car herself at high speed, pursued by two motorcycle cops, rival suitors for her affection. The violence at the Sennett studio increased with the burlesque melodrama *The Fatal Taxicab* (var. *The Faithful Taxicab*, 1913): Mabel's rival lovers snatch her back and forth between a speeding taxicab and an automobile. In the slapstick comedies that followed, cars dropped off cliffs, were parked in the tops of trees, or simply fell apart. Probably the most well-known vehicular violence was inflicted on the Keystone Kops' paddy wagon. In *The Surf Girl* (1916), the paddy wagon is too high to go under a doorway, so the cab and the body separate, and half of it grows legs and walks off. In other films, the Keystone Kops accompanied their paddy wagon over cliffs or off the pier into the Pacific.

The Sennett studio was a training ground, or at least a starting point for most comedy directors and stars of the early 1910s, but it was soon equaled, and in some instances surpassed, by the Hal Roach Studios. By the 1920s, most producers of slapstick comedies occasionally or even frequently used the demolition of cars as a sure-fire gag, and therefore I will refer to a number of comedies that were not from the Sennett studio. The movie palaces of the 1920s catered to a middle-class audience, and that audience had a thorough familiarity with the pleasures and pains of owning and driving an automobile. In 1919 *'Twas Henry's Fault*, produced by Al Christie, showed how the mass production of the Model T affected people's lives. It also portrayed sensitivities to car status, with the cheap Ford car ranked at the bottom: a young married couple dream of owning a car, but he has higher ambitions than she does. She saves up her grocery money and surprises him with the purchase of a Model T. He is unhappy because he is teased at the office and, anyway, the tin lizzy breaks down too easily. In the end, however, the Model T ends up towing the more expensive car. In the films *Don't Park Here* (1919), with Monty Banks and Charlie Dorety, and *Don't Park There* (1924), with Will Rogers, it is clear that

110

the number of cars were beginning to outnumber parking places. Will Rogers had to go all the way to Alaska looking for a parking space.

It is likewise evident from the movies that the cheaply made Ford cars needed plenty of repairs. The new profession of auto mechanic expanded to meet demand. The point of the comedies about them is that these mechanics, like the owners of the cars, know nothing about the work except how to take cars apart, not how to put them back together. In fact the Model T had fewer parts than its predecessors, as a result of Ford's methods of production efficiency, one of which was to manufacture components that combined several parts into one. For slapstick comedy, car "repair" is only another way to destroy the Model T. Fatty Arbuckle and Buster Keaton in *The Garage* (1919) use a turntable for working on cars, but mostly rotate themselves instead, while a rental car falls to pieces in front of the garage. "I didn't want a collapsible model," the customer complains. In *All Wet* (1924), Charley Chase's car is fully immersed in a mud puddle and comes apart when the incompetent mechanic tries to tow it; the tow vehicle also comes apart after Charley improbably repairs his own car under water. In *Fully Insured* (1923), a Hal Roach film, Snub Pollard is a garage mechanic who cheerfully demolishes a taxicab. In *The Mechanic* (1924), Jimmy Aubrey is the mechanic in the "Henry Ford Garage," where, in spite of the famous name, cars are always mistreated. In *Lizzies of the Field* (1924), Billy Bevan in a dream drives his bed to his job as a mechanic. A rival garage stands across the street from the one where he works and the mechanics compete for the cars brought in for repair. At the peak of the contest the rivals pull on the same car until it is stretched out to twice its original length. In *Wandering Willies* (1926), a car receives the opposite treatment (this time not by incompetent mechanics but by an incompetent driver), when it is compressed like an accordion between two streetcars. A wonderful example of the absurdity and despair that characterizes many of the incompetent mechanic comedies may be found in *Don't Tell Everything* (1927), a Hal Roach production. Max Davidson's touring car is in the garage for repairs. The mechanic has taken out a lot of parts and, when he sees Max approaching, hastily sweeps them under the car. As the car falls apart, a street-cleaning truck lets a flood of water into the gutter, sweeping the car – in pieces – down the curb-side sewer drain as Max slides into the gutter flat on his stomach and peers hopelessly into the drain.

Judging from slapstick comedies produced during the first decade or two of the mass intrusion of the affordable automobile into American life, we might conclude that people reacted to these transformative events with apprehension, pride, and considerable ingenuity, tempered by resignation. Alice Howell in *One Wet Night* (1924) asks her soaking wet spouse after he arrives home in the "puddle jumper" of which he is so proud: "Is Henry building submarines now?" That freedom, that first delightful control over one's own rapid movement was soon constrained by traffic and traffic laws and traffic cops and poor roads, as well as cars that fell apart, not to mention the high price of gas at the pump, a shocking 25–30 cents per gallon in 1916, and rising.

In 1911 the Supreme Court split up Standard Oil, charging restraint of trade in contravention of the Sherman Anti-Trust Act. As the oil barons were squeezing profits out of the gas station pumps, the nation's car enthusiasts hoped to find an alternate fuel: in January 1913 the International Association of Auto Clubs offered a $100,000 prize for the best alternate fuel for the internal combustion engine. I have not investigated the results of this contest, but I have observed that slapstick comedies were highly imaginative at proposing substitutes. In the Sennett film, *Skylarking* (1923), an inventor "with an idea to keep Fords off the earth" devises "Victor Edison's Self Raising Air Car," a car with a hot-air balloon attached and a propeller behind that can lift the car above street traffic. In *Get Out and Get Under* (1920), Harold Lloyd observes the transformation of a drug addict when he takes a hit, and lifts the man's hypodermic to put the drug in the tank of his Model T, which, newly energized, takes off without him. In *Go As You Please* (1920), Snub Pollard tries pouring beer in his tank, which results in the car staggering drunkenly as it moves. In *It's a Gift* (1923), Snub Pollard again, a Rube Goldberg kind of inventor, fuels his own vehicle with a huge magnet that pulls him along behind other people's cars. He is invited by an oil company to invent a more powerful fuel. We don't learn the ingredients, but a drop of his concoction is strong enough to cause a whole fleet of automobiles to go into a frenzy like that of a disturbed ants' nest, until they all collide and explode. These films were made at the Hal Roach Studios, which may have surpassed Sennett in the production of automobile destruction, if we take into consideration such masterful comedies as the Laurel and Hardy film *Two Tars* (1928), when the boys precipitate a riot of mass destruction during an enormous traffic jam. Still, the Sennett studio came up with a great example of the gas substitute proposals in 1925, in *Super-Hooper-Dyne Lizzies*, which was directed by Del Lord from a script by Frank Capra. An inventor (Andy Clyde) has found yet another cheap alternate fuel: he powers all the cars in town with radio waves, or "the hot air wasted on radio speeches," sometimes resulting in automobiles taking off on their own without their drivers or dragging them behind, but nonetheless enabling car owners to thumb their noses at high-priced gas to the annoyance of the oil company. This idea was so timely that it was copied in 1926 in *Wireless Lizzie*, where Walter Hiers plays another inventor who uses a radio to power cars.

Returning to *Super-Hooper-Dyne Lizzies*, Billy Bevan finds himself out of gas thanks to the wicked machinations of the big oilman, who is after Billy's girl. Bevan begins to push the girl's empty and powerless car from the back, head bent to the task. His car bumps into a parked car, and then another, without his knowledge, until he is engaged in the task of pushing a curving line of at least seven cars ahead of him. This is a prolonged sequence, and slow-paced for a Sennett film. The chain of cars pushes through an intersection and around it, to the confusion of a traffic policeman, and is followed by a growing group of fast-walking men in business suits in pursuit of their vehicles but never catching up with the slow but dogged Billy Bevan. Up a steep hill, Bevan, still unknowing, his head down, pushes the train of cars, slowly, until it reaches the top and each car in turn goes over a cliff and smashes into the last. The bewildered Bevan only discovers the facts when his own car comes to teeter on the brink. I would like to argue that long before Albert Camus wrote *The Myth of Sisyphus*, Mack Sennett gave us the metaphor for man's fate in the modern age.

## notes

1. Michael Pollak, "F.Y.I.," *New York Times*, City Weekly Desk section, February 4 (2007): 2.
2. Mikhail Bakunin, in *Deutsche Jahrbücher*, October (1842), cited in James Mark Leier, *Bakunin: The Creative Passion* (New York: Thomas Dunne Books, 2006), 98.

# "uproarious inventions"

the keystone film company,

modernity, and the art of the

motor

s e v e n

r o b   k i n g

*The mechanical truth, in short, was sometimes first spoken
in jest.*

(Lewis Mumford, *Technics and Civilization*[1])

In October 1917, the film magazine *Photoplay* published an essay describing
a recent "improvement in ... slapstick comedy." Whereas "the old slapstick effect" had formerly been achieved with "the familiar pie," argued
writer Alfred Cohn, one studio had, in recent years, developed a new
slapstick style centered upon "the super-stunt in which the camera is the
chief performer, aided by derricks and piano wires." The "chief policy" of
that studio, Cohn wrote, was "to 'thrill 'em as well as make 'em laugh'"
by "hitting the victim with an auto or blowing him up with a bomb."[2]
Cohn did not mention the company by name because he did not have to;
any movie fan would have known he was referring to the Keystone Film
Company. Nor was he alone in making these observations. As another
critic had noted two years previously, "Almost every Keystone comedy
contains at least two or three mechanical or spectacular surprises,"

adding that "the secrets of many of these would be worth fortunes to less resourceful competitors."[3] Certainly no other aspect of the studio's output ever received such unanimous praise, as, week after week, reviewers wrote in amazement of the films' "mechanical contrivances," "trick, mechanical effects," and "uproarious inventions."[4]

One of the things for which Keystone is best remembered is, indeed, mechanical and spectacular surprise, "super-stunts" featuring the haywire tin lizzies, out-of-control police wagons, somersaulting planes, and other contraptions in which the studio's films abounded from the mid-1910s on. Of course, as many historians have noted, the desire to see machine technology not simply in utilitarian terms, but as a source of enjoyment and fascination in its own right provided the basis for a very wide range of entertainments during this period, not only at Keystone. Whether manifest in the mechanical rides at Coney Island, in the "invention" cartoons of Rube Goldberg, in the cult of the automobile, or even in the public's fascination with cinema itself, technological innovation had become the core of a vernacular tradition whose influence extended across cultural hierarchies and social divisions. Already by 1900, new technical institutes and engineering schools were proliferating nationwide, including Stevens Institute of Technology (1870), the Case School of Applied Science (1880), and Carnegie Technical Schools (1900). Figures of straightforward growth signal a burgeoning fascination for mechanical invention: the record of 23,000 patents issued by the US Patent Office during the entire 1850s had been equaled if not exceeded every single *year* from 1882 onwards.[5] These were decades of intense industrialization and technological progress: few people were left unaffected by the speed and scale of change.

Keystone's "mechanical contrivances" clearly take their place in this context. Yet, more than mere symptoms of a historical moment, they also provide a touchstone against which to weigh the changing function of popular comedy during what has come to be known as American cinema's "transitional" era (roughly speaking, the period spanning the shift from the "cinema of attractions" to the consolidation of classical film practices, between 1908 and 1917). As *Moving Picture World* critic Louis Reeves Harrison suggested in 1916, the success of the studio's uproarious inventions lay in their ability to "delight *all* classes," and to address fascinations shared by a majority of the film-going public.[6] Whereas Keystone's earliest films had once been disparaged as vulgar fare intended only for working men and "friends of burlesque," mechanical spectacle allowed Keystone to build a cross-class public for its films and draw filmgoers into a new world of mass culture.[7] They thus participated in the emergence of a distinctly modern comic form — one that may have played a key role in mediating the experience of mechanization for audiences whose own encounters with technology, I will suggest, often betrayed startling ambivalences.

Throughout, my aim here is to argue for the significance of Keystone slapstick – a crucial instance of what Miriam Hansen has termed the "aesthetic horizon" of American modernity[8] – to a discussion of the formation of mass culture and its relation to turn-of-the-century technological advance. As Frankfurt School theorist Theodor Adorno suggested, one of the characteristics of mass culture has been the primacy of technique and technology over issues of social meaning. The "ultimate expression" of modern culture's technological underpinnings, he wrote in a late essay, is a growing concern with "the technical 'how,'" with virtuoso technique and technological achievement.[9] The point has direct applicability to the American situation, where the popularization of a "machine aesthetic" during the early twentieth century often came at the cost of the social and political themes that had infused the work of earlier Progressive artists.[10] To paraphrase Adorno, the technical "how" of mass culture increasingly supplanted the social "what" of Progressive-era creativity. Something similar can be seen at Keystone, as the studio's emphasis on mechanical effects transformed the films' earlier engagement with the fantasies and experiences of the working class. Understanding those displacements not only sets in relief technology's role in creating new forms of cultural consensus; it also suggests how that consensus has continued to frame recent debates about early cinema and modernity.

## "they have no explanation – they simply are": stunts, tricks, and the operational aesthetic

Back when Keystone debuted, in the fall of 1912, slapstick cinema had been in the doldrums, only just beginning its recovery from a four-year slump in comic film production; Keystone's dizzying rise to success no doubt owed much to the perceived weakness of its competition.[11] By the middle of the decade, however, the situation was different: the studio's popularity had helped spark an industry-wide resurgence in film comedy, with the result that Keystone was now, ironically, fighting to retain its prominence against competitors who aped its formula for broad slapstick and genre parody (and who, in certain cases, poached Keystone's leading talent – notably Essanay's acquisition of Charlie Chaplin in December 1914). Indeed, several of the studio's most recognizable players were, by this point, either moving on or fading out: Mabel Normand would quit the company in 1916 to star in five-reel "light comedy dramas," the first of which, *Mickey*, would not be released until 1918; Roscoe Arbuckle declined in productivity over the course of 1916 and was signed to the Paramount label early the following year; and Ford Sterling, who had returned to Sennett's fold following a disappointing year at Universal in 1914, never regained the popularity of his early "Dutch" roles at Keystone. Thus, an initial proposal: Keystone's "uproarious inventions" need to be understood as showmanship, a new tactic of product differentiation in an era of changing stars and growing competition. Thus, also, some initial questions: What did this emphasis on sensational effects entail for the making of the studio's films (the level of production) and, more importantly, how did audiences and the trade press respond to those changes (the level of consumption)?

The new direction first became clear in early 1915, when, following a 50 percent budget increase for each film (raising the available funds per two-reel picture to around $10,000), Keystone's filmmakers immediately set to work on the pathbreaking *The Cannon Ball* (June 1915) – the studio's first full-fledged example of what might be termed an "effects" comedy.[12] Advertised to exhibitors as "The First Big Mack Sennett Keystone Special" and "The Most Spectacular Comedy Ever Made," *The Cannon Ball* broke new ground for Keystone through its sustained concatenation of absurd stunts, explosions, and improbable actions.[13] At one point in the film, a well-hidden use of piano wires (to lift objects in the air) creates a tracking shot in which the villain (Chester Conklin) is doggedly pursued by an errant cannonball; elsewhere, double exposure and piano wires combine to show a policeman flying across rooftops, dragged by a second hurtling cannonball; finally, miniature models create the film's thrilling climax, in which the hero (Charles Arling) uses the cannon to explode a bridge, sending Conklin tumbling into the river below. "The Keystone company is in topknotch form in this number," commented the approving reviewer in *Moving Picture World*.[14]

The level of attention the film garnered in the trade press was, admittedly, nothing special; yet, in retrospect, it is evident that *The Cannon Ball* marked a turning point of sorts at Keystone. Evident also was studio head Mack Sennett's willingness to support these developments, as production budgets were increasingly funneled toward the purchase of new technical tools and gadgetry. Already by the spring of 1915 construction had begun on a $35,000 frame building, housing a 140-foot by 75-foot outdoor stage equipped for stunt work and sensational effects. A 20-foot by 40-foot water tank at its center would serve Keystone's filmmakers for various purposes over the following years, yielding scenes in which rooms filled up with water (*Ambrose's Nasty Temper*, April 1915) and houses floated out to sea (*Fatty and Mabel Adrift*, January 1916). The new building also housed a "garage of sufficient size for eight or ten big autos," supplying storage space for the studio's growing stable of flivvers and police wagons.[15]

This process of expansion only accelerated following the summer of 1915, when Keystone deserted its distributor, Mutual Film Corporation, to align itself with Harry Aitken's newly formed Triangle Film Corporation, of which it was a founding member.[16] Immediately launched was a lavish studio upgrade that enabled the purchase of yet more tools and contraptions. As *Motion Picture News* reported in late November 1915, "air equipment [has been bought for] the Keystone plant, a Wright model 'B' aeroplane which is in addition to the monoplane with a Rotary Motor made by Joe Murray of the Keystone publicity department."[17] That same year filmmakers also began work on an elaborate "panorama" device for the filming of chase sequences – a rotating painted backdrop in front of which performers would run on a treadmill. The principle behind this apparatus eventually became the basis for the most unusual and unique contraption ever to grace Sennett's lot: the "Cyclorama." An enormous revolving drum measuring 109 feet in diameter and 25 feet in height, driven by three separate engines and capable of speeds of up to 35 miles per hour, the Cyclorama was, in the words of one of Sennett's child actors, "like a big merry-go-round in a fun park."[18] In an era of industrial expansion and rationalization, the Keystone lot had come to resemble nothing less than a funfair, a carnivalesque reflection of a mechanized world.

In fact, by 1916 Keystone had remade itself into an industry leader in innovative special effects and stuntwork, a base for a number of filmmakers (and frequent collaborators) who began experimenting with the studio's new resources. Among these, for instance, was Coy Watson, a long-standing Sennett employee whose inventive work with piano wires and other devices earned him the studio nickname "Fire, Wire and Water

Figure 7.1

The "Cyclorama" c. early 1920s. Courtesy of the Academy of Motion Picture Arts and Sciences

Watson." Other innovations were contributed by Fred W. Jackman, a cameraman at Keystone since 1913 and the studio's resident photographic effects specialist. But it would be director Walter Wright who played the crucial role in fusing these disparate innovations into the new, effects-laden approach that became the hallmark of Keystone's later films. As a report in one trade journal enthused,

> Walter Wright is the Keystone's "trick" director. If you want to make a close-up of an aeroplane 5,000 feet above the sea, or of a man escaping from a sunken submarine, or any little thing of that sort, [Wright] can tell you how to do it.[19]

Wright's reputation as the studio's stunt specialist was chiefly established by two films released close together in late 1915/early 1916, *Saved by Wireless* (November 1915) and *Dizzy Heights and Daring Hearts* (January 1916), each one an extravagant spectacle of modern machinery, trick photography, and breathtaking stuntwork. The latter film, in particular, astonished critics with its imaginative use of Keystone's new planes. "[It] is a marvelous stunt picture," commented the *New York Tribune*. "Air ships are made to loop the loop, turn turtle, walk on their hind legs and do all the thousand and one tricks incapable of accomplishment except by the aerial fleet used by Mack Sennett."[20] Such thrilling effects were, for the most part, accomplished through camera work (notably, a rotating camera); but *Dizzy Heights* also included the most stunning scene of authentically staged spectacle in Keystone's entire output. For the climax, the studio purchased a 200-foot industrial smokestack at a deserted Inglewood factory and dynamited it for the cameras (an event that drew hundreds of observers).[21] The resulting footage was then cut in with studio-shot footage in which, thanks to deft use of piano wires and a chimney-top set, the heroine appears to fly down and rescue her beloved from atop the smokestack seconds before it explodes. "Melodrama in its wildest moments," observed one critic, "has pictured nothing more thrilling than the ascent of the tall chimney and the nerve-tingling incidents of rescue that follow."[22]

To modern viewers watching these films almost a century after their first release, Keystone's "thrilling" effects likely appear rather obvious, perhaps even clumsily so. The important question, however, concerns the films' original audiences: Were *they* aware that camera trickery was involved? To be sure, Keystone's filmmakers never denied their use of special effects, and they knew their audiences were savvy enough to differentiate real stunts from trick photography. "Now and then we do a trick film," confessed comedian/director Roscoe Arbuckle, "but everyone knows it is a trick when they see it — there is no bunk about it."[23] Keystone's special effects, it would appear, evoked pleasure not because they

convinced audiences of their authenticity, but because they inspired won-
derment in the representational possibilities of cinema and delight in
being "taken in" by skilful trickery. In the eyes of contemporary critics
the Keystone studio appeared as a magician's chest, delighting audiences
with trick work that "completely mystifies the uninitiated"; the films'
special effects were "impossible feats" which "have no explanation – they
simply are."[24] The pleasure of Keystone's "uproarious inventions" was the
pleasure of the trick: audiences knew their eyes were being deceived, yet
they delighted in their own mystification.

Recent work by Ben Singer points to a useful comparison here with the
"sensation scenes" of turn-of-the-century stage melodrama. As Singer
suggests, the elaborate scenography of the popular melodramatic stage –
often used to render quite extraordinary spectacles, anything from Alpine
avalanches to hot-air balloon battles – appealed to audiences not by allowing them to suspend their disbelief (as if they were witnessing something
real) but rather, like Keystone, by engaging their "'how to' interest in the
medium's materials and its representational potentials."[25] Keystone's
uniqueness in this respect was not that it imported this kind of interest to
cinema – the "trick" comedies and animations of J. Stuart Blackton, Emile
Cohl, and others were the obvious pioneers here – but that as it exploited
it was key to the studio's brand identity.[26] Sennett and his filmmakers were
well aware that a carefully manipulated veil of secrecy concerning production methods would not only stimulate audience curiosity, but give them
competitive advantage over others who, like Vitagraph's Larry Semon,
were beginning to experiment with similar effects. A *Photoplay* cartoon from
March 1917 represents the Keystone studio as a heavily defended fortress,
barricaded against "spies" sent by less-resourceful filmmakers. Keystone's
trick effects, we are led to understand, were equivalent to state secrets in a
time of war: "It's easier to get into Germany than it is to get into the Keystone in these piping times of trick stunts," the caption reads. One further
gets a sense of the value Sennett personally placed on such secrecy from a
letter he wrote to Adolph Zukor in December 1917, shortly after joining
Zukor's Paramount organization that summer. "We do our utmost here
to keep any and all of our mechanical contrivances a studio secret,"
Sennett insisted, explaining:

> Can you imagine, as an illustration, a magician explain-
> ing to his audience how a trick is done and then going
> ahead and doing it? Naturally there ceases to be the
> required illusion; therefore it is of no interest to the
> spectators whatever.[27]

Sennett and his filmmakers, the letter suggests, were akin to "magicians";
the studio's special effects were "tricks" or "illusions," the success of
which depended on the audience's inability to figure them out.

It is vital to realize that, in making these claims, Sennett was placing himself and his filmmakers in a tradition of American entertainers skilled in the practice of pleasurable deception – a tradition encompassing stage illusionists like Harry Houdini and extending back to P. T. Barnum, who had invited mid-nineteenth-century viewers to debate whether his attractions were genuine or hoaxes. This kind of entertainment strategy, labeled the "operational aesthetic" by historian Neil Harris, was characteristic of an age of intense public fascination with the way things worked, and it appealed to a delight in problem-solving and observing technical operations. Like Houdini's impossible escapes, Keystone's operational aesthetic addressed the amateur's desire to understand technical processes at a time when technological advancement far outstripped the average individual's understanding or control. The studio's trick effects invited audiences to examine and debate how they were accomplished – to match wits with Keystone's filmmakers – all the better to "mystify the uninitiated." The spectacle of technology was pervaded by a species of glamour, in the original etymological sense of magical spell.

One can in fact see Keystone's operational aesthetic at work in the very structure of the films' comic action. A common tendency, fully developed in the studio's post-1914 output, was to stage elaborate race-to-the-rescue climaxes in which multiple modes of transport intersect along chaotic, criss-crossed paths of pursuit – for instance, a car versus a police wagon versus two handcarts versus a runaway safe in *Only a Messenger Boy* (August 1915), a plane versus a yacht versus a car versus a (temporarily) airborne motorbike in *Saved by Wireless* (November 1915), and a car versus a motorbike versus a bicycle versus two horse-drawn carts versus sprinting policemen in *Thirst* (July 1917), to cite only three variations on this motif. Technology thus became a model for comic action in which narrative logic was replaced by the haywire circuitry of modern technology. In one sense, such sequences continue Sennett's frequent parodies of the race-to-the-rescue melodramas of his former boss at Biograph, D. W. Griffith. Yet, in their absurdist concatenation of mechanical devices, they point also in the direction of cartoonist Rube Goldberg, whose famous "invention" drawings likewise invited the American public to trace nonsensical sequences of cause and effect through the image of the machine. As contemporary critics put it, Keystone's rapid, criss-crossing action addressed the film-goers' desire to keep abreast of "the general destination of what is going on," and it "bewildered" them with "the rapid succession of the unexpected."[28] The very speed of the action forestalled adequate comprehension. From around *The Cannon Ball* onward, in fact, Keystone's films were edited far more rapidly than its previous releases, with an average shot length of around 4.5 seconds that, for *Moving Picture World* critic Louis Reeves Harrison at least, was simply too fast to follow: "The movement is very fast, too fast at times for the average spectator" (on *Cactus Nell*,

June 1917); "We are lost, in fact, as to the general destination of what is going on" (on *A Dog Catcher's Love*, June 1917); "There is plot enough to supply a high comedy, but it soon becomes submerged in the swift farce, too swift at times" (on *Whose Baby?*, July 1917).[29] What Keystone's "uproarious inventions" achieved at the level of spectacle, the studio's "swift farces" thus accomplished at the level of narrative: both challenged viewers to make active sense of mechanical process, only to submit them to the passive delights of amused befuddlement.

The enormous acclaim this style of comedy received nonetheless suggests how greatly it appealed to the emotional needs of diverse film-goers. Technological spectacle possessed a mass basis precisely because it addressed interests that were widely shared in a technocratic society; as such, it provided a framework within which Keystone's filmmakers could tailor their output to tastes and enthusiasms linking different classes of audience. The point comes to be of particular importance when we recall American slapstick's roots in the popular festivities, saloon entertainments, and burlesque houses of late nineteenth-century male working-class culture: if, in inevitable consequence, film slapstick was typically viewed as a "low" cinematic form, then Keystone's mechanical displays laid the foundations for a new slapstick style that transcended the genre's disreputable origins. Such, at least, was suggested by the reviews of *Moving Picture World* critic Louis Reeves Harrison, who frequently praised Keystone's stunts and trick work precisely on this count. Appealing to gender-coded notions of respectability, Harrison described the action of *Crooked to the End* (December 1915) as "bound to make some excitable member of any mixed [i.e., mixed-gender] audience hysterical."[30] *Dizzy Heights and Daring Hearts*, meanwhile, was said to contain "marvels of ingenuity which delight all classes."[31] Despite the roughhouse antics of *The Great Vacuum Robbery* (December 1915), Harrison noted elsewhere, even refined viewers would discover much "of real merit" in the film's "original conception of robbing a bank through vacuum tubes."[32] But the point was made most succinctly in an open letter from one Keystone fan to Mack Sennett, printed in the *Philadelphia Public Ledger*. "Much has been said about the vulgarity of the Keystone comedies, and few people grasp the ingenuity of the mechanical devices," began the writer, concluding simply, "What could be more clever and less vulgar?"[33] In effect, technological spectacle redeemed physical comedy for a cross-class audience: where once genteel critics had been offended by slapstick's "vulgarity," they now were able to celebrate the "ingenuity" of its mechanical devices. The spectacle of modern technology thus formed a crystallizing point for a new mass culture that engaged the interests and experiences of an overwhelming majority of the population. The relevant questions to ask next, however, are: What kinds of experiences were being engaged here? To what end?

## "the most astonishing bit of mechanical tomfoolery that ever happened": warfare, funfairs, and fetishism

What made Keystone's operational aesthetic so popular at this historical moment was a conjunction of concerns about the meanings of modern technology, and about the social and human costs of modernity. Perhaps more than any other development in turn-of-the-century culture, the embrace of mechanization displayed a Janus face. Already by the 1880s technological growth in the United States had entered a new phase – a "second industrial revolution," it has been called – spurring a utopian faith in industrial progress whose monuments included the Brooklyn Bridge and the railroad. Yet the very speed of industrialization exacted a stiff price in terms of social discontent, a crisis of discomposure and shock which observers attributed to increased nervous stimulation, what New York reformer Michael Davis labeled "hyperstimulus."[34] Alongside the din of cheers on behalf of technology as a horn of plenty, there also existed sinister expressions of technological cataclysm, in which machines were envisioned as instruments of destruction, as in the technologically induced holocaust that closes Mark Twain's 1889 novel, *A Connecticut Yankee in King Arthur's Court*, or the dystopic vision of future technocracy in Ignatius Donnelly's *Caesar's Column*, published the same year. A succession of titles such as George Miller Beard's *American Nervousness* (1881) and John Girdner's *Newyorkitis* (1901) viewed the pace of the modern technological environment as a disease whose symptoms included anything from neurasthenia to baldness and tooth decay.[35] Modernity appeared to many much in the guise of a juggernaut, a runaway engine of uncontrollable power that crushed all that stood before it. Whether manifest in late nineteenth-century paintings of trains thrusting out into a virgin landscape (the "machine in the garden" of Leo Marx's famous study) or in magazine illustrations of streetcars leaving streams of injured pedestrians in their wake, the juggernaut provided a template for envisioning the irrationality and unstoppable onrush of a mechanized, industrial society.[36]

Against this backdrop of concerns Keystone's mechanical contrivances remystified technology as a source of pleasure, not anxiety, offering carnivalesque images of out-of-control machinery that bracketed off the more distressing aspects of American culture's encounters with the machine. The point emerges clearly from a discussion of Keystone's 1915 Christmas special, *A Submarine Pirate*, a four-reel comedy whose five-month production period represents the single greatest expenditure of time on any Keystone release.[37] Little known now, *A Submarine Pirate* was in fact the most financially and critically successful of the studio's films outside of its 1914 feature, *Tillie's Punctured Romance*. Critics were unanimous in offering the most positive reviews that any Keystone film had ever received, describing it as "quite unusual if not marvellous," "one of the best examples of [Sennett's] art yet shown," and "the most astonishing bit of mechanical tomfoolery that ever happened."[38] According to a report in *The Triangle*, the film even received the unusual distinction of being selected by William Randolph Hearst to show at a high-toned Thanksgiving Day party: "Triangle plays apparently appeal to all classes," the writer smugly surmised.[39]

What appealed "to all classes" was once again the spectacle of technological process. As promotional material proclaimed, *A Submarine Pirate* offered viewers an opportunity to see for themselves a "naval submersible of the latest American type" which the US Navy had loaned to Keystone for exterior sequences.[40] The film, it was claimed,

> displays submarine work pictorially in such detailed fashion as has never before been seen on the screen.... It is like being right in the inside of things to see the views of the interior of the submarine with all its mysterious wires, switches and gears.[41]

Triangle exhibitors, for their part, were advised to be-deck theater lobbies with torpedo and periscope props that would "reflect the characteristics of the movie," while critics, too, boosted the film's technological appeal, praising its display of "interesting methods of handling Uncle Sam's submersibles."[42]

At the time when *A Submarine Pirate* was released, there was indeed exceptional public interest in "submersibles," albeit not for reasons that had much to do with comedy. The sinking of the ocean liner *Lusitania* by a German U-boat on May 7, 1915 had provoked a widespread outcry which, while it did not precipitate American entry into the war, nevertheless fostered US government support for new defense programs and boosted public anxiety about the nation's military preparedness. Over 1,200 lives had been lost in an incident that newspapers freely described with words like "insane," "madness," and "brutality."[43] This, one would imagine, was hardly fit subject matter for slapstick comedy, especially since two more passenger liners had fallen victim to the same fate within months of the *Lusitania*. The paradox, then, is that a comedy so explicitly grounded in the tragedies of mid-1915 should have proved so enormously popular – even with the US Navy, which announced that it would screen *A Submarine Pirate* for recruiting purposes in light of America's possible entry into the war.

How, then, to transform such events into comedy? The answer offered by *A Submarine Pirate* involves a careful substitution, a rewriting of submarine technology from the perspective of a purely operational fascination. From the moment the waiter first boards the vessel (at the beginning of the third reel), the submarine is presented as an entirely technological space, its interior bristling with gears, levers, dials, wheels, and other contraptions. The waiter descends into this interior and there follows a paradigmatic instance of Keystone's operational aesthetic, as a naval officer patiently explains how each instrument functions. Cutting between interior and exterior shots, the film now shows the submarine responding to the waiter's control, submerging and resurfacing as he pushes the levers this way and that. This "Lesson in Submerging" (as an inter-title describes it) served as a key attraction in the film, the point at which – to quote from the film's publicity campaign – viewers were able to witness the

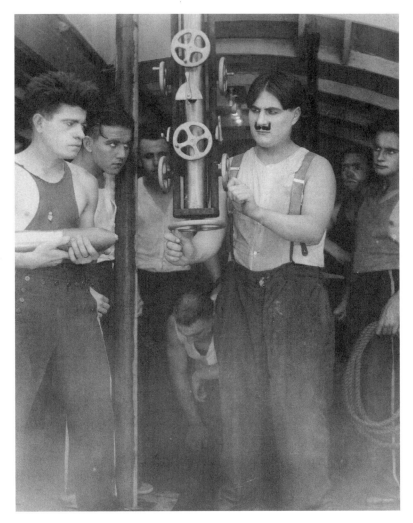

Figure 7.2

The waiter (Syd Chaplin) receives a "Lesson in Submerging." Production still from *A Submarine Pirate* (1915). Courtesy of the Wisconsin Historical Society (Image ID 43916)

craft's "mysterious wires, switches and gears." Coming at the very center of this four-reel comedy, the scene stages the central confrontation between clown and machine through the display of modes of operation and control, inviting the spectator to view the submarine not as an instrument of war, but as a source of technical amusement. In effect, the submarine's technology becomes a fetish, precisely analogous to Marx's definition of commodity fetishism as a displacement of desire from human relations onto material objects: substituting for the memory of the *Lusitania*, which contemporary movie-goers surely brought to their experience of the film, *A Submarine Pirate* invites an enchanted fascination with "mysterious" gears, dials, and levers.

It is this substitution upon which the film's success as comedy depends. Rather than engage the vessel's more sinister associations, the film offers instead the pleasures of technological gadgetry. In quick succession, there now unfolds a series of burlesque piratical exploits in which the submarine sinks a passenger liner and then gets caught in a comic battle with a gunboat. Twice the vessel expels the hapless waiter into the surrounding waters, and each time it becomes more a microcosmic amusement park than a machine of war. The first time, the waiter is launched out of the submarine on the end of a torpedo, sending him skimming across the ocean surface in a fashion akin to the then-popular "Shoot-the-Chutes" water slides. In the second instance – the film's final scene – the submarine spins round and round, sending the waiter flying through a port-hole; the use of a revolving set here recalls Steeplechase Park's famous "Barrel of Fun," a rotating cylinder that rolled customers off their feet as they entered the park.[44] The film ends with an image of comic mechanical entrapment: a close-up of the waiter mugging frenetically, his head underwater. A coda to the waiter's fate, a big fake fish swims into shot and bites him on the nose.

*A Submarine Pirate*, then, is a film that envisions the submarine less as an instrument of militaristic destruction, more as a vehicle for amusing exploits. If part of the fear evoked by the sinking of the *Lusitania* was a sense of technological uncontrollability – the realization that the machines to which people daily entrusted their lives were unable to protect them, that they could even lead them into the paths of other machines in the service of warfare and destruction – then *A Submarine Pirate* negotiated those fears by redefining human subjection to technology as pleasurable spectacle. Viewed thus, Keystone's mechanical contrivances take their place as symptoms of a far broader, fetishizing compulsion in turn-of-the-century popular culture to revisit technological cataclysm as amusing display. From Currier & Ives lithographs of steamboat explosions to amusement park disaster shows recreating tenement fires and naval battles, a wide range of popular entertainments sought to redefine technological trauma according to the pleasure principle. If technology awoke dystopian fears in many, still it could be enjoyed as a source of kinetic sensation and spectacle, as films like *A Submarine Pirate* make clear. The amusement parks and summer resorts that had become big business in America by the early 1900s likewise substituted the thrills of the roller coaster for the shocks of technological devastation. Coney Island's "Leap-Frog Railway," for example, played upon popular fears of railroad accidents by hurtling two electric cars toward each other, each filled with up to 40 people. At the last moment, one of the cars sloped up along a curved set of rails, over the roof of the other and back down behind it.[45] The very technologies that workers encountered at the factory – and that had, in many instances, put them out of work – could be returned to them as forms of commercial pleasure: some amusement park rides were directly inspired by industrial machinery, beginning with Coney Island's 1884 "Switchback Railroad," an early form of roller coaster based on the gravity-powered coal cars used for mining. At the amusement park, observed modernist artist Joseph Stella, machines were transformed into instruments of visceral delight, "generating for the first time, not anguish and pain, but violent, dangerous pleasures."[46] A symbol of the new mass culture, the roller coaster became the dialectical counterpart to the negative perception of technology as juggernaut.

Such amusements provide the context against which the meaning of Keystone's mechanical contrivances emerges clearly. The psychic principle that could transform a train wreck into a roller coaster was obviously the same as that which could revisit the *Lusitania* tragedy as slapstick comedy. What Coney Island invited the public to experience directly, Keystone comedies allowed audiences to enjoy reciprocally as immersive spectacle; the pervasive "tricks and traps" of the studio's films, noted a critic for the *Philadelphia Public Ledger*, were "apt to leave the [viewer] delirious, gasping, but unsatiated."[47] Evidently there was more involved here than mere contiguity or historical parallelism. We are dealing, rather, with *homology* in the precise sense suggested by Raymond Williams, that is, a link between different specific practices as "directly related expressions of and responses to a general historical process."[48] If Keystone and Coney shared a vision of the world as a crazy machine, then this was not because (or not merely because) that vision exploited technology's commercial possibilities as a new source of amusement, but, more important, because it played a key role, across a range of cultural practices, in transfiguring the experience of modernity and modernization. At Keystone as at Coney, the image of the world as a crazy machine was a fetish for the modern era, in which cogwheels, levers, and gears meshed to such exhilarating ends that there remained not the slightest gap for confronting the costs of a mechanized environment.

## "a contraction of the zygomatic muscles": modernity, mechanics, and the philosophy of laughter

Here, however, one has to venture a step further by asking, not simply what, but *who* was being omitted in this picture? Put another way, how might the operational mindset have served as an ideology within existing relations of social power and disenfranchisement? And how, if at all, did the figurative association of machines with pleasure contribute forms of representation that submerged class distinctions in an ostensibly homogeneous mass culture? The fetish character of modern mass culture was noted by a large number of sociological thinkers around the turn of the century, although for most, like Thorstein Veblen, this was associated with the circulation of commodities within a consumer economy. Yet there were others for whom the reification of modern life was rather to be traced to its technicist tendencies. When, during World War I, the great art dealer René Gimpel toured America, he discovered a cult of technical effectiveness virtually unknown in Europe, and which he implicitly associated with the disenfranchisement of industrial labor,

> a materialism that took the form of a cult of the machine that was, strictly speaking, alarming, in make-shift villages no longer centered on a church ... but on a factory, a mineshaft, or a railway station, and often deserted overnight.[49]

Likewise for Theodor Adorno, in later decades, America's fascination with "cultic" images of technology – the "technological veil," as he put it – had come to constitute a ritual of mass delusion, a form of disavowal in confronting the consequences of modernity.[50]

The mystique of technology was indeed a particular hallmark of early twentieth-century American culture, its impact felt across the entire spectrum of cultural production. Diverse and different as it was in form and content, American literary and artistic production of the period shared a commitment to an abstract, mechanical conception of force. Writing in 1906, the noted American historian Henry Adams proposed a "Dynamic Theory of History" in which social and political process was now to be apprehended as the development and economy of "forces" and "attractions": "Man is a force; so is the sun; so is a mathematical point."[51] In the wake of the Armory Show of 1913, American modernists seized on the machine as a figure for new aesthetic experiments – and, in the process, abandoned the social focus of earlier Ashcan painters like George Bellows and John Sloan.[52] Around the same period, Lewis Hine's famous photographs of factory laborers grew increasingly less concerned with the problem of labor in its social dimension, emphasizing instead the artful symmetries of factory machinery.[53] Whether manifest in Coney Island or

Keystone, in the work of native-born modernists like Joseph Stella or European immigrés like Francis Picabia, cultural discourse on mechanization represented a disavowal of the social implications of the new technologies and an unwillingness to engage the experiences of workers, who bore the full brunt of modernity's impact. As historian Alan Trachtenberg suggests, America's fascination with the machine dimmed awareness of the transformation of labor, the radical dehumanization of the workforce, that each technological advance represented.[54] One needs to speak, then, of a deterritorialization of the social perspective of Progressive-era creativity by the technicist perspective of modernity: if the machine was a fetish for modernity, then it was a fetish predicated on a certain displacement of working-class horizons of experience and a muting of reformist discourse on class difference.

More than one cultural historian has observed these changes. Less commonly noted are their implications for the comic sensibility of the new mass culture. As Henry Jenkins has shown, contemporary attitudes to physical comedy had begun to change. Slapstick's low reputation as a comic form associated with the traditions of workers and immigrants was superseded by a new appreciation focused instead on the mechanics of its physical action – what musical comedy playwright George M. Cohan termed the "mechanics of emotion."[55] Under the aegis of a developing interest in reflexology, a pseudoscience of comic "mechanics" came to dominate debates on comedy during this period. Social scientists began to embark on quantitative surveys measuring human receptiveness to jokes and other bits of comic business. French philosopher Henri Bergson – who was nearly mobbed by his American fans when he spoke at Columbia University in 1912 – likewise argued for a mechanistic definition of humor, suggesting that laughter erupted whenever someone behaved in a mechanical way, like a wind-up person no longer under intelligent control.[56] Mack Sennett himself contributed to the discourse in a 1914 interview, in which he discussed laughter in terms of a "contraction of the ... zygomatic muscles" and a brightening of the eyes "result[ing] from these muscular contractions."[57] What this actually means – and whether Sennett actually said it – is, of course, anyone's guess. But it does indicate the extent to which contemporary discussions of comedy had, by the mid-1910s, joined hands with a technicist vision of culture. Redefined through a language of reflex and mechanical force, popular comic traditions were increasingly disassociated from their origins in working-class and immigrant cultures.

The Keystone Film Company was deeply complicit with the new sensibility. The emphasis on "mechanical contrivances" effectively dissolved Keystone's earlier connection to the culture and values of the lower classes. Prior to the studio's association with Triangle, Keystone's comedians had generally portrayed the dispossessed, tramps and immigrants in particular: of the 77 comedies released by Keystone during the first six months of 1915, at least 23 (just under one-third) can be positively identified in which the central comic protagonist is defined as a member of the lower classes. By 1916, however, that emphasis was gone. During the last six months of that year, only three of the studio's releases centered upon ethnic or working-class clowns, as Keystone's formula for rapid, knockabout action was increasingly combined with opulent, decidedly middle-class settings. In one sense, a growing focus on mechanics was a direct consequence of this shift in class dynamics, as several Keystone comedies began exploiting the growing middle-class automobile culture as comic material – for example, *His Auto Ruination* (February 1916) and *Wife and Auto Trouble* (March 1916). Yet the studio's 1916 releases also saw the emergence of a new type of comic protagonist, one that marked unmistakably the adaptation of Keystone's output to modern technics: the tinkerer or inventor. Substituting in part for the studio's earlier gallery of tramps and ethnic stereotypes, the new Keystone protagonist was now as likely a young and dashing inventor who, as romantic lead, successfully rescued his sweetheart from peril through some innovative gadget or other – an "aeroplane life saving device" in *The Love Comet* (May 1916), a "wireless spark plug" in *Hearts and Sparks* (June 1916), even – more mundanely – a new kind of tram fender in *A Scoundrel's Toll* (November 1916).[58] Implicit in this development was an ideologically revealing switch in the relation of Keystone's protagonists to the means of production; unlike the worker, the inventor controls new technologies, rather than being controlled by them. *The Love Comet* provides a particularly effective example of the process. A remake of the earlier, Mutual-period Keystone film, *Hearts and Planets* (February 1915), the film substitutes a youthful, well-heeled inventor (Joseph Belmont) in the role initially taken by Chester Conklin's lumpen "Walrus" character. Both films center upon a wealthy old astronomer's disapproval of his daughter's love choice and the prank played by the two lovers, who set off fireworks to fool the astronomer into believing a meteor storm is under way. But whereas the father's disapproval is, in the earlier film, predicated on class difference and the daughter's incompatibility with Walrus, the remake instead links the disapproval to business reasons and the young man's failure to get financial backing for his new invention.[59] Such instances of explicit substitution are admittedly rare – another example, in which the switch occurs within the bounds of a single film, would be *A Clever Dummy* (July 1917), where a lowly janitor disguises himself as an automaton and, in the process, transforms the class-oriented comedy of the film's opening scenes into the more mechanically derived slapstick of robotic impersonation.[60] These instances, however, are nonetheless revelatory of the broader logic linking Keystone's aesthetic of uproarious inventions to the growing cross-class appeal of this style of slapstick. As Progressive-era discourse on class faded, so Keystone's proletarian clowns had begun to transform and disappear, no longer able to represent the fantasies of their audiences. Accordingly, comedy came to imply an engagement with society based more on fantasies of technical possibility than on the fractures of class difference.

A brief synthesis suggests itself in this regard, drawing together the various aspects of the foregoing discussion. For it is clear that the connections linking Keystone's slapstick mechanics to mass culture involved at least two related vectors: one involving issues of representation (what was and what was not shown); the other involving issues of critical evaluation (how these representations were assessed and perceived). In respect of the former, "uproarious inventions" partook in the integrative schema of an emergent mass culture that, as later described by Theodor Adorno, evaded explicit representations of conflict by directing its energies toward technical virtuosity and "mechanical and astonishing display" (thus the turn away from depictions of class difference); in respect of the latter, they served also to establish new standards of critical assessment for what had formerly been disparaged as "low" comedy, a displacement from the vocabulary of social hierarchy ("low," "rough," etc.) to the more abstract language of amazement, fascination, and physical reflex ("bewildered," "ingenuity," "muscular contractions," etc.).[61] The extraordinary success of this comic style was thus filled with ironies that illuminate the ambiguous role of technology in the formation of modern mass culture. "Uproarious inventions" provided Keystone's filmmakers with a means of satisfying collective desires, but they did so by mystifying technological processes and obfuscating mechanization's troubling implications. Integrating the spectacle of modern machinery into slapstick's carnivalesque ethic of pleasurable disorder, Keystone defined new images of technology that appealed across class boundaries; but it also surrendered the assertions of working-class identity that had previously accompanied such disorder. Public fascination with technological innovation was a key *topos* of modernity, but one that promoted shared modes of perception that obscured recognition of the social differences on which that culture was founded.

This last point calls for a postscript, since it points to a possible revaluation of what film historians have termed the "modernity thesis" – the position, advanced by Miriam Hansen, Ben Singer, Tom Gunning, and others, that investigates early cinema against the historical context of urban modernity.[62] In a certain sense, Keystone's mechanical contrivances are obvious grist for the mill of this kind of approach, highly suggestive of early film's congruence with the technological advances of the modern era. But there is also a sense, I would argue, in which they invite a rethinking of turn-of-the-century technological spectacle, not only as a *symptom* of modernity (Singer), but crucially as part of its *social discourse*, exercising a real political function in terms of social relations and hierar-chies of power. Arguably, one of the major weaknesses of the modernity thesis has been its avoidance of just such a reading; the tendency is rather to erect a base-structure determinism that isolates cinematic representa-tions of technology as responses to "modernity," broadly construed. Modernity is thus characterized as, in some sense, the ontological grounding of early cinematic form – whether posited in terms of a linear relation of cause and effect (again, Singer) or through more flexible assumptions of "influence" and "response" (e.g., Gunning) – without comparable attention paid to modernity's role as a cultural ideology, itself determined by concrete relations of social power. A more material-ist level of analysis, by contrast, requires precisely the shift of accent that asks not only *how* early cinema was shaped by the context of modernity – the base-superstructure version of the modernity thesis – but also *what social interests* were served by cinema's participation in those developments. This chapter has been, in part, an attempt to begin this shift, to resituate the spectacle of technological modernity, as mediated by cinema, against the forms and processes of the society that governed technology's meaning. The point to be made here is that such a move enables us to discern the logic of an ideological omission which, as a kind of fatal blind spot, was at work in turn-of-the-century encounters with technology; that blind spot concerned the question of class difference and the repre-sentability of class struggle in an era of nascent mass culture.

These are assertions, not proofs. The extent to which this picture can be generalized requires further research. Yet it is not perversity that leads me, by way of conclusion, to offer this picture as a curb against develop-ing trends in early film history. The conception of modernity which pre-vails today within academic film circles – with its emphasis on phenomenological categories like "shock," "sensation," and "force" – corresponds term for term with the language with which modernity was itself described at the turn of the century. In a very real sense, the con-temporary historiography of early cinema has, knowingly or not, answered to Henry Adams' already-quoted call for a history focused on the "dynamics of Forces," and, to this extent, falls squarely within the parameters of modernity's own discourse about itself. Rather than simply parrot that discourse, we need to look behind it, to investigate the histor-ical connections linking terms like "force" and "attraction" to the techni-cist perspective of modernity, and to think about the social processes that underlie that perspective. As I have suggested here, technology formed the cornerstone of a new mass culture that muted representations of class difference by directing its energies toward "mechanical and astonish-ing display." Keystone's "uproarious inventions" were constituent ele-ments of that process, harbingers of new patterns of cultural consensus. Not only did they replace the "old slapstick effect" formerly achieved with the "familiar pie," as one critic wrote; they also uprooted the American slapstick tradition from its origins in popular, working-class culture and experience.

## notes

1. Lewis Mumford, *Technics and Civilization* (New York: Harcourt and Brace, 1934), 101.
2. Alfred A. Cohn, " 'Writing' Slapstick," *Photoplay*, October (1917): 117.
3. "Three-Minute Visit to Keystone Studio," *The Triangle*, November 27 (1915): 6.
4. Review of *Bathtub Perils*, *Moving Picture World*, June 24 (1916): 2259; "The Seventh Knickerbocker Triangle Program," *Motion Picture News*, November 27 (1915): 92; "The Shadow Stage," *Photoplay*, May (1916): 109.
5. Figures taken from John F. Kasson, *Civilizing the Machine: Technology and Republican Values in America, 1776–1900* (New York: Penguin Books, 1976), 183–184; Alan Trachtenberg, *The Incorporation of America: Culture and Society in the Gilded Age* (New York: Hill and Wang, 1983), 64.
6. "Triangle Program," *Moving Picture World*, January 1 (1916): 91 (emphasis added).
7. The reference to "friends of burlesque" is from a description of Keystone's *Riley and Schultz* in "Comments on the Films," *Moving Picture World*, October 12 (1912): 144.
8. Miriam Hansen, "The Mass Production of the Senses: Classical Cinema as Vernacular Modernism," *Modernism/Modernity* 6.2 (1999): 69.
9. Theodor Adorno, "The Schema of Mass Culture," in *The Culture Industry*, edited by J. M. Bernstein (London: Routledge, 1991), 79.
10. See, for instance, Robert Crunden, *American Salons: Encounters with European Modernism, 1885–1917* (New York: Oxford University Press, 1993), esp. Introduction; Kasson, *Civilizing the Machine*, chapter 4; and Trachtenberg, *Incorporation of America*, chapter 2.
11. On the slump in comedy production, see Eileen Bowser, *The Transformation of Cinema, 1907–1915* (Berkeley: University of California Press, 1990), 179.
12. Figures on the budget increase have been calculated from Keystone Film Company, Cash Book, 28 September 1912 to 24 April 1924, Aitken Bros. Papers, Wisconsin State Historical Society (hereafter ABP).
13. Advertisement for *The Cannon Ball*, *Moving Picture World*, June 5 (1915), 563.
14. "Comments on the Films," *Moving Picture World*, June 19 (1915): 1940.
15. "Work on New Keystone Studio is a Rush Job," *Motion Picture News*, May 29 (1915): 44. My description of the new Keystone studio facilities also draws on the following sources: "Sennett Razes Mountain for Keystone Studio," *The Triangle*, October 30 (1915): 7; "In and Out of West Coast Studios," *Motion Picture News*, November 6 (1915): 69; "Rebuild Keystone Studio by Aid of Laughs," *Motion Picture News*, July 22 (1916): 402–403; "Facts about the Sennett Studios," *c.*1923/1924, General Files, Mack Sennett Collection, Margaret Herrick Library (hereafter MSC).
16. For more on Triangle, see my article, " 'Made for the Masses with an Appeal to the Classes': The Triangle Film Corporation and the Failure of Highbrow Film Culture," *Cinema Journal* 44.2 (2005): 3–33.
17. "In and Out of West Coast Studios," *Motion Picture News*, November 27 (1915): 76.

18. Coy Watson, Jr., *The Keystone Kid: Tales from Early Hollywood* (Santa Monica: Santa Monica Press, 2001), 110. Information on the "Cyclorama" is drawn from Watson, 110–115, and "Facts about the Sennett Studios," MSC.

19. "Three-Minute Visit to Keystone Studio," *The Triangle*, November 27 (1915): 6.

20. Review quoted in "Telegram Predicts Long Run for 'Quixote,'" *The Triangle*, January 8 (1916): 8.

21. "Keystoners Preparing Thrills and Laughs," *The Triangle*, December 11 (1915): 4; "In and Out of Los Angeles Studios," *Motion Picture News*, December 18 (1915): 73.

22. "Triangle Program," *Moving Picture World*, January 1 (1916): 91.

23. "Why Aren't We Killed?" *Photoplay*, April (1916): 84.

24. "Triangle Program," *Moving Picture World*, January 1 (1916): 91; "Triangle Turns the First Birthday Mark," *Motion Picture News*, November 18 (1916): 3128.

25. Ben Singer, *Melodrama and Modernity: Early Sensational Cinema and Its Contexts* (New York: Columbia University Press, 2001), 182.

26. See Donald Crafton, *Before Mickey: The Animated Film, 1898–1928* (Chicago: Chicago University Press, 1993), esp. chapters 1–3.

27. Mack Sennett to Adolph Zukor, December 13, 1917, Correspondence Folder (1915–1919), General Files, MSC.

28. "Triangle Program," *Moving Picture World*, July 7 (1917): 80.

29. "Triangle Program," *Moving Picture World*, June 16 (1917): 1798; "Triangle Program," *Moving Picture World*, July 7 (1917): 80; "Triangle Program," *Moving Picture World*, July 14 (1917): 255. My calculation of average shot lengths should be taken as an estimate only, based on a sample of 29 Keystone films produced under Triangle. Only around 30 percent of Keystone's Triangle releases survive (according to my findings, 36 out of 119), and, of these, many exist only in heavily re-edited and/or fragmentary form.

30. "Triangle Program," *Moving Picture World*, December 4 (1915): 1848.

31. "Triangle Program," *Moving Picture World*, January 1 (1916): 91.

32. "Triangle Program," *Moving Picture World*, November 27 (1915): 1679.

33. "Sennett Gets Open Letter from Keystone Fan," *The Triangle*, November 27 (1915): 1.

34. Michael M. Davis, *The Exploitation of Pleasure* (New York: Russell Sage Foundation, 1911), 33, 36, quoted in Singer, *Melodrama and Modernity*, 65.

35. See Stephen Kern, *The Culture of Time and Space, 1880–1918* (Cambridge, MA: Harvard University Press, 1983), 124–130.

36. Leo Marx, *The Machine in the Garden: Technology and the Pastoral Ideal in America* (London: Oxford University Press, 1964). On dystopian motifs in turn-of-the-century magazines, see Singer, *Melodrama and Modernity*, 69–90. For the image of modernity as juggernaut, see Anthony Giddens, *The Consequences of Modernity* (Stanford: Stanford University Press, 1990), 139. As Giddens explains in a footnote, the term juggernaut

> comes from the Hindi *Jagannâth*, "lord of the world," and is a title of Krishna; an idol of this deity was taken each year through the streets on a huge car, which followers are said to have thrown themselves under, to be crushed beneath the wheels.

(139)

37. "Production Report," *A Submarine Pirate*, ABP.

38. "Seventh Knickerbocker Triangle Program," *Motion Picture News*, November 27 (1915): 92; review of *A Submarine Pirate, Moving Picture World*, November 27 (1915): 1681; "The Shadow Stage," *Photoplay*, February (1916): 104.

39. "New York Elite Gives Private Triangle Show," *The Triangle*, December 4 (1915): 5.

40. "Prominent Comedians at Keystone Studios," *The Triangle*, November 13 (1915): 5.

41. "Triangle Film Shows Working of Submarine," *The Triangle*, November 13 (1915): 7.

42. "Bally-Hoo Display for Syd Chaplin Comedy," *The Triangle*, December 18 (1915): 5; reviews of *A Submarine Pirate* quoted in *The Triangle*, December 4 (1915): 5.

43. See, for example, "War by Assassination," *New York Times*, May 8 (1915): 14; "Submarines Alter Marine War Code," *New York Times*, May 9 (1915): 5.

44. For "Shoot-the-Chutes" and the "Barrel of Fun," see John F. Kasson, *Amusing the Million: Coney Island at the Turn of the Century* (New York: Hill and Wang, 1978), 60, 78–79.

45. On the "Leap-Frog Railway," see ibid., 74.

46. Joseph Stella, "Discovery of America: Autobiographical Notes," *Art News* 59 (November 1960), 64, quoted in ibid., 88.

47. "Sennett Sends Us Three Fine Farces," *Philadelphia Public Ledger*, February 28, 1917, quoted in an advertisement for the Keystone Film Company, *Motion Picture News*, March 31 (1917): 1931.

48. Raymond Williams, *Marxism and Literature* (New York: Oxford University Press, 1977), 104.

49. René Gimpel, *Le Journal d'un Collectionneur* (Paris: Calmann-Levy, 1963), quoted in Paul Virilio, *The Art of the Motor*, trans. Julie Rose (Minneapolis: University of Minnesota Press, 1995), 77.

50. Theodor Adorno, "Perennial Fashion – Jazz," in *Prisms*, trans. Samuel Weber and Shierry Weber (Cambridge, MA: MIT Press, 1967), 125.

51. Henry Adams, *The Education of Henry Adams* (Boston: Houghton Mifflin, 1961 [1906]), 474.

52. For an account of the impact of the Armory Show, see Crunden, *American Salons*, esp. 357–382.

53. Peter Seixas, "Lewis Hine: From 'Social' to 'Interpretive' Photographer," *American Quarterly* 39.3 (1987): 381–409.

54. Trachtenberg, *Incorporation of America*, 55.

55. On Cohan and the "mechanics of emotion," see Henry Jenkins, *What Made Pistachio Nuts? Early Sound Comedy and the Vaudeville Aesthetic* (New York: Columbia University Press, 1992), 32–37.

56. Henri Bergson, *Laughter: An Essay on the Meaning of the Comic*, trans. Cloudesley Brereton and Fred Rothwell (London: Macmillan, 1911 [1900]).

57. "Putting the Laugh in Laughter," *Reel Life*, May 30 (1914): 20.

58. Quoted phrases taken from "Synopsis," *The Love Comet*, ABP; "Comments on the Films," *Moving Picture World*, July 8 (1916): 306.

59. As the synopsis of this lost film describes the opening scenes: "The youth makes a bad landing [in demonstrating his airplane device], capitalists lose interest and leave the grounds. Girl rushes to assist youth but father separates them, takes girl home." "Synopsis," *The Love Comet*.

60. See my discussion of the film in *The Fun Factory: The Keystone Film Company and the Emergence of Mass Culture* (Berkeley: University of California Press, 2009), 201–209.
61. Adorno, "The Schema of Mass Culture," 87.
62. For a useful survey of the literature, see Tom Gunning's entry on "modernity and early cinema" in Richard Abel, ed., *The Encyclopedia of Early Cinema* (London: Routledge, 2004), 439–442.

rob king

# mechanisms of

# laughter

## the devices of slapstick

e i g h t

t o m   g u n n i n g

*For JB, one more time.*

In the first FIAF Slapstick Symposium at the Museum of Modern Art in 1985 Eileen Bowser quoted humorist Robert Benchley about laughter:

> In order to laugh at something, it is necessary
>
> 1.  to know what you are laughing at,
> 2.  to know why you are laughing,
> 3.  to ask some people why they think you are laughing,
> 4.  to jot down a few notes,
> 5.  to laugh.[1]

The antithesis between theory and laughter, reflection and guffaws endures. Certain theories, such as Benchley's, may make us laugh, but we have little confidence that laughter can explain itself. More importantly, it isn't obvious that laughter needs to be explained – laughter just *is*. To explain laughter seems to be destructive of its effect. This opposition between laughter and explanation goes beyond the belief that many have that poetry, or perhaps art in general, can never be completely explicated, or the broader claim that explication of an affect cannot, indeed should not, attempt to mime the affect it explains. But the antithesis between laughter and explication goes deeper. The forms dedicated to producing laughter – jokes, gags, comic situations – are understood as *nonsense*, profoundly and fundamentally a reversal and undermining of sense, logic, or explanation.

Comedy as a narrative or dramatic genre can, of course, be considered separately from laughter. The enduring narrative structures of comedy often involve the establishment or restoration of order (usually through the formation of a romantic couple, or the creation of a new society based on youthful pleasure), rather than simply the overturning of conventions and rules of reason. This pattern is often traced back to New Comedy, and has a long history, including its melding with forms of Romance, its development by dramatists such as Shakespeare and Gozzi, or filmmakers like Cukor, Hawks, and Capra. Further, the analysis of the comic mode or genre by critics and philosophers like Northrop Frye and Stanley Cavell has produced something that could be called a philosophy of comedy.[2] But if we turn to the micro-level, less the narrative structures than the devices of comedy, its building blocks and laugh-getters – gags, jokes, pratfalls, grimaces, the costume and make-up of clowns, sight gags, and burlesque actions – then the logic of destruction rather than construction predominates.

Philosopher Henri Bergson related laughter to the mechanical being engrafted onto the living. Life, Bergson claimed, was supple and organic, and mechanical actions violated these qualities. Laughter operates as a social censure, ridiculing such unnatural behavior.[3] I want to explore Bergson's insight that a relation exists between laughter and the mechanical separately from his theoretical explanation of that relation. As a theorist, I have become increasingly suspicious of the drive to provide a single explanation for a complex phenomenon with multiple determinants. Bergson's explanation of the phenomenon of laughter as an expression of an impulse to overcome the mechanical and inert aspects of human behavior in favor of the flexible and vital displays this sort of singular focus. However, Bergson's essay highlights the affinity that gags and jokes have with the mechanical. In a previous essay on early film comedy and gags I claimed that gags could be thought of as machines that produce nothing other than a process that destroys itself – crazy machines.[4] Crazy machines are complex devices that appear rationally designed to achieve a purpose, but suddenly and comically assert a counter-will of their own, thwarting the purpose of the protagonist (who thereby becomes a comedian). Gags are devices that explode, collapse, or fail in some spectacular manner. The self-destructing machine provides a vivid image of the dynamics of a gag. A structural analysis of gags and jokes (and therefore not only visual gags) might best describe them as an unexpected undermining of an apparent purpose, a detouring, if not derailing, of a rational system of discourse or action. The gag suddenly interrupts, or radically redefines, the apparent predictability of an action or system, leaving its original goals shattered and in tatters.

This formulation reflects the most profound philosophical discussion of laughter I am aware of, from Immanuel Kant's *Critique of Judgment* of 1790: "Laughter is an affection arising from a strained expectation being suddenly reduced to nothing."[5] For Kant, laughter results when a determined sense of purpose and system becomes suddenly destroyed. Kant offers the image of the burst bubble: "the bubble of our expectation was extended to the full and suddenly went off into nothing."[6] A sudden unexpected physical response can generate laughter as well as a crazy machine. Noël Carroll's claim that Edison's 1894 *Record of a Sneeze*, arguably the first motion picture, recorded a gag seems inspired by Kant's description.[7] Indeed, one immediately sees why cartoonist (and early film animator) Winsor McCay selected the character Little Sammy Sneeze, a child subject to sudden and unpredictable fits of sneezing, as the basis for one of his greatest comic strips — in each strip the hapless Sammy triggers disasters (from upsetting his father's checkers game to stampeding elephants in a circus parade) by sneezing at inopportune moments.[8] Kant himself describes laughter as a psycho-physiological reaction, in which the body and mind operate like a machine breaking down:

> The mind looks back in order to try it over again, and
> thus by a rapidly succeeding tension and relaxation it is
> jerked to and fro and put in oscillation. As the snap-
> ping of what was, as it were, tightening up the string
> takes place suddenly (not by a gradual loosening), the
> oscillation must bring about a mental movement and a
> sympathetic internal movement of the body.[9]

While few today could take this explanation literally as a description of either psychological or physiological processes, it vividly images the conversion of purposeful motion into a pure dithering and breakdown. It vividly describes, I think, the scenography of a gag and its dysfunctional mechanical nature.

The principle of sudden collapse of a built-up expectation can be translated into a variety of situations. Besides actual machines or involuntary bodily reactions, recalcitrant objects can block or defeat purposes unexpectedly. With their seemingly intentional resistance to human purposes, such demonic objects often resemble crazy machines, as their resistance becomes sustained and seemingly purposeful — for example, Chaplin's mechanical bed in *One AM* (1916). Bergson's description of the comic body as mechanical describes moments when the body seems to carry out its own program, divorced from conscious control and purpose, such as Chaplin's drunken behavior in the same film, unable to carry out the everyday actions of turning a key in the door or climbing the stairs. Crazy machines create gags in which purposes are thwarted and new scenarios of systematic frustration seem to take over.[10] But beyond describing the illogic of the gag structure, machines in their literal form appear again and again in silent comedy. In silent cinema, machines tend to fall apart or explode rather than accomplishing the purposes for which they are designed.

The machine normally embodies the instrumental logic of human behavior. A machine misused or turned against itself becomes a gag. In my account of the earliest gag films (brief films from the turn of the century, often consisting of only a single shot), I described a number of fairly simple devices (especially the use of tightened strings and threads – recalling Kant's description – mischievously tied to various objects and triggering a series of collapses, falls, and other disasters) as machines.[11] Thus crazy machines, even if elementary ones, appear with the very first comic films. These very simple contraptions – strings tied to washing machine mangles, or to doorknobs – present the essence of a machine gag in introducing a kink or pitfall between agent and purpose. Therefore I want first to explore simple mechanical devices and the gags they trigger, before driving into the complex apparatuses of the industrial age.

Comedy hardly needed to wait for the Machine Age to manufacture gags. *Commedia dell'arte* clowns based many of their gags – or *lazzi* – on the comic inversion of simple tools: using a rake to comb hair; walking a ladder as if it were a pair of stilts; even using a fake peep show box to conceal a love affair.[12] As early as the seventeenth century *commedia* Harlequins used the hinged and expanding device known as a zigzag, much as Buster Keaton (for one) used it centuries later to bop policemen in *Cops* from 1922. I will start my consideration of gag contraptions with an extremely primitive device, which gives its name to the genre: the slapstick. The slapstick originated in the *commedia dell'arte* in the form of the *battacio*, a club or wooden sword used in comic beatings. But as the stage weapon transformed into the slapstick, it became a primitive machine, one that produced a special effect. Wikipedia, the online encyclopedia, defines the slapstick as "a club-like object composed of two wooden slats [hinged at one end] so that, when struck, it produced a loud smacking noise."[13] Although it might be worthwhile to undertake further philological investigation, the slapstick undoubtedly gave its name to the dominant genre of silent comedy, and the knockabout vaudeville and clown acts that preceded cinema, because of the high degree of physical violence – slapping, bopping, and especially ass-kicking – that many comedians cultivated.

As a device, the slapstick exemplifies a simple sort of crazy machine. With its hinged wooden slats, the slapstick serves as an elementary device for producing a loud noise (indeed, the slapstick exists today primarily as a percussion instrument obtainable from musical supply companies). But besides functioning effectively as a noisemaker, the slapstick also qualifies as a trick device, rather than a purposeful tool. On stage or in the circus ring, the slapstick looked like and was employed as a weapon, a tool for beating an opponent. Here the tricky machinery enters in. As Wikipedia puts it: "Little force, however, is transferred from the object — called the 'slap stick' in English — to the person being struck, allowing actors to strike each other repeatedly with great audio effect while causing very little actual damage."[14] The hinged slats allow energy to be displaced from the apparent purpose of striking a victim to the creation of a sound effect; the loud noise produced seems to indicate the force (and probably the painful effect) of the blow. The slapstick acts an archetypal machine of displacement in which an instrument detours from its original purpose into a strong sensual effect — it makes a lot of noise, but actually works less efficiently as a pain-inflicting weapon. Part of the amusement the slapstick offers lies in the exaggerated noise it generates, making the viewer aware that the slaps are not really painful, but are nonetheless intense in their sensual effects. As a gag, it produces the collapse of purpose into a noisy nothing, like an exploding bubble.

The slapstick, then, presents a rather minimal form of a crazy machine, a seemingly purposeful device, which in fact detours that purpose into a spectacular but destructive or purposeless end, triggering laughter. But machines in slapstick comedy need not be so simple. Indeed, the most memorable gag machines from the later classic period tend to be grandiose and complex. Keaton displays the greatest fascination with large-scale machines, from locomotives (*Our Hospitality*, 1923; *The General*, 1927) to large mechanical ships (*The Navigator*, 1924; *Steamboat Bill Jr.*, 1928) to his *Electric House* (1922) or even the cinematic apparatus itself (*Sherlock Jr.*, 1924). Aspects of scale, as well as mechanical skill, dominate Keaton's relation to machines in his features, but in many ways it is the elaborate gadgets devised to handle everyday tasks (such as setting the table or serving a meal) in the two-reel *The Electric House* that provide the most revealing treatment of Keaton's mechanical humor. In his films (as apparently also in real life, according to biographer Rudi Blesh) Keaton delighted in devising crazy machines, elaborate contraptions that accomplished rather minor tasks through complex means.[15] His inspiration may come from the comic inventions created by the great cartoonist Rube Goldberg (or perhaps these two comic geniuses simply shared a common grasp of the gag possibilities of machines that actually did very little, but in the most complicated way possible). Parallel to the exploding or collapsing machines (and sometimes converging with them), these crazy contraptions (actually called in the vernacular "rubegoldbergs") are marked not only by their absurdity, but by their delightful, handyman, jerry-rigged quality.[16] The inventions that Goldberg featured in his newspaper cartoons from 1914 to 1964 were made up partly of everyday objects. Our pleasure in these sight gags comes from their illogical legibility: we can see how they are put together (or could be taken apart) and they have their own peculiar logic. Goldberg devices operate like machines, with interconnecting or interacting parts. But it is the absurd nature of this interaction, and often absurdly small results (for instance, cooling a bowl of soup, tying a knot in a piece of string, or scratching a mosquito bite) that make them recall Kant's formulation of a "tensed expectation suddenly reduced to nothing."

The complex mechanical humor of later silent slapstick involves more than just bigger and better machines. Even the one- and two-reel comedies of the 1910s, let alone the later features, moved from the simple unfolding of gags that marked the comedies of the era of the cinema of attractions (before 1907) to films which attempted to string gags together with a greater sense of coherence. In these later films the machine becomes the center of a larger gag scenography, in which performance, other objects, and the unfolding of action all work together. A great comic gag sequence works, well, like clockwork, but a clock that could never tell you the right time and might blow up in your face.

Like the amusement park rides of the turn of the century, silent film comedies take the technology of modern industrialism and convert them into toys, forms of amusement, even spectacles of harmless destruction, rather than instrumental production. This can be traced back to the earlier gag films. Two early British trick comedies exemplify the way the crazy machine served as ur-form for the gag, predating the later more elaborate forms: Cecil Hepworth's *How it Feels to be Run Over* and *Explosion of a Motor Car* (both 1900). In both films the automobile, the twentieth century's exemplary machine, triggers a disaster that seems to destroy or damage the car itself, its occupants, and possibly bystanders. Instead of creating terror or pity, these explosions or collisions not only destroy the machine, but redirect our reactions from concern or horror to surprise and amusement.

While these short films inaugurate a long tradition of cinematic car collisions, they also partake of early cinema's fascination with destruction and explosions generally. Indeed, explosions were so frequent in early films that Eileen Bowser actually considered them as a minor genre in 1902 and 1903 (with such films as *The Finish of Bridget McKeen, How Bridget Built the Fire, They Found the Leak, A Pipe Story of the Fourth, Algy's Glorious Fourth of July, The Poet's Revenge*).[17] This brief but intense genre included both trick films and actualities (e.g., *A Mighty Tumble* (1901), which documented the explosive destruction of a multi-story building). All of these films climax with a grand explosion, unexpected by the protagonist, which destroys surroundings, and most often the protagonists as well.

While we associate trick filmmaker Georges Méliès primarily with magical disappearance and transformations, the prevalence of explosions in Méliès' films needs more acknowledgment. Think of the ultimate effect of enlargement/inflation in *The Man with the Rubber Head* (1901) or the explosive nature of the Selenite bodies in *A Trip to the Moon* (1902). In fact, when machines appear in Méliès' films they tend to become involved in collisions and explosions (think of the train that falls off the tracks; the touring car that plows through the wall of the tourist inn; the submarine that explodes in *The Impossible Voyage* in 1904; or the cars that run over and flatten people in *Paris to Monte Carlo* from 1905). Within the fictional world of Méliès' films, technology may appear as an extension of magic (while through his filmmaking Méliès creates magic through an extension of technology). In spite of critical claims that Méliès initiated cinematic science fiction, the scientists and inventions that appear in his films primarily provide a basis for satirical farce in which modern machines misfunction and often explode with comic results. Rather than a pioneer of science fiction, Méliès should finally be acknowledged as one of the true fathers of slapstick and silent comedy.

In fact, Méliès' scenography and performance styles reach back to the *commedia*, as does the long tradition of pantomime comedy on which he drew. Méliès continues the late nineteenth-century tradition of trick farce, exemplified by the Hanlon Brothers, nineteenth-century stage comedians whose acrobatic antics and trick machines directly inspired both Méliès and Keaton (their theatrical act, "Voyage en Suisse," with its "Railroad Disaster where no one is hurt — it's only done for fun" undoubtedly inspired the Alps sequence of Méliès' *The Impossible Voyage*, while the dive through a human body that Keaton performs in *Sherlock Jr.*, often cited as an example of Keaton's surrealism, derived directly from a Hanlon trick).[18] While histories of silent comedy usually anoint the great Max Linder as the point of origin of silent clowns, the tradition of destructive comedy springing from Méliès was most thoroughly developed by Gaumont's anarchic comedian, Jean Durand, whose character Onésime wandered through a chaotic universe of collapsing buildings and cosmic collisions, giving cinematic expression to the Hanlon Brothers' violent use of trick sets and acrobatics.[19] Comedy, and especially a comedy based on destruction and mayhem, infected the world of early cinema broadly, including such genres as the trick film. As the car collides with — or bursts through — the screen in Hepworth's *How It Feels*, early cinema's ontological thirst for apocalypse looms at us from the screen. In the accounts of early spectatorship such fantasies of destruction haunted early film viewers of both actualities and staged films.

Besides Maxim Gorky's 1896 invocation of the Lumière train emerging from the screen and "crushing into dust and into broken fragments this hall," my colleague Yuri Tsivian has drawn our attention to the cinematic musing of the great Russian symbolist author, Andrei Bely, inspired, most likely, by watching the English trick comedies *The ? Motorist* (Walter Booth, 1906) and *That Fatal Sneeze* (Hepworth, 1907) (this latter film possibly inspired by McCay's comic strip).[20] Bely's modernist masterpiece of 1913, his novel *Petersburg*, literally revolved around an explosion as the main character is given a time bomb by a terrorist organization that intends to destroy his father. First, let's quote Bely's wonderful description of *The ? Motorist*:

> Crrump! The car smashes through a wall and drives through someone's peaceful living room. Crunch! It smashes through the wall and calmly drives on down the street. It's funny but it's not at all funny. Walls and peaceful domesticity cannot protect us from the arrival of the unknown, can they? ... And the driver — Death in a top hat — is baring his teeth and rushing towards us.[21]

After describing the action of *That Fatal Sneeze*, a film in which an involuntary sneeze causes a series of disasters, ending with the explosion of the man himself, Bely concludes:

> [M]an is a cloud of smoke. He catches a cold, he sneezes and bursts; ... the cinematograph has crossed the borders of reality. More than the preachings of scholars and wise men, this has demonstrated to everyone what reality is: it is a lady suffering from a cold who sneezes and explodes.[22]

Bely's sense of a political and metaphysical apocalypse (which also structures *Petersburg* and the unfilmed script he adapted from it) may have been uniquely Russian. But the fascination with an explosive reality populated early cinema across borders, national and generic.

Early film comedy evoked this explosive nature of reality quite directly, even careening into the spectator's space. Attractions in early cinema — with their burst of presence — operate like little explosions. The longer forms of gag comedy before Keystone mainly consist of a concatenation of these small explosions, ending usually with a truly climactic one (like *That Fatal Sneeze*).[23] But gradually a more complex scenography arises in which the explosive logic builds within a scene, creating a sense of interlocking gags. These elaborated sequences are the clockwork mechanisms I mentioned earlier, in which the comic energy seems to hold off and become re-routed, creating a sort of suspense that renders the final explosion even more effective. I will analyze two examples, both centered on the complex possibilities of the automobile as exemplary machine.

Locomotives, the ultimate machine of the nineteenth century, do play a role in slapstick comedies (most obviously in Keaton's films, but also in Keystone's parody of melodramas such as *Teddy at the Throttle* (1917)), but automobiles generally possessed more comic possibilities, while trains provided the ideal prop for melodrama. Perhaps the connection of cars to individuals, or their more frangible structure gives them a comic edge, a sense of burlesque as opposed to the train as emblem of fate (think of Abel Gance's fateful reworking of Oedipus among the train tracks in *La Roue* (1923)); or the force of history (the train as the engine of revolution in Alexi Dovzenko's *Arsenal* (1928) or Fernando de Fuentes' *Let's Go with Pancho Villa* (1936)). Since film historians have turned a great deal of attention to Keystone — including the brilliant chapter in this collection by Rob King — I will not dwell on the succession of Sennett-inspired rallies, collisions, and general collapse of metal and glass. The cars at Keystone seem primarily avatars of speed (and its inverse, collision). In the 1920s the rise of a more personalized, comedian-based comic structure focused more on the car's role as prized possession, an emblem of the burgeoning consumer culture and the sign of the new middle-class family. This more individualized concern with the car collides, often explosively, with its more traditional relation to speed and danger.

As we examine specific machines in specific comedies, rather than taking them as emblems of the gag structure itself, the nature of the individual machine takes on greater importance, and a comic filmmaker can derive a variety of associations from them. Speed and collision form the baseline of car comedies.[24] Whether a car evokes the skill of professional racers, the mobility desired by young lovers, the container of the nuclear family, or the prized object of a consumer society depends on narrative and historical context. Harold Lloyd may represent the most typically middle class of the great comedians of the American silent cinema, but the apparently conformist nature of his "glasses" characters (after his abandonment of his earlier tramp character, Lonesome Luke) allowed his fine-tuned sense of mechanical chaos to penetrate deeply into the fabric of American domesticity. And the car lies at the center of his comic subversion.

Rather than simply delighting in speed and courting the danger of collision, Lloyd's 1924 feature, *Hot Water*, places the new family car centrally among the repressions and frustrations of modern domestic living, so that the machine stages the violation of rules and regulations without ever supplying the liberation of the open road. If the car is first presented as a vehicle of romantic love for a young married couple, domesticity arrives with a vengeance as Harold's in-laws pile into their imagined get-away car. I have always felt that in American cinema of the classical era, across genres, a car primarily signifies family coherence even as it seems to offer escape. Narratively speaking, the car in the 1920s seems to enact a dialectic of freedom and containment that drives much of American cinema. Driving a car (as opposed to the locomotive which is always confined to its track) allows for erratic trajectories as the driver's attention becomes distracted; but in these comedies of civilization and its discontents, the ultimate superego, the traffic cop lurks at nearly every corner. Car travel increasingly had to follow not only a series of rules and regulations, but also to negotiate a complex pattern of signals and signs, whose ambiguous misinterpretation could trigger gags. Harold's momentary delight in the joys of the open road in *Hot Water* soon turns from a lighthearted impromptu race into a pursuit by the forces of law in a world where many pleasures, even accidental ones, are forbidden.

But I would argue that Lloyd's best construction of a gag sequence around a car comes in his short film, *Get Out and Get Under* (1920). The automobile as a complex machine with many parts supplied a gamut of gag possibilities for Lloyd, but also provided a way to bring them together in a carefully constructed (once again, like clockwork) comic sequence. In this sequence Lloyd fully explores the possibility of the car as a crazy machine, as a gag device. If the gag machine is one that does not accomplish its intended purpose, clearly a car stalling opens up the rich opportunities for gags. An attempt to get the car started again, Lloyd understood, could be even richer.

Interestingly, Lloyd opens the sequence with a gag form I usually associate with more abstract comedians, such as Jacques Tati or Keaton, what I call a refused gag, where the audience sees the possibilities of a gag, is cued to expect it (the string is artfully tightened), but it doesn't happen.[25] Here Lloyd toys with an old-fashioned explosion gag, as he uses a match to see if there is gas in the car's tank. But Lloyd refuses us this gag – the car never explodes; he is after a more developed scenario, rather than a simple bang. But the invocation of the explosion genre accents his comic sophistication and historical sense of the development of gag scenography.

Even in this early short film, Lloyd's "glasses" character introduces the context of middle-class respectability and plays with the repressions that often bring his films close to a comedy of manners (as when he places the nearby old maid's hands over her ears so she won't hear him cursing out his car when it won't start). But this sequence primarily mines the slapstick absurdity of crazy machines, carefully coordinating the variety of gag possibilities that the stalled machine offers. As the sequence opens, Lloyd installs his stalled car front and center. After turning the crank fails, he gets to work, taking off and placing his straw-hat, emblem of middle-class sportiness, on the car's running board as he raises the car hood to examine the problem.

The sequence moves into gear as a young black boy emerges from a nearby saloon. Certainly even a comparatively innocent use of an African-American character like this one evokes the racist context of American culture in the 1920s, as much a part of white middle-class life as a car or a straw hat, and we all (I hope) feel a bit uncomfortable as we watch this stereotyped character enter. However, without mitigating that laugh-killing racist context, we also recognize this small boy as the heir of the potentate of early gag comedy, the mischievous boy. And, if the boy's role as the lord of comic misrule were not immediately evident, he proudly bears the scepter of slapstick comedy – the banana. Rather than being intent on mischief, however, the boy displays the same curiosity about the machine (as Kenneth Anger describes it in his notes for his 1963 masterpiece, *Scorpio Rising*, "masculine fascination with the Thing that Goes")[26] that Lloyd has, and mirrors his actions. However, after being repelled from the scene of action, the boy (accidentally on purpose?) discards his essential device, the banana peel, leaving slapstick's emblem in Lloyd's pathway. Thus, as the car starts to shudder into mechanical life, and Lloyd responds by rushing to the driver's seat, like clockwork, he steps on the peel. Of course, when Harold recovers, the car has stalled again. The boy, imp of the perverse, has created his own counter-machinic assembly to Lloyd's purposeful one. He continues to thwart the bond between man and machine that Harold wants to forge. Bouncing with his boyish energy on the running board, he makes the car jounce in a manner that causes Harold to mistake boypower for horsepower, the careful selection of camera angles providing one of the sight gags of mis-interpretation that Noël Carroll describes so well.[27] As he climbs in this time, no banana peel slips between foot and ground, but Lloyd steps firmly onto, and demolishes, his straw hat. Likewise, when Harold finally "gets out and gets under," crawling under his car to see if the fuel line is the problem, another avatar of instinctive behavior emerges: a puppy that licks Lloyd's face as he tries to maintain the concentration the machine demands.

The next stage of this sequence involves Harold being literally swallowed by his car as he works his way under the hood. Although the psychoanalyt-ical meaning of return to the womb probably occurs to modern viewers, this actually harks back to the breakaway props of the Hanlon Brothers. Harold's subsequent emergence from the auto brings on another sticky-face joke (ice cream is dropped on Harold's face by the boy, rather than doggie saliva, a gag that is topped off by another banana peel pratfall as Harold chases the boy away). These sticky-face gags link the machine gags to the other main source of gags, the biological rather than the mechanical, invoking an infantile body not yet under conscious control.

In an extended comic sequence such as this, the concatenation of gags builds expectations of a "big finish" to use the vaudeville and circus term for the climatic ending of an act. Lloyd supplies one by briefly changing dramatic registers and expectations with the entrance of a shady character, who we see injecting himself with a drug via a hypodermic, which unexpectedly transforms him from a strung-out derelict to a peppy and dapper middle-class figure. While the entrance of this potential villain cues us to expect a switch into melodramatic action (a car theft most likely), Lloyd again comically inverts expectations. Not only does the transformation of the shady character deftly satirize middle-class mores, but the respectable "glasses" character himself performs the only criminal act, picking the junkie's pocket for his syringe, which he uses on his tin lizzy. A good shot of heroin, cocaine, or a speedball was all this crazy machine needed, and it responds with a jolt and takes off without its driver.

The concept of the "automobile," the vehicle that supplies its own motive power, supplied the premise of many silent comedy sequences as cars take off and drive themselves. *Hot Water* includes a sequence of the car driving itself with Harold in hot pursuit; and, in the climax of *Get Out and Get Under*, Lloyd performs a wonderful *pas de deux* between his own speed and acrobatic dexterity and the frequently running away car. The beauty of this sequence, like that of the best of Chaplin, Keaton, Lloyd, or Semon, involves the dynamic interaction of the human body and the machine, in which the machine becomes humanized with an apparent will of its own and the human mechanized as it strives to catch or control the errant machine. As I have stated elsewhere, the impression of this mechanization of the human (or perhaps better, the human's merging with the machine in a crazy machine assembly) recalls less Bergson's mockery of the inflexibility and absurdity of the human body, and more the way the mechanical endows the human with a sense of grace, perfection, and even freedom.[28] Although Lloyd, in the climax of *Get Out and Get Under*, seems to achieve blissful oneness with his car, his driving seems liberated from the narrative purpose of getting him to the amateur theatrical performance that originally prompted his car trip. Instead, as he careens past traffic cops and subdivides a political parade, Lloyd becomes a demon of energy, an infernal machine, rather than a frustrated middle-class guy rushing to a late appointment. The detours on his journey supply the gags (as Donald Crafton famously put it in his classical essay from the first Slapstick Symposium: "Gags are the potholes, detours and flat tires encountered by the tin lizzy of the narrative on its way to the end of the film").[29] Lloyd drives his car onto a freight train, across open fields, and sliding down hills (without its driver again). But what I want to stress is not simply the way purposes are foiled, but the almost perfect matching up of incidents with gag logic. The whole world seems to be in motion, and once Lloyd catches the rhythm of this motion it serves him well. He can hop on and off his car in order to rearrange signs; he can use a moving van or a camper's tent to conceal himself (both Harold and his car now being swallowed by these objects), or attach himself to a trolley car in order to emerge once more from his hiding place. No longer simply at the mercy of the machine, he seems to have let go of his individual middle-class ego and become part of a larger crazy machine that works perfectly – as long as you don't care if it actually accomplishes anything. The film ends with Lloyd actually arriving at the amateur theatrical just in time to take a bow at the curtain call then drive off with his sweetheart, uprooting a fire hydrant in the process and leaving a well-dressed crowd soaked as the film's closing gesture.

Comedy, like most of art, plays with ambivalence. Rather than making a simple statement, comedy explores the experience of contradiction, the way life and the world defeats the best-conceived purposes. Like a sense of humor in daily life, a comic mode may allow characters to cope with obstacles, but it is not always simply adaptive. Few aspects of modern life (if indeed it is an aspect, rather than the center, of modern life) evoke such ambivalence as technology. If technology is founded in an instrumental mindset, one that challenges nature and bends it to human purposes, comic thinking inverts that mode. It may allow us to adjust to the minor collapses of the machines of daily life with humor, or it may present a comic utopia in which men and machines seem to merge. Or it may envision for us the precarious nature of modern reality as, in Bely's words, "a lady suffering from a cold who sneezes and explodes." In all these cases the gag functions by its playful inversion of the machine from a means to an end to a humorous demonstration of the way purposes go astray and produce laughter.

## notes

1. Eileen Bowser, "Introduction," in Eileen Bowser, ed., *The Slapstick Symposium* (Brussels: FIAF, 1988), i.
2. Northrop Frye, "The Argument of Comedy," in D. A. Robinson, ed., *English Institute Essays 1948* (New York: Columbia University Press, 1949); Stanley Cavell, *The Pursuits of Happiness: The Hollywood Comedy of Remarriage* (Cambridge, MA: Harvard University Press, 1981).
3. Henri Bergson, *Laughter: An Essay on the Meaning of the Comic*, trans. Cloudesley Brereton and Fred Rothwell (Los Angeles: Green Integer, 1999).
4. Tom Gunning, "Crazy Machines in the Garden of Forking Paths: Mischief Gags and the Origins of American Film Comedy," in Kristine B. Karnick and Henry Jenkins, eds., *Classical Hollywood Comedy* (New York: Routledge, 1994), 87–105.
5. Immanuel Kant, *The Critique of Judgment*, trans. James Creed Meredith (Oxford: Oxford University Press, 1980), 199.
6. Ibid., 200.
7. Noël Carroll, "Notes on the Sight Gag," in *Theorizing the Moving Image* (New York: Cambridge University Press, 1996), 146–157.

8. Little Sammy Sneeze is reproduced in black and white, in Winsor McCay, *Early Works* (Miamiburg: Checker BPG, 2003), 107–171.

9. Kant, *Critique of Judgment*, 201.

10. Rob King has insightfully pointed out that some of my examples of "devices" are closer to tools than to machines, since machines involve a greater degree of automation than the manual work enabled by a tool. This is an important distinction and I basically agree with it. However, my focus in this section lies more on the idea of an instrumental project into which either the tool or the machine can fit, and the way this project becomes inverted in gags. More than the uniquely modern aspect of the machine, I want to relate gags to the inverting of purposes and projects, but most of my devices create a scenario in which several moving or separate parts interact, such as the hinged slapstick or the zigzag. In order to show how slapstick gags derived from a pre-industrial world, I am highlighting the role of instrumental logic, more than advanced technology. However, my discussion of the car and the interacting parts of the more developed gag scenarios that ends this chapter deals with an unambiguously modern and mechanical environment.

11. Gunning, "Crazy Machines."

12. Mel Gordon, *The Comic Routines of the Commedia dell'Arte* (Baltimore: Johns Hopkins University Press, 1983). The zigzag is illustrated on page 30.

13. http://en.wikipedia.org/wiki/Slapstick.

14. Ibid.

15. Rudi Blesch, *Keaton* (New York: Macmillan, 1966), 349–350.

16. See Maynard Frank Wolfe, *Rube Goldberg Inventions* (New York: Simon and Schuster, 2000). According to Wolfe (10), the term "rubegoldberg" first appeared in Webster's *New World Dictionary*.

17. Eileen Bowser, "Preparation for Brighton: The American Contribution," in *Cinema, 1900–1906: An Analytical Study* (Brussels: FIAF, 1982), 7.

18. John A. McKinven, *The Hanlon Brothers: Their Amazing Acrobatics, Pantomimes and Stage Spectacles* (Glenview: David Meyer Magic Books, 1998).

19. See Francis Lacassin, *Alla Ricerca di Jean Durand* (Bologna: Cineteca Bologna, 2004).

20. Maxim Gorky, "Lumière Review," in Jay Leyda, *Kino: A History of the Russian and Soviet Film* (London: George Allen and Unwin, 1960), 407–409; Yuri Tsivian, *Early Russian Cinema and its Cultural Reception* (London: Routledge, 1994), 151.

21. Ibid., 151.

22. Ibid.

23. On the cinematic attractions and their sense of a burst of presence, see my chapter, "'Now You See it, Now You Don't': The Temporality of the Cinema of Attractions," in Richard Abel, ed., *Silent Cinema* (New Brunswick: Rutgers, 1995), 71–84.

24. Karen Beckman's forthcoming work (from Duke University Press) on car crashes in the cinema, *Little Bastard*, will provide perhaps the definitive treatment of this theme.

25. It was Kristin Thompson's artful essay on Tati's *Playtime* in *Breaking the Glass Armor: Neoformalist Film Analysis* (Princeton: Princeton University Press, 1988), 247–262, that made me aware of refused gags.

26. Quoted in Alice L. Hutchinson, *Kenneth Anger* (London: Black Dog Publishing, 2004), 130.

27. Carroll, "Notes on the Sight Gag."
28. Tom Gunning, "Buster Keaton or The Work of Comedy in the Age of Mechanical Reproduction," in Frank Krutnik, ed., *Hollywood Comedians: The Film Reader* (New York: Routledge, 2003), 73–77.
29. Don Crafton, "Pie and Chase: Gag, Spectacle and Narrative in Slapstick Comedy," in Bowser, ed., *The Slapstick Symposium*, 49–59.

# slapstick

# skyscrapers

### an architecture of attractions

nine

s t e v e n   j a c o b s

## skyscrapers, slapstick, and the modernity thesis

The image of Harold Lloyd dangling from a clock attached to the face of a skyscraper is by general agreement the most famous shot of American silent comedy. According to Richard Schickel,

> no illustrated history of the movies – indeed, of the social history of twentieth-century America – seemed complete without that famous still from *Safety Last* [1923] of Lloyd hanging from the hands of a clock, its face itself dangling from the huge timepiece's main-spring, some twelve stories above a busy downtown street.[1]

Other slapstick protagonists, such as Buster Keaton and Laurel and Hardy, climbed and defied skyscrapers as well. Keaton even confronted skyscrapers off-screen. When he came to New York for the opening of his *Seven Chances* in April 1925, there was a gag photograph of him and his wife taken standing on the rooftop of the Biltmore Hotel. The photo bore the caption: "Natalie Talmadge, his wife, is urging him to be careful."[2] Carefulness, however, was a meaningless concept to slapstick protagonists. It was precisely the confrontation of vulnerable bodies with the thrills of heights and the wonders of architectural progress that provided the genre with its most powerful images. This chapter deals with the lure and popularity of these images by investigating the ways in which they resonate with other contemporary skyscraper imagery.

Prior to World War I, at the start of the golden age of slapstick comedy, skyscrapers had already become tokens of urban modernity.[3] High-rise buildings had become synecdoches of the metropolis, the image of the skyscraper city providing a key locus of early twentieth-century modernization. Accommodating thousands of office workers in innovative pieces of engineering, high-rise buildings became the emblems of capitalism, industrialization, rationalization, standardization, and Taylorism. Furthermore, skyscraper cities defined an environment shaped by new technologies, new means of transportation and communication, and new forms of popular entertainment (such as cinema). Accumulating floors and rows of windows, skyscrapers became the vertical equivalent of the grid plan of the modern city and its endless crowded streets. Veritable machines of urban density, skyscrapers were also important components of an environment that generated a new subjective experience. According to leading scholars of urban modernity, such as Georg Simmel, Siegfried Kracauer, and Walter Benjamin, this perceptual modality was determined by the profusion of physical and perceptual shocks of the modern urban environment, characterized in terms of speed, chaos, fragmentation, and disorientation. The kaleidoscopic spectacle of high-rise buildings combined with hectic traffic, flickering street signs, raging crowds, colorful window displays, glaring billboards, and loud advertisements resulted in a mental state that Simmel defined as an "intensification of nervous stimulation." According to Benjamin, the modern metropolis was a cultural constellation in which, through the confrontation with anonymous crowds and motorized traffic, "shock experience has become the norm."[4]

Skyscrapers contributed to the creation of such an environment determined by bombardments of multiple shocks. They were not only landmarks dominating the urban environment, they were also stunning visual objects that incorporated the fragmentary and kaleidoscopic nature of the metropolis. According to architectural historian Manfredo Tafuri, early twentieth-century American skyscrapers were hybrid constructions, which generated an "orgy of forms" characterized by an "optimistic merging of the influences of late-romantic European culture and Hollywood taste."[5] Furthermore, for many architectural critics of the first decades of the twentieth century, the proliferation of tall buildings resulted in urban "chaos" or in "a mere formless urban jumble."[6] Sky-scrapers, in short, enacted on a grand architectural scale the conflict between individualism and civic life, which urban sociologists had marked as the central issue of the modern metropolis. This chaotic juxtaposition, however, resulted in a new kind of urban spectacle. According to Tafuri, skyscraper cities presented themselves as "a variety theater, through which eccentricity becomes an institution, a mode of collective behavior."[7]

Several scholars have connected this perceptual modus of the modern metropolis with the development of cinema as well.[8] On the one hand, cinema incorporated the dynamics and stimulus–response mechanisms of big-city life, its flickering and disjointed projections of movement cor-responding to the receptive disposition of the city-dweller. On the other hand, the modern city was itself described in cinematic terms, interpreted as a scopic device based on a cinematic logic of multiple points of view, of an alternation of acceleration and deceleration. This was particularly the case for specific genres, such as so-called city symphonies and slapstick comedy. City symphonies, such as *Manhatta* (Strand and Sheeler, 1921), *Rien que les heures* (Cavalcanti, 1926), *Berlin: Symphony of a Metropolis* (Rutt-mann, 1927), or *The Man with the Movie Camera* (Vertov, 1929), not only depicted the spaces and programs of modern urbanity, they also appro-priated emphatically the dynamics, sensory hyperstimulation, and shock experiences of big city life.[9] Although its engagement with modernity was clearly different, slapstick comedy, as well, adopted the innervations that many forms of modern popular entertainment borrowed from the new metropolitan environment. With its fascination for mechanical speed, physical action, and consecutive thrills, slapstick comedy embraced the logics of what Tom Gunning has called a "cinema of attractions," a cine-matic paradigm that preferred the immediate stimulation of shocks and surprise effects over narrative coherence.[10] Furthermore, slapstick took some icons of urban modernity as favorite motifs. This is certainly the case with the car, for instance, which slapstick frequently turned into one of its crazy machines, which both celebrated and desecrated symbols of technological and industrial progress.[11] Engendering speed, which the American silent comedy applauded anyhow, cars provided slapstick stunts with ever-changing backgrounds. Often, within the context of a single sequence, backgrounds consist of a continuous alternation of met-ropolitan, suburban, and natural landscapes. At a dazzling speed, the characters move through the streets of Los Angeles, which was already developing into a horizontal urban grid determined by the car.[12] The surreal dimensions of slapstick chases remind us of the fact that the motif of the car drive was immediately recognized as a convenient instrument to construct cinematic space. The car, after all, sets itself the same task as cinema: breaking spatio-temporal limitations. Not coincidentally, speeding cars turned up frequently in Griffith's parallel-edited, last-minute rescue sequences. In addition, car chases invoked the use of long tracking shots, which gave the chase the functional elegance of the trajectory of a bullet and which subjected the world to a simple system of geometric coordinates. Like the car, the skyscraper was another late nineteenth-century feature of technological progress that defined the spatial logics of the urban environment. Cars and skyscrapers were the horizontal and vertical vectors of modern rationalized space enthusiastically explored by slapstick film, which we first and foremost associate with long shots showing bodies and objects moving rapidly through space.

### *three ages*, the manhattan skyline, and skyscraper imagery

In contrast with cars, skyscrapers appeared only quite late in slapstick comedy. Although tall buildings occur sporadically in early productions – the Keystone Kops, for instance, climb rooftops and beam structures high above the ground in *The Lion and the Girl* (1916) – slapstick's most famous and spectacular skyscraper scenes date from the 1920s. This coincided with a new building boom of skyscrapers, which was no longer restricted to the archetypal skyscraper cities of New York and Chicago. Both the 1916 New York Zoning law, which generated a new skyscraper typology and a true vertical aesthetic, and the 1922 worldwide competition for the Chicago Tribune Tower fostered architectural and civic debates in both the trade and popular press.[13] The skyscraper, in short, became the symbol of the "roaring twenties" and renditions of it increased dramatically throughout the decade.[14]

Tellingly, Buster Keaton adopted the skyscraper as an emblem of the era in his *Three Ages* (1923). To establish the modern episode in this film, which also comprises scenes set in prehistoric times and Ancient Rome, Keaton selected the still image of a skyline filled with skyscrapers. A title card connects an assembly of skyscrapers with "the present age of speed, need, and greed." This association with "greed" was inherently connected with the skyscraper building type from its inception in the late nineteenth century. Skyscrapers, after all, were the creations of corporate capitalism. Their rise coincided with new forms of management and changes in the corporate hierarchies of big business.[15] They also marked the emergence of a tightly packed central business district that came to symbolize not only New York, but eventually the American city in general. Consequently, appreciation of the skyscraper was closely tied to changing perceptions of corporate capitalism. For some commentators, skyscrapers symbolized the efficiency and optimism of the American economy. According to R. W. Sexton, author of a 1928 photographic survey of new tall office buildings, "honesty, fearlessness and prosperity" not only characterized American business, but these qualities "lend themselves readily to architectural expression." For Sexton, "the high standards which American business maintains" were expressed best in the "good architectural design" of the new tall office buildings.[16] For others, skyscrapers were the monstrous architectural manifestations of the failures of American capitalism and the inhumanity of big business. Dwarfing pedestrians and robbing them of light and air, skyscrapers were regarded as monuments to dangerous prosperity, pride, carelessness, and greed. According to leading contemporary critics, tall office buildings represented "rampant individualism" and a blatant disregard for both urban context and collective effect.[17]

The precise location of the establishing shot in the modern episode of Keaton's *Three Ages* is telling. Although the entire film, including its spectacular skyscraper stunt scene, was shot in Los Angeles, the image offers us a view of lower Manhattan's financial district and some of the structures that played an important part in the architectural history of the skyscraper: the Singer tower designed by Ernest Flagg (1908), the Municipal Building by McKim, Mead & White (1914), the Woolworth Building by Cass Gilbert (1913), and the City Investing Building by Francis H. Kimball (1908). Echoing the inter-title in Keaton's film, an architectural historian has labeled the City Investing Building and its 500,000 square feet of office floor area as "a monument to pure greed."[18] When Keaton made *Three Ages* in 1923, the impressive juxtaposition of the Singer Tower, the Municipal Building, and the Woolworth Building, among many other high-rise structures, had already featured in numerous photographs, prints, and postcard views. As a result, Keaton could use the image of the lower Manhattan skyline as a convenient establishing shot for the modern metropolis and even the modern era. Moreover, by 1923, the denunciation of skyscrapers as products of base materialism and symbols of capitalism incarnate was certainly no longer the dominant opinion. On the contrary, by the 1920s, the skyscraper had become one of the most cherished motifs of American modernist painters and photographers.[19] In addition, the New York skyscraper featured prominently in the photographs and photomontages of European avant-garde artists. Some of the iconic works of constructivism, for instance, made use of virtually the same view as Keaton's establishing shot in *Three Ages*. A famous example is Paul Citroën's montage entitled *Metropolis* (1923), which includes, in its top-left corner, a view showing the Woolworth Building and the Municipal Building. In addition, the Woolworth Building, the Singer Tower, and the City Investing Building feature prominently in a 1926 photomontage by Kazimir Malevich, which shows a Suprematist skyscraper project inserted in the lower Manhattan skyline. Leading European modernist architects were also fascinated by the daring achievements of the designers and constructors of Manhattan's tall buildings.[20] Skyscrapers fill the pages, for instance, of *Amerika* (1926), the book of photographs made by Erich Mendelsohn during his trip to the United States.[21] Le Corbusier, who described Manhattan as a "catastrophe féerique" (an enchanting catastrophe) could not conceal his fascination for the American metropolis and its skyscrapers in his writings – some of them published in journals such as *L'Esprit nouveau* and *Plans*, which also paid attention to the latest products of American film comedy.[22] Finally, American skyscrapers also proliferated in popular visual culture, such as comic strips, both in America (e.g., Winsor McCay's *Little Nemo*, 1908) and Europe (e.g., Hergé's *Tintin en Amérique*, 1931).

Last but not least, the worldwide reputation of the New York skyscraper no doubt rested to a large extent on its cinematic appeal. Numerous turn-of-the-twentieth-century Edison and Biograph actualities had cherished the street life and skyline of lower Manhattan, many of which were shot from windows and rooftops.[23] The 1902 American Mutoscope & Biograph film, *Panorama of the Flatiron Building*, for instance, celebrated the completion of this landmark skyscraper, the great height of which provided the narrative. A vertical panning shot starts at street level and moves upward along the structure, culminating at the roof. Later on, in the 1920s, both European and American directors were fascinated by the enchantment of tall buildings. Fritz Lang, for instance, told repeatedly that he conceived *Metropolis* in 1924, when he caught a first glimpse of the New York skyline from the deck of his ship.[24] Unmistakably, the urban imagery of *Metropolis* refers to the famous visionary drawings of New York as a future skyscraper city by designers or illustrators such as Harvey Willey Corbett and Harry M. Pettit at the beginning of the twentieth century. Skyscrapers, of course, were also prominent motifs in the aforementioned city symphonies, many of which take New York's architecture as their theme. The very same towers that mark the establishing shot in Keaton's *Three Ages* are also celebrated in *Manhatta* (1921) by Paul Strand and Charles Sheeler. In these city symphonies, high-rise buildings provide for numerous extreme high-angle, bird's-eye views, and diagonal camera set-ups calling to mind the high modernism of constructivist photography. This was demonstrated by Robert Florey, who even dedicated an entire film to the building type with his 1929 *Skyscraper Symphony*. The film opens with a series of stationary oblique views of high-rise buildings, dissolving into each other, before disorienting camera movements scan the surfaces of the endless facades. In Florey's film, it seems as if the buildings themselves start to dance – an image prefiguring the famous skyscraper ballet in Busby Berkeley's *42nd Street* (1933).

Such enthusiastic explorations of the visual potential of the skyscraper by artists, architects, and filmmakers indicate that, by the time Keaton presented it as a symbol of "speed, need, and greed," the building type was no longer generally seen as a petrified expression of diabolic powers.

Rather, the building type now elicited a growing range of responses, from social critique to aesthetic experiment. Such ambivalence is evidenced in several films of the mid-1920s, such as King Vidor's *The Crowd* (1928), in which social commentary and aesthetic play are combined in a single montage sequence of bustling streets and skyscrapers, which is followed by the famous crane shot of a vast office space filled with endless rows of clerks. Again showing the same towers of Keaton's establishing shot, Vidor's skyscraper sequence denotes a new world of haunting loneliness and alienation, even as it symbolizes a world of opportunities and a celebration of the exaltation of modern city life. This ambivalence also characterizes Keaton's *Three Ages*. The skyscrapers are presented as symbols of greed, but they are also transformed into fascinating machines partaking in spectacular stunts, which celebrate the thrills of the modern metropolis.

## vulgar fun, thrills, and crazy machines

Even before slapstick protagonists created spectacular skyscraper scenes, high-rise buildings provided inspiration for new forms of popular entertainment upon which slapstick film would draw. First, right from the start, skyscrapers were connected with forms of vulgar, physical humor. Since new skyscrapers, such as Daniel H. Burnham's spectacular Flatiron Building (1902), created gusts of wind blowing up women's dresses, they became places of attraction that provided much amusement for the voyeurs of the city. Like other tourist attractions, postcards were even made of these accidental exposures to the public gaze.[25] One of these, entitled "I am seeing great things," bears striking similarities to the so-called "teasers" that were popular in early cinema, such as Edwin Porter's *What Happened on Twenty-Third Street, New York City* (Edison Manufacturing Company, 1901), which, like the postcard, catches a young woman whose light summer dress is blown upward above her knees.[26]

Second, skyscrapers also fueled the growing urban market in sensational thrills, as discussed by Ben Singer.[27] Their sheer height was an attraction in itself. Several landmark skyscrapers, such as the Singer Tower, contained observation decks. In addition, the popular press was fascinated by the new dangers high-rise buildings entailed. Suicide leaps from rooftops and skyscraper workplace accidents, for instance, preoccupied sensational newspapers at the beginning of the century. Some of these falls evoked a kind of uncontrollable danger lurking in the modern urban environment. Slapstick comedy rewardingly employed this thrill of height, which was also incorporated in other forms of modern popular culture, such as the thrilling mechanical rides included in popular amusement parks. In addition, the skyscraper city created its own class of modern urban acrobats, the so-called "human flies" who climbed the faces of skyscrapers. One of these was Harry Gardiner, who successfully climbed over 700 buildings in Europe and North America, usually wearing ordinary street clothes and using no special equipment. In November 1918 Gardiner climbed the Bank of Hamilton, Ontario. Almost foreshadowing Harold Lloyd, the bespectacled Gardiner stuck his head into one of the open windows and signed some insurance papers. Lloyd himself got the idea for *Safety Last* when he saw one of these human flies, a certain Bill Strother, climbing the Brockman Building in Los Angeles.[28]

Third, skyscrapers not only provided models of vulgar fun and modern thrills but were also in keeping with slapstick's fascination for crazy machines. With their revolutionary iron and steel framing, elevators, and electrical illuminations, skyscrapers were often described and enthusiastically heralded as machines. They originated thanks to the introduction of the mechanical elevator and, like cars, were commonly associated with speed; in fact, some of the most famous examples presented themselves as elegantly designed "structure[s] that incorporate[d] velocity" within themselves.[29] Skyscrapers also often caused amazement by the speed of their construction.[30] In addition, although static objects themselves, skyscrapers also generated movement and rhythm. In the early twentieth century, many artists and writers began to comment on the accelerated movement of crowds among the skyscrapers. In his 1912 book, *The Great New York*, author and illustrator Joseph Pennell, for instance, noted the "tumult and excitement" on the "curb market" in Wall Street.[31] Drawing people together, skyscrapers were machines of density. They contributed to the development of a new metropolitan lifestyle that architect Rem Koolhaas has called "the culture of congestion."[32] According to Koolhaas, the combination of human density, new technologies, and the interiorization of shock experiences, resulted in an outrageous but unformulated movement, "Manhattanism," of which the skyscraper became the ultimate architectural embodiment. With its superposition of independent levels with autonomous programs, the skyscraper operated as a surrealist *machine à habiter*, not unlike the numerous crazy architectural machines in slapstick cinema, such as the dwelling of Snub Pollard in *It's a Gift* (Hugh Fay, 1923) or several houses of Buster Keaton, whom Gilles Deleuze has called "l'architect dadaïste par excellence."[33] Koolhaas' interpretation of the New York skyscraper as a structure combining modern technology, fantasy, and ecstasy reminds one of the interiors in Keaton's *The Scarecrow* (1920) and *The Electric House* (1922), or the prefab house in *One Week* (1920), in which Keaton invented deconstructivist architecture *avant la lettre*. In *Delirious New York* (1978), Koolhaas interprets New York skyscrapers, such as the 1931 Downtown Athletic Club, as similarly complicated architectural gadgets. Containing a full spectrum of facilities, such as dining rooms, squash courts, Turkish Baths, gymnasiums, an eight-bed station for artificial sunbathing, a library, a swimming pool occupying the entire twelfth floor, and an indoor golf course on the seventh, the Downtown Athletic Club offered metropolitan bachelors a full array of superimposed facilities. The skyscraper, which Koolhaas calls a "constructivist social condenser" and "an incubators for adults," was conceived as an architectural mechanism that restores the human body – just like slapstick's crazy machines, which were perfectly adapted to the acrobatic bodies of the slapstick characters. In similar words, Manfredo Tafuri has called the American skyscraper "a scenic toy rich with ludic valencies" and he described their lobbies as "true and proper *boîtes à surprises*."[34]

## linearity and the architecture of attractions

The Downtown Athletic Club provides a paradigm of the logic of the skyscraper, which is first and foremost a neutral superposition of independent levels. Koolhaas refers to a remarkable 1909 cartoon published in *Life*, which shows a slender steel structure supporting 84 horizontal planes, all the size of the original plot. Each of these artificial levels contains a detached country house with a garden. "From now on," Koolhaas writes, "each metropolitan lot accommodates an unforeseeable and unstable combination of simultaneous activities, which makes architecture less an act of foresight than before, and planning an act of only limited prediction. It has become impossible to *plot* culture."[35] For Koolhaas, what is striking is that a popular magazine such as *Life* intuited the promise of the skyscraper at a time when architectural magazines were still devoted to Beaux-Arts. But slapstick comedy also embraced those possibilities. From this perspective, the building in the *Life* cartoon acts like a slapstick gag machine. Its *promenade architectural* is no more than a simple, straight vertical line – reminiscent of the slapstick chase, which integrates a series of gags into a continuous spatial system. Its succession of independent units can be compared with the lurching stop-and-start rhythm of silent comedy. In short, the skyscraper can be considered an *architecture of attractions*. Instead of the integrated and organic architectural unity of the traditional building, the structure of the skyscraper answers perfectly to the structure of a cinema of attractions: on every level, another program, another encounter, another gag; on each floor, at each strata, a fragmentary "montage of attractions." Koolhaas' description of the Downtown Athletic Club as a machine for metropolitan bachelors answers perfectly to Donald Crafton's description of slapstick as a dialectic of the pie (explosive, show-stopping gags) and the chase (elements of narrative development).[36] In the Downtown Athletic Club, the chase has been replaced by the linear and vertical structure of the skyscraper, whereas the successive surprising programs on every floor provide the users with the explosive attractions. "In an abstract choreography," Koolhaas writes, "the

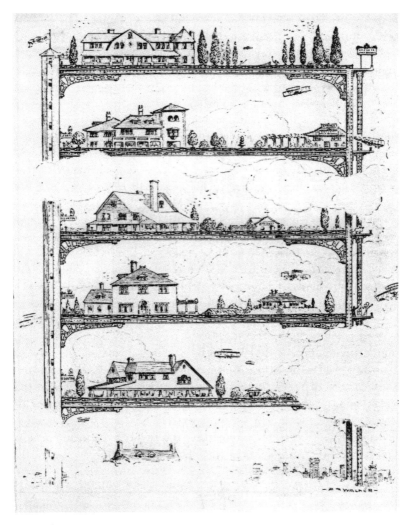

Figure 9.1

*Life* (October 1909). According to Rem Koolhaas, "each metropolitan lot accommodates an unforeseeable and unstable combination of simultaneous activities"

building's athletes shuttle up and down between its 38 'plots' – in a sequence as random as only an elevator man can make it – each equipped with techno-psychic apparatus for the men's own redesign."[37]

Slapstick comedy tactfully exploited the skyscraper's combination of simple linear organization and surprising juxtaposition of functions. The modern episode of "speed, need, and greed" in *Three Ages* is marked by a famous rooftop jump that ends with a fall through canvas window awnings, onto a swinging drainpipe and down to a fire station on the first floor. Performed on a set built atop the Hill Street Tunnel, Keaton's dangerous stunt creates the illusion that he is working high off the ground.[38] In *The Cameraman* (1928), by contrast, Keaton makes fun of the repetition of interchangeable floor levels and the vertical movement between them. In his Manhattan apartment, Buster eagerly waits for a phone call from a girl. When the phone rings on a lower floor, a vertical crane shot follows the acrobatic Buster dashing up and down his apartment stairs. Repeatedly, he oversteps his mark, ending up in the basement or on the roof of the building, before he zigzags between the traffic along Fifth Avenue to meet his girl. In other films, Keaton made skilful use of other skyscraper paraphernalia, such as elevators and fire escapes. In *The Goat* (1921), Buster exploits an elevator to transform a tall building into one of slapstick's crazy machines. To evade his pursuer, Buster nails the floor counter arrow to brake the elevator. Later, he steers the arrow past all numbers, launching the elevator through the roof like a surreal rocket.

The combination of a linear trajectory with the succession of ever-changing programs and functions also marks Harold Lloyd's famous climb in *Safety Last*. To impress his girlfriend, Lloyd's character decides to risk everything for a $1,000 prize offered to anyone who can lure more customers to the department store where he works. His idea is to have his roommate, the human fly Bill Strother, climb the building. The roommate, however, is chased by a cop and Lloyd himself is forced to substitute as the climber. The plan is that the roommate will replace him on the second floor, or the third, or the next one, but Lloyd ends up having to scale the entire building. In *Safety Last*, which is characterized by an unusually tight story line, the skyscraper ascent veritably becomes the vertical equivalent of the chase. Like the chase film, Lloyd's climb offers a model of spatial linearity, but also a succession of frenzied actions: as Scott O'Dell notes, "in *Safety Last* each sequence dove-tails into its logical successor. The absence of cutbacks and parallel action is noticeable."[39] Climbing the building and encountering a series of obstacles, Lloyd transforms the architecture into a vertical stack of thrills in which the protagonist finds himself clinging to ledges, decorations, flagpoles, and clocks. Lloyd himself spoke of the "thrill picture" — a film comedy, in which, according to Walter Kerr, "laughter depends not so much on the quality of the joke as on the fact that it occurs when an audience's nerves are so titillatingly ravaged that response comes on the double."[40] Although the ingredients of thrill comedy were also part of Sennett's formula, Lloyd and producer Hal Roach amplified and intensified it. The skyscraper, no doubt, became the thrill comedy's fetish object. According to Donald McCaffrey, the thrill comedy "depended for its laughs on dangerous incidents atop a high building."[41] Lloyd pictures such as *Safety Last*, *Look Out Below* (1919), *High and Dizzy* (1920), *Never Weaken* (1921), *Welcome Danger* (1929), and *Feet First* (1930), remind us of the thrilling aspect that architects recognized in the skyscraper building itself. In his seminal and often-quoted 1896 essay, *The Tall Building Artistically Considered*, architect and skyscraper pioneer Louis Sullivan wrote that

> the loftiness of the skyscraper is to the artist-nature its thrilling aspect.... It must be tall, every inch of it tall. The force and power of altitude must be in it, the glory and pride of exaltation must be in it. It must be every inch a proud and soaring thing, rising in sheer exultation that from bottom to top it is a unit without a single dissenting line – that it is the new, the unexpected, the eloquent peroration of most bald, most sinister, most forbidding conditions.[42]

Lloyd's thrill pictures not only play on the danger of heights, they also give evidence of the exultation spoken of by Sullivan. In Lloyd's stunning skyscraper scenes, the simple danger of gravity contributes to their thrilling character. Lloyd's acrobatic talents as well as his vulnerability are emphasized throughout the entire climbing scene, since the street below, with its cars, streetcars, and pedestrians, is in view in virtually every shot. Even medium shots and close-ups of Lloyd's terror-stricken face are angled to show us exactly where he is and what may happen to him. Lloyd and Roach as well as the directors of the film, Fred Newmeyer and Sam Taylor, kept the thrill in every shot. Unmistakably, the entire scene is breathtaking because it was so evidently shot on location without photographic trick effects. Although the filmmakers skillfully exaggerated the height by selecting dramatic camera angles and using a set built atop an existing building, the scene nonetheless displays real tall buildings and real streets.[43] The long shots show not Lloyd but Bill Strother, who climbed the International Bank Building on Temple and Spring Streets with four cameras under the direction of Roach. The scene of Harold hanging on a clock was shot on top of a tall building at 908–910 Broadway, where a platform was built near the edge. According to Roach, several Los Angeles skyscrapers such as the Los Angeles Investment Company, the Western Costume Building, the Merchant's National Bank Building, and the Washington Building were employed for publicity stills.[44] Several of these office buildings were located on Spring Street, which was the site of major skyscraper building booms in the years 1900–1917 and from the early 1920s through 1931 successively.[45] Most of these 10- to 12-story office buildings utilized the imagery of classical Beaux Arts, turning Spring Street into the "Wall Street of the West," as it was called. *Safety Last* "may thus be viewed as one of the first full-length urban films in the United States to advertise Los Angeles, not New York, as a site for commerce and modernity."[46]

*Safety Last*, of course, presented Los Angeles in the first place as a skyscraper city. For Lloyd, whose glasses character embodies the values of the

American middle classes much more than Chaplin's tramp and Keaton's aloof stone face, the tall office building and the department store were a natural habitat. Described as "the quintessential achiever in the era of Harding normalcy and Coolidge prosperity" and outfitted with horn-rimmed glasses and a business suit, Lloyd established himself as the office clerk or the "young urban professional" who populated the new down-town skyscrapers.[47] Given this perspective, the fact that Lloyd gets entangled in a clock is not a coincidence. Earlier in the film, the punctuality of his character is emphasized – he is a product of mechanized time and Taylorization, which determined the rationale not only of skyscraper offices but also of slapstick itself. In short, the main character in *Safety Last* blends perfectly with the background of the high-rise department store where he works. Lloyd's character even literally embodies the capitalist success ethos of "upward mobility" since he hopes to rise to the top of the department-store business – a dream that comes true, but only architecturally: he climbs the building instead of the business hierarchy. In so doing, he even becomes a human billboard since his stunt is meant to promote consumerism. By acting as a company advertisement, Merrill Schleier observes, Lloyd subscribes to corporate ideology: "In order to be a fully integrated, middle-class man, he had to battle the era's monument to modernity, the skyscraper, and win."[48]

## heroes on steel skeletons

Nicknamed "the king of daredevil comedy," Lloyd confronted skyscraper architecture in some of his earlier two-reel shorts, such as *Look Out Below*, which, like the rooftop sequence in Keaton's *Three Ages*, was shot on top of the Hill Street Tunnel in downtown Los Angeles. Another spectacular skyscraper scene can be found in *Never Weaken*, which opens with a title card stating that "each crowded skyscraper holds a budding romance. It's the one and only thing the janitor can't smash." In both films, Lloyd ends up on the structural steel skeleton of an incomplete skyscraper.

Laurel and Hardy climbed the steel skeletons of high-rise buildings as well. In *Liberty* (1929), they play two escaped convicts who hastily change clothes in a getaway car, and end up wearing each other's pants. A cop chases them to a construction site, where they escape by riding an elevator to the top floor of an unfinished building. Shot on a scaffold on top of the roof of the Western Costume Company building in downtown Los Angeles, the film shows the two comedians finally switching pants atop the girders, high above the street. The image of Laurel and Hardy on a construction site is remarkable, since, for one thing, they were more typically associated with the systematic *destruction* of machines and buildings rather than with their *construction*. Furthermore, the spectacular imagery of Lloyd and Laurel and Hardy balancing on steel girders reminds us of the fact that, in the 1920s, the erection of a skyscraper was often regarded as an attraction in itself. Construction sites, steel skeletons, and scaffolds became veritable sidewalk shows, and artists and photographers presented them as emblems of modernity.[49] These three-dimensional grids were so shockingly modern that, when the buildings were actually built, they had to be concealed behind a façade with historical references. The steel skeletons, by contrast, evoke the modern abstract space of the European avant-garde that resulted in the post-war skyscraper with the glass curtain wall. Provided with clambering bodies, slapstick skyscrapers under construction are also reminiscent of constructivist theater sets, which were populated by actors who based their "biomechanics" on the movements of slapstick acting. In addition, the images of slapstick actors balancing on steel girders high above the street also resonate with those of real skyscraper builders, who were called "cowboys of the skies."[50] Answering to the constructivist notion of an organic unity between man and machine, construction workers were lauded as new American folk heroes, who demonstrated that tall buildings did not necessarily crush the spirit of the individual. This theme was later developed by photographer Lewis Hine, in his famous series of pictures of the construction of the Empire State Building (1931). Defying gravity, these sky laborers seemed to share the acrobatic skills of slapstick characters. According to Scott Bukatman, Hine's sky laborers prefigured the superheroes of the new decade, who extended the exploration of the skyscraper city that slapstick comedy had so eagerly started.[51] Buster Keaton, Harold Lloyd, and Laurel and Hardy thus paved the way for Superman and Batman, who also defied gravity among the skyscrapers. Like the slapstick urbanites, the superheroes of the 1930s "could suffer the brutalizing shocks of modernity with neither broken bones nor neurasthenic breakdowns" by turning the city's skyscrapers into an architecture of attractions.[52]

## notes

1. Richard Schickel, "Harold Lloyd," in Stuart Byron and Elisabeth Weis, eds., *The National Society of Film Critics on Movie Comedy* (New York: Grossman Publishers, 1977), 10.
2. See Tom Dardis, *Keaton: The Man Who Wouldn't Lie Down* (London: Virgin Books, 1979), 115.
3. See Merrill Schleier, *The Skyscraper in American Art 1890–1931* (New York: Da Capo Press, 1986); and Roberta Moudry, ed., *The American Skyscraper: Cultural Histories* (New York: Cambridge University Press, 2005).
4. See Georg Simmel, "The Metropolis and Mental Life" (1903), in *Simmel on Culture*, edited by David Frisby and Mike Featherstone (London: Sage, 1997), 173–185; Walter Benjamin, "Über einige Motive bei Baudelaire" (1939), in *Gesammelte Schriften* I, 2 (Frankfurt am Main: Suhrkamp, 1991),

614. For more on this topic, see Ghent Urban Studies Team (GUST), ed., *The Urban Condition: Space, Community, and Self in the Contemporary Metropolis* (Rotterdam: 010 Publishers, 1999).

5. Manfredo Tafuri, "The New Babylon: The Yellow Giants and the Myth of Americanism (Expressionism, Jazz Style, Skyscrapers 1913–30)," in *The Sphere and the Labyrinth: Avant-Gardes and Architecture from Piranesi to the 1970s* (Cambridge, MA: MIT Press, 1990), 180.

6. Keith D. Revell, "Law Makes Order: The Search for Ensemble in the Skyscraper City, 1890–1930," in Moudry, ed., *The American Skyscraper*, 41.

7. Tafuri, "The New Babylon," 181.

8. See Miriam Hansen, "Early Silent Cinema: Whose Public Sphere?," *New German Critique*, 29 (1983), 147–184; Anke Gleber, *The Art of Taking a Walk: Flanerie, Literature, and Film in Weimar Culture* (Princeton: Princeton University Press, 1999); and Tom Gunning, "Modernity and Cinema: A Culture of Shocks and Flows," in Murray Pomerance, ed., *Cinema and Modernity* (New Brunswick: Rutgers University Press, 2006), 297–315.

9. See Eric Barnouw, "Images at Work," *Documentary: A History of the Non-Fiction Film* (Oxford: Oxford University Press, 1983), 33–81; Jean-Paul Colleyn, "La ville-rythme: les symphonies urbaines," in François Niney, ed., *Visions Urbaines: Villes d'Europe à l'écran* (Paris: Centre Georges Pompidou, 1994), 23–27; David Macrae, "Ruttmann, Rhythm and Reality: A Response to Siegfried Kracauer's Interpretation of *Berlin: the Symphony of a Great City*," in Dietrick Scheunemann, ed., *Expressionist Film: New Perspectives* (Rochester, NY: Camden House, 2003); and Helmut Weihsmann, "The City in Twilight: Charting the Genre of the City-Film 1900–1930," in François Penz and Maureen Thomas, eds., *Cinema & Architecture: Méliès, Mallet-Stevens, Multimedia* (London: BFI, 1997), 8–27.

10. Tom Gunning, "Cinema of Attractions: Early Film, Its Spectator and the Avant-Garde," in Thomas Elsaesser and Adam Barker, eds., *Early Cinema: Space, Frame, Narrative* (London: BFI, 1990), 56–62.

11. Cecelia Tichi, *Shifting Gears: Technology, Literature, Culture in Modernist America* (Chapel Hill: University of North Carolina Press, 1987), 230–245. See also Steven Jacobs, "From Flaneur to Chauffeur: Driving through Cinematic Cities," in Christian Emden, Catherine Keen, and David Midgley, eds., *Imagining the City* (Oxford: Peter Lang, 2006), 213–228.

12. See Robert M. Fogelson, *The Fragmented Metropolis: Los Angeles 1850–1930* (Berkeley: University of California Press, 1967). On the relation between early twentieth-century urban planning and the slapstick chase, see Charles Wolfe's contribution to this volume.

13. See Revell, "Law Makes Order," 47–54; and Merrill Schleier, *The Skyscraper in American Art*, 70.

14. See Larry R. Ford, *Cities and Buildings: Skyscrapers, Skid Rows, and Suburbs* (Baltimore: Johns Hopkins University Press, 1994), 36; and Schleier, *The Skyscraper in American Art*, 69.

15. For the relation between skyscrapers and corporate capitalism, see Kenneth Turney Gibbs, *Business Architectural Imagery in America, 1870–1930* (Ann Arbor: UMI Research Press, 1984); and Carol Willis, *Form Follows Finance: Skyscrapers and Skylines in New York and Chicago* (New York: Princeton Architectural Press, 1995).

16. R. W. Sexton, *American Commercial Buildings of Today* (New York, Architectural Book Publishing Company, 1928), 2.

17. Montgomery Schuyler, "To Curb the Skyscraper," *Architectural Record* 24

(1908): 300; Charles H. Caffin, "The Beautifying of Cities," *World's Work* 3 (1901): 1429.

18. Sarah Bradford Landau and Carl W. Condit, *Rise of the New York Skyscraper 1865–1913* (New Haven: Yale University Press, 1996), 323, 374, 381–391. See also Robert A. M. Stern, Gregory Gilmartin, and John Massengale, *New York 1900: Metropolitan Architecture and Urbanism 1890–1915* (New York: Rizzoli, 1995).

19. Schleier, *The Skyscraper in American Art*.

20. Jean-Louis Cohen and Hubert Damisch, eds., *Américanisme et modernité: L'idéal américain dans l'architecture* (Paris: Flammarion, 1993); Jean-Louis Cohen, *Scenes of the World to Come: European Architecture and the American Challenge 1893–1960* (Paris: Flammarion/Montreal: Canadian Centre for Architecture, 1995).

21. Erich Mendelsohn, *Amerika: Bilderbuch eines Architekten* (Berlin, Rudolf Mosse, 1926).

22. See also Le Corbusier, *Quand les cathédrales étaient blanches: voyage au pays des timides* (1937) (Paris: Benoël Gonthier, 1983).

23. See, for instance, *Lower Broadway* (Robert K. Bonine, 1902), *Beginning of a Skyscraper* (Robert K. Bonine, 1902), *Panorama from Times Building, New York* (Wallace McCutcheon, 1905), *Panorama from the Tower of the Brooklyn Bridge* (Billy Bitzer, 1903) – all American Mutoscope and Biograph Co. productions. Similarly, Edison produced films such as *Skyscrapers of New York City from North River* (J. B. Smith, 1903).

24. Patrick McGilligan, *Fritz Lang: The Nature of the Beast* (New York: St Martin's Press, 1997), 104.

25. Schleier, *The Skyscraper in American Art*, 50.

26. See Jay Leyda and Charles Musser, *Before Hollywood: Turn-of-the-Century American Film* (New York: Hudson Hills Press, 1987), 110.

27. Ben Singer, *Melodrama and Modernity: Early Sensational Cinema and Its Context* (New York: Columbia University Press, 2001), 81–90.

28. Jeffrey Vance and Suzanne Lloyd, *Harold Lloyd: Master Comedian* (New York: Harry N. Abrams, 2002), 90–99.

29. Tafuri, "The New Babylon," 177.

30. Gail Fenske, "The Beaux-Arts Architect and the Skyscraper: Cass Gilbert, the Professional Engineer, and the Rationalization of Construction in Chicago and New York," in Moudry, ed., *The American Skyscraper*, 33–34.

31. Joseph Pennell, *The Great New York* (Boston: Le Roy Phillips, 1912), n.p. See also Schleier, *The Skyscraper in American Art*, 32.

32. Rem Koolhaas, *Delirious New York: A Retroactive Manifesto for Manhattan* (New York: Monacelli Press, 1994 [1978]), 81–160.

33. Gilles Deleuze, *Cinéma: 1. L'Image-Mouvement* (Paris: Les Editions de Minuit, 1983), 240.

34. Tafuri, "The New Babylon," 180–181.

35. Koolhaas, *Delirious New York*, 85.

36. Donald Crafton, "Pie and Chase: Gag, Spectacle, and Narrative in Slapstick Comedy," in Kristine Brunovska Karnick and Henry Jenkins, eds., *Classical Hollywood Comedy* (New York: Routledge, 1994), 106–119.

37. Koolhaas, *Delirious New York*, 157.

38. John Bengtson, *Silent Echoes: Discovering Early Hollywood through the Films of Buster Keaton* (Santa Monica: Santa Monica Press, 2000), 128–129.

39. Scott O'Dell, "Safety Last," in Richard Dyer McCann, ed., *The Silent Comedians* (Metuchen: The Scarecrow Press, 1993), 223.

40. Walter Kerr, *The Silent Clowns* (New York: Da Capo Press, 1975), 197.

41. Donald W. McCaffrey, *4 Great Comedians: Chaplin, Lloyd, Keaton, Langdon* (London: A. Zwemmer, 1968), 65.

42. Louis Sullivan, "The Tall Building Artistically Considered" (1896), in *The Public Papers*, edited by Robert Twombly (Chicago: University of Chicago Press, 1988), 108.

43. Vance and Lloyd, *Harold Lloyd*, 90–99.

44. Annette M. D'Agostino, *Harold Lloyd: A Bio-Bibliography* (Westpoint: Greenwood Press, 1994), 306–314.

45. David Gebhard and Robert Winter, *Los Angeles: An Architectural Guide* (Salt Lake City: Gibbs-Smith Publisher, 1994), 216.

46. Merrill Schleier, "Harold Lloyd's *Safety Last* (1923): Gendered Celebration of Los Angeles's Modernity," in Julia Halam, Robert Kronenburg, Richard Koeck, and Les Roberts, eds., *Cities in Film: Architecture, Urban Space, and the Moving Image* (Liverpool: University of Liverpool, 2008), 244.

47. Richard Koszarski, *An Evening's Entertainment: The Age of the Silent Feature Picture 1915–1928* (New York: Charles Scribner's Sons, 1990), 306. See also Frank Krutnik, "A Spanner in the Works? Genre, Narrative and the Hollywood Comedian," in Karnick and Jenkins, eds., *Classical Hollywood Comedy* (New York: Routledge, 1994), 19.

48. Schleier, "Harold Lloyd's *Safety Last*," 245.

49. Schleier, *The Skyscraper in American Art*, 25–27.

50. Schleier, *The Skyscraper in American Art*, 26.

51. Scott Bukatman, *Matters of Gravity: Special Effects and Supermen in the 20th Century* (Durham, NC: Duke University Press, 2003), 196–202.

52. Bukatman, *Matters of Gravity*, 202.

steven jacobs

# california slapstick

# revisited*

c h a r l e s   w o l f e

Addressing the first Slapstick Symposium held at the Museum of Modern
Art in New York in 1985, the late film historian Jay Leyda proposed that
film scholars adopt the label "California Slapstick" to describe a style of
physical comedy that linked the films of Sennett, Chaplin, Arbuckle,
Keaton, and others during the years 1912 to 1928. The central ingredients
of this comedy, he contended, were "violence, acrobatics, embarrassment,
and irrationality." Making light of the fondness of academics for categories derived from art history, Leyda joked that "students who love to apply
the term 'expressionist' to any film that hasn't yet been labeled could
easily change my suggested term to 'expressionist slapstick.' Do, if that
will make you happier."[1] A serious argument, however, can be discerned
in the particular term Leyda chose for talking about these films. In the
remarks to follow I wish to explore the utility of the label "California
slapstick," both as short hand for a subgenre of silent film comedy and as
an invitation to more systematic thinking about the role of social geography in comedy films made in a particular place and period. In effect, I
want to press harder on the concept of California – particularly Southern

California – as a materially specific region for the production of slapstick comedy, with primary focus on the development of the forms and themes of the comic chase.

I have come to this topic through researching the production histories of silent comedies by Buster Keaton, and will be using two passages from Keaton's 1920 two-reeler, *The Scarecrow*, to explain my central ideas. But I believe these ideas have wider relevance and application. Investigating the production of films from the silent era can be difficult work. In the case of Keaton, for example, the lack of studio records, scripts, notes or other written documents is a substantial barrier to understanding precisely how and under what conditions a given film was planned, shot, and assembled. Scattered recollections and trade press reports provide clues, and sometimes good stories, but the reliability of these accounts is often in question. Anyone with an interest in the production of silent comedy in California therefore can only be grateful for the remarkable detective work of John Bengtson, who in two recent books examines the production sites of many of Keaton's and Chaplin's films.[2] Armed with video discs, production stills, fire insurance maps, and other public images and documents, with great skill and shrewdness Bengtson has identified a wide range of locations beyond the studio where scenes and sequences were shot. His meticulous research provides a new perspective on the way in which comic ideas were generated and refined in specific physical locations, and a different kind of guide to the changing environment of Los Angeles and Orange Counties, as well as more remote locations, in the 1910s and 1920s.

Among other things, locating the history of slapstick comedy in relation to social geography – to the ways in which a terrain is delineated, inhabited, and administered; its resources identified, marshaled, and allocated; its surfaces built up and made available for human movement and settlement – requires us to focus on the production of early comic films in both practical and conceptual ways. Implicit in the concept of "California slapstick" as I will expand on it here are four interrelated premises.

First, elements of the material environment – topography, modes of transportation, traffic corridors, grading and landscaping, parks, residential and commercial buildings, interior and exterior architectural design – are not only important backdrops to the staging of physical comedy, but may be seen to have shaped the development of comedy forms and themes in distinctive ways. The label "California slapstick" is valuable in part because it encourages us to examine the comedies in relation to environmental conditions in rural, suburban, and urban locations, and how these in turn took particular shape in response to land use practices and policies in Southern California between 1890 and 1930, a period of rapid industrialization and extraordinary population growth. The sites where motion picture production companies were established, as well as the neighboring locations favored by filmmakers for the staging and recording of comic events, can be profitably studied in relation to these historical patterns. It is commonplace in writing on early US film history to attribute the settlement of the motion picture industry on the west coast at least in part to the combination of topographical diversity and temperate climate that Southern California offered. However, California slapstick should be conceived not simply as a convenient response to the favorable conditions for location filmmaking, but as a subgenre of comedy that articulated new relations among a variety of residential, agricultural, industrial, and recreational settings. Comedy performers and filmmakers who migrated to Southern California in the 1910s confronted the physical effects of economic and political practices that had guided urban development in the region over the course of several decades. With this in mind, I wish to consider how the physical environment they encountered may have come to inform the stylistic design and thematic import of the slapstick chase.

Second, slapstick films are valuable to us today in part for the photographic record that they provide. On the occasion of the first Slapstick Symposium, Ron Magliozzi of the Film Study Center at MoMA emphasized this point in his report on the Slapstick Identification Seminar that accompanied the conference, noting:

> The fact that so many of these films are shot on location, on the real streets of Hollywood and its vicinity is significant. There is rare beauty in these fresh new palm trees, the garden paths, the city streets, store fronts, the street lights, a glimpse now and then of a non-actor moving or staring in the distance.... A record of everyday reality in the twenties is always present in these films.[3]

The late architectural historian Reyner Banham once described silent comedies shot in Los Angeles as "an archive of urban scenery around 1914–27 such as no other city in the world possesses."[4] No doubt for many viewers today the fascination of these comedies follows at least in part from this archival dimension, a sense that traces of a once visible but now vanished world have been unveiled. Despite recent claims that the referential authenticity of the photograph has diminished in the digital era, new technologies may prove to deepen rather than dampen this fascination. As Bengtson emphasizes, digital video technology has provided additional tools to search a moving image for documentary evidence.[5] Combined with other sources of information, such scrutiny functions as a form of historical forensics, enabling the reconstruction of an otherwise undocumented act of picture-taking through attention to the smallest particulars of a stilled image. This includes, perhaps especially includes, incidental details: a half-hidden street sign, an irregular pattern to a rooftop or window frame, a distant city water tower, a distinctive line to a mountain ridge. Bengtson's detective work depends on his – and our – enduring confidence that images can be scanned and analyzed for clues of this kind.

My third assumption is that these comedy films construct imaginary worlds. The social places that we infer from these slapstick comedies are also always in some sense different than the material spaces they document, constituting yet another, fictional terrain. In framing and linking different images, in accelerating and decelerating movement, in establishing and developing characters that move through and across synthetically collocated spaces, slapstick chases can be said to exploit a cinematic geography that bends physical reality and torques social logic. This is a principal reason, of course, that comic chases are capable of provoking laughter. Critics have long explained the attractions of slapstick comedy in terms of a tension between the factual dimension of on-location performances and cinematography, and the transformational capacities of the medium based on film stock, camera optics, recording and projection speeds, patterns of editing, and the absence of recorded sound.[6] The notion of California slapstick explored below thus depends not only on an understanding of how physical environments impinge on the filming of comic action, but on the formal and stylistic structures through which such action coheres into pleasurable fictional patterns, articulating relations among moving bodies and varied settings in new ways.

Finally, I assume that the "California" in California slapstick refers not only to a geographic region, but to a cultural idea, a terrain that at the turn of the century was routinely promoted for both its great physical beauty and future prospects, and associated in popular myth with the possibility of personal and social transformation. Made newly fertile and verdant by major water projects, the semi-arid coastal region of Southern California was often described by Anglo-American journalists and boosters alike as a new kind of paradise, at once arcadian and utopian, combining the wonders of unspoiled nature with the marvels of modern engineering.[7] Linking "California" to the comedy term "slapstick" serves not simply to denote a geographic location but to evoke an atmosphere of open-air, freewheeling lunacy found in many of the films, a sense that the myth of California, under the pressures of modernization, was capable of courting its own unraveling. I am interested, in short, in charting the relationship between material conditions and comic forms, in the way in which the social geography of California was neither faithfully reconstructed nor willfully dispensed with, but re-imagined for the comic chase.

This double sense of California as both a physical place and cultural symbol is captured in Leyda's brief discussion of the subgenre. He defends his choice of "California slapstick" over a plausible alternative, "Holly-wood slapstick," partly on the grounds that the former is geographically "more exact," since Sennett's work alone covered locations stretching from San Francisco in the north to the Mexican border in the south. Leyda's insistence on this point should remind us of the dispersed quality not simply of the locations selected for filming, but of the film studios themselves during the early years of California filmmaking. A map of settled California companies producing comedies in the 1910s would extend at least as far north as Niles, near Oakland, where beginning in the fall of 1912 the west coast branch of Essanay produced rural comedies set in the fictional town of Snakeville, featuring Augustus Carney, Victor Potel, Harry Todd, and Margaret Joslin, as well as five of Charlie Chaplin's two-reelers in the winter of 1915;[8] proceed south along the coastline to Santa Barbara, where the American Film Company, beginning in 1913, produced "Calamity Ann" western comedies with Louise Lester, in 1914 short slapstick "Heine" comedies with George Field, and in 1916 features starring the "Dutch" comedians Clarence Kolb and Max Dill;[9] and then farther south and inland to Santa Paula, where the St. Louis Motion Picture Company briefly made Premier western comedies with Lillian Hamilton.[10] Moreover, the location of production companies across Los Angeles and Orange Counties greatly exceeded the physical boundaries of Hollywood, a late nineteenth-century Cahuenga Valley real estate devel-opment that was incorporated as a city in 1903 and absorbed by the greater city of Los Angeles in 1910.

More is at stake in Leyda's comments than the need for a wider geo-graphical compass, however. "Hollywood as a term," he cautions, "has become so over-used and worn-out, selling everything from shampoos to diets, that no one listens to it any more."[11] While Leyda does not elaborate further, it seems clear that "California" slapstick connotes for him a kind of filmmaking that emerged antecedent to, and developed on the margins of, a Hollywood system of production that came to be synonymous with entrenched commercialism. Slapstick comedy shorts were produced by a wide number of small, economically shaky production companies – many in and out of business in a matter of a few years – located physically and symbolically on the periphery of the major studios that took root during the late 1910s and 1920s. In ways not unlike "dot.com" internet companies 80 years later in "Silicon Valley" (another geographically sym-bolic California site), the economic model for these smaller companies often involved low-end entrepreneurship and a high tolerance for risk. Retrospectively applying the label "Hollywood" to all slapstick comedies

173

filmed in Southern California, Leyda's comments imply, would be to obscure the eccentric relationship of some companies to the more powerful centers of production. Thinking of these films as works of "California slapstick," in contrast, opens up a space between these films and the conventional production practices of Hollywood, while drawing our attention to the physical terrain where many slapstick comedies were shot.

Note, however, that "California" as an adjective also *narrows* the focus of what typically has been described not as "Hollywood" but rather "American" slapstick.[12] The label provides a regionally specific rather than national cultural frame. Leyda's quick genealogy of California slapstick emphasizes its debt to popular comedy traditions from other countries. He describes California slapstick as a "furnace ... mixing various ores and chemicals," including elements of *commedia dell'arte*, vaudeville, burlesque, circus, music hall, comic films from Italy and France, and society dramas from the east coast and Europe. Satire, he notes in an acerbic aside, could only come from outside California. Regional specificity, in this way, is understood in relation to comic practices that traveled across regional and national cultural boundaries. While only implicit in Leyda's comments, this aspect of his "fresh definition" of American film comedy has new resonance today when the question of national film cultures – once a bedrock principle of film historiography – has been complicated by a new interest in micro-regional, macro-regional, and transnational cultural formations and flows.

We need only turn to Vachel Lindsay's 1916 treatise, *The Art of the Moving Picture*, to appreciate the degree to which, by the mid-1910s, the identity of California was thoroughly bound up in its symbolic relation to the United States as a whole, and filmmaking in California had come to be seen as a projection of nationalist utopian longing. In a chapter entitled "California and America," Lindsay cites the capacity of California-based filmmakers to explore and exploit the unique resources of the local environment as a model for regionally specific and diverse filmmaking.[13] "Let us hope," he declares, "that every region will develop the silent photographic pageant in local form." At the same time Lindsay argues that the iconographic beauty and power of the films produced in California opened up the possibility of revising American cultural identity along entirely new geographical coordinates. "People who revere the Pilgrim Fathers of 1620," Lindsay observes, "have often wished those gentlemen had moored their bark in the region of Los Angeles rather than Plymouth Rock, that Boston had been founded there. At last that landing has been achieved."[14] To those who deemed California too thin on history to represent America, Lindsay advises that this "apparent thinness" was in fact shared with the "routine photoplay, which at times is as shallow in its thought as the shadow it throws upon the screen," but this coincidence of region and medium made it "thrillingly possible for the state and the art to acquire spiritual tradition and depth together."[15] It was true, he allows, that with filmmaking now relocated to the west the "panoramic tendency" of motion pictures "runs wild." But "in the hands of masters" a proclivity for the "sweeping gesture" and a "passion for the coast-line" could become sources of strength, given the intense sensory qualities of California as a *visual* environment.[16] "It is possible for Los Angeles to lay hold of the motion picture as our national text-book in Art," Lindsay concludes, "as Boston appropriated to herself the guardianship of the national text-books of Literature.... Edison is the new Gutenberg. He has invented the new printing. The state that realizes this may lead the soul of America, day after to-morrow."[17]

Florid descriptions of this kind may seem wholly incompatible with the characteristics that Leyda imputes to California slapstick – violence, acrobatics, embarrassment, irrationality – but such an incongruity could also serve the ironic attitude the films often adopt.[18] Much as Sennett's comedies can productively be thought of as subversive responses to the propriety of contemporaneous moral melodramas, California slapstick can be seen to have taken as a target the kind of romantic sentiments that Lindsay fulsomely espoused, while at the same time exploiting the liberating energy of moving pictures that Lindsay also embraced.[19] Flowery sentiments, after all, were embedded in the popular rhetoric of California boosterism, from the railroad era of the late nineteenth century through the 1920s, with its recurring theme, "The Land of Sunshine," promoted through magazines, tourist guides, and packing crate labels depicting fruit orchards, palm trees, beaches, and snow-capped mountains backed by clear skies. These sentiments are explicitly undercut at the very outset of Keaton's 1927 feature, *College*, which opens with the mock poetic titles, "On the sunkist slopes of the Pacific, where land and water meet–/California," followed by a shot of classmates scurrying for shelter on commencement day at Union High School, amid gale-force winds and rain, while an oblivious Buster escorts his mother to the ceremony. Or consider how booster imagery of fruit picking and packing in California is undermined in the Hal Roach–Stan Laurel comedy short, *Oranges and Lemons* (1923). In an opening title, Stan is introduced as an "Orange packer – sunkist sap with a sunny smile – and a foggy mind." A tiny sombrero emphasizes the lack of brain power and alludes to an otherwise elided Mexican workforce. An orange grove and distant mountain range signal the California setting. Featuring no plot development of significance, the premise provides an opportunity for 12 minutes of escalating violence among the employees, constructed around the standard slapstick principle of tit-for-tat, and integrating various devices that mechanize agricultural work at the small packing plant, where nature's orchard has been turned into an automated workplace. Utopian visions of industrial manufacture in a California landscape are challenged by the comic breakdown of social manners as expressed through retaliatory slapstick violence and repetitive motions put to non-utilitarian ends.

Still, critiques of this kind came from within the new "American" cultural formation that Lindsay attributed to filmmaking in California, not from without. For Gilbert Seldes, for example, the comedies of émigrés Sennett and Chaplin were part and parcel of an exuberant national sensibility to which movie slapstick made in California gave full expression. The fact that many slapstick comedies *shot* in California were not explicitly *set* in California may account for the kind of geographic slippage that occurs when Lindsay speaks of the region as "California-as-America" in the process of "re-becoming," a broader national project not bound by the kind of topographical and environmental specificity that made the "golden state" an attractive site for romantic projections in the first place. In comedy shorts of the 1910s and 1920s, locations often represent a variety of generic settings, rural to urban, even while incidental elements of the *mise-en-scène* – a recognizable mountain range, a palm tree, a California bungalow, an identifying store front sign – give greater geographic specificity to the image. The point I wish to stress here is not the common one: that the ease with which regional locations were re-imagined as *other* places left Los Angeles as a city without a coherent identity of its own. This line of reasoning can lead to the dematerializing of Los Angeles, rendering it as a postmodern simulacrum, or an enigma, an unknowable place.[20] Rather, this geographic slippage should encourage us to consider how the imagery of a more general "American" modernity was envisioned not as an international commercial center, such as New York City, or heavily industrialized city, such as Pittsburgh or Detroit, but was drawn from the variegated land, town, and cityscapes of Los Angeles and Orange Counties, and how patterns of movement in chase comedies may have provided a comic template for imagining transport between rural and urban settings in other regions of the United States as well.

## urban planning: the los angeles model

Urban historians have long stressed the unique aspects of the growth of Los Angeles as a metropolitan center in the late nineteenth and early twentieth centuries.[21] At the time of the US conquest of Mexican California in 1848, administrative boundaries largely followed the property lines of large, self-sufficient *ranchos* deeded to *Californios* by Spanish and Mexican authorities after the collapse of the mission system. Over the next three decades, the *ranchos* were slowly sold off, and Spanish and Mexican cultural spaces were gradually resettled by Anglo ranchers, farmers, merchants, and manufacturers migrating from the east. As late as the 1870s, the terrain remained predominantly rural, with citrus groves, vineyards, and wheat farms dotting the semi-arid flatlands and valleys. Between 1880 and 1930, however, the population of Los Angeles mushroomed from 11,000 to 1.2 million in the city; in the metropolitan area, from 33,000 to 2.3 million.[22] This growth was fueled by several factors: the decision of the Southern Pacific and Santa Fe railroad lines to make Los Angeles – rather than San Diego – its central hub; the infamous Mulholland Owens River Water project, approved in 1907 and completed in 1913, which secured the water necessary for these metropolitan ambitions to be realized; the annexation and development of the harbor districts of San Pedro and Wilmington in 1909, giving the city of Los Angeles its first natural harbor; and the concurrent growth of the motion picture and oil industries in the 1910s and 1920s.[23] Downtown expanded in a southwesterly direction. Heavy industry emerged in the south and southeast and along the waterfront, at a distance from the downtown area. Residential properties were carved out of agricultural land in all directions. With this growth, vast tracts of land became privately subdivided, transforming rural areas into blocks of suburban real estate, with little centralized regulation or review.

By 1930 the structure of Los Angeles differed from other US cities because of its decentralized industrial and commercial districts, and the array of residential, low-density subdivisions dominated by single-family homes. This dispersion was favored by topography, particularly the immense Los Angeles basin, which extended from the foothills to the ocean, and the wide valleys to the northwest and east. Growth proceeded not concentrically from downtown to outlying areas, the common course in other cities, but in a patchwork fashion, at various points along the branches of a developing transportation infrastructure. Horse-drawn street cars yielded to the inter-urban Pacific Electric Railway, which connected isolated communities in a network of rails, and in turn competed with paved and graded roads for automobiles, the registration of which grew from 20,000 in 1910 to 800,000 in 1930, higher per capita than any other city in the United States.[24] The aesthetics of suburban and urban real estate, and of traffic to, through, and around these interconnected subdivisions, was shaped by the recurring application of a traditional urban "grid" pattern, with perpendicular, intersecting streets and rectangular lots. Local zoning laws and restricted covenants secured a sense of privilege for white homeowners, many transplanted from the rural Midwest. This suburbanization, in turn, has been cited by urban historians as a model for future, mid-twentieth-century urban development in other regions, despite differences in climate, topography, and natural resources.[25] If New York City was the American commercial metropolis par excellence, Los Angeles was in the process of becoming another kind of urban center: non-hierarchical and dispersed; its grid of streets broken up by foothills with snaking switchbacks and canyon passes; its once agricultural basin increasingly claimed by housing developments and light industry, and crossed by rail lines and boulevards that ran to the coast, with links to Pacific trade.

This topographically variegated, expansive, and decentralized urban space, I am proposing, readily accommodated location slapstick comedy, with its extended trajectories across diverse and distant settings compressed, extended, and reordered through editing in highly variable ways. By focusing on the local, specific, and largely vanished sites where Keaton's silent comedies were produced, Bengtson has made a vital contribution to our understanding of how such trajectories were invented in Keaton's films. At the same time, we should seek to understand the relation of these filmmaking activities to wider patterns of demographic and environmental transformation, involving migration, transportation, land management, and industrial development. By studying the locations that figured in the production of Keaton's comedies in relation to the fictions of comic placement and displacement that the films compose, a new understanding of California slapstick comes into view.

## keaton and *the scarecrow*

Keaton's first contact with California came as a vaudeville performer, touring west coast theaters with his family in the mid-1910s. Los Angeles, in fact, would be the final stop of the long-running family vaudeville act. After a brief tour of second-tier vaudeville houses from Vancouver to San Francisco in the fall of 1916, the act broke up the following January in Los Angeles, prompting Keaton's return to New York City to look for work as a solo stage performer. By the end of the year he was back in Los Angeles as a member of Roscoe Arbuckle's Comique film company, which he had joined in March, and which moved to Southern California in the fall of 1917. During Keaton's partnership with Arbuckle, Comique rented production facilities in three west coast locations, forming the corners of a broad triangle across the Los Angeles metropolitan area. The first was the Horkheimer Brothers' Balboa Amusement Producing Company, established in 1912 in Long Beach, southeast of Los Angeles proper, which served as the base of operations for the making *A Country Hero*, *The Bellboy*, and *The Cook* (all 1918), and from which Arbuckle and Keaton traveled to the nearby San Gabriel Canyon for the filming of *Out West* and *Moonshine* (both 1918), and to the Hot Springs Health Resort in Arrowhead for *Good Night, Nurse* (1918). In the fall of 1918 Arbuckle moved the company briefly to the short-lived Diando (formerly Kalem) studio in Glendale, then to his old neighborhood in Edendale, near the old Selig and Keystone lots on Allesandro Street, two miles north of downtown Los Angeles. *Back Stage* was filmed at 1723 Allesandro, principally indoors, marking Keaton's return to Comique in 1919 after a ten-month stretch in the military. Keaton's final two shorts with Arbuckle – *The Hayseed* (1919) and *The Garage* (1920) – were made at the Henry Lehrman Studio in Culver City, and in surrounding neighborhoods, including the town of Palms, which served as the setting for many comedies produced by another Culver City resident, Hal Roach.[26]

After inheriting the Comique company from Arbuckle in 1920, Keaton filmed short comedies in locations ranging in the south to Newport Beach and Balboa Island on the Orange County coast, and in the north to San Francisco, the principal location for a climactic chase sequence in *Daydreams* (1922), and Truckee, in the Sierra Nevadas, where exteriors for *The Frozen North* (1922) and *The Balloonatic* (1923) were filmed. Closer to home, the rock-laden hillsides of the Iverson Movie Ranch, in the northwest corner of the San Fernando Valley, provided key settings for *The Paleface* (1921) and *Balloonatic*, and for the prehistoric story of *Three Ages* (1923). The principal zone for shooting, however, was Los Angeles' extended basin, with the epicenter of production at the Keaton studio in central Hollywood, located one block south of Santa Monica Boulevard at 1025 Lillian Way. The studio had been previously occupied by the Climax film company, by Chaplin during his brief period at Mutual, and then by Metro, whose large stages, administration building, and two backlots were built in 1918 and lay directly to the south of Keaton's much smaller facility.[27] Downtown Los Angeles was approximately 6 miles to the east. Here the city's grid of streets, nestled between Bunker Hill and Boyle Heights, was squeezed into various triangular and trapezoidal patterns, attractive features for the geometric, urban choreography Keaton composed in short films such as *The Goat* (1921) and *Cops* (1922), with diagonal movements cutting across the matrix of traffic pathways. Parcels of land immediately surrounding the Keaton studio were more uniformly rectilinear, but also less uniformly built up than downtown. Lining the streets were small bungalows, storefronts, a school house, a firehouse/police station, a lemon distribution plant one block north, wooded areas and shrubbery, and, especially early in Keaton's tenure, many vacant, undeveloped lots. One can imagine that, for Keaton, the seacoast communities of Newport (the principal location for *The Boat* (1921) and briefly seen at the end of *The Scarecrow*) and Venice (featured in the openings to *The High Sign* (1921) and *The Balloonatic*) brought to mind his family's retreat in Muskegon, Michigan, near Lake Michigan Park, where he spent his teenage summers and developed a passion for amusing vehicles and gadgets of a kind featured in these films. Geographic expanse is most evident in those shorts premised on Buster's nomadic wandering, as in *The Paleface*, or nomadic dreaming, as in *The Frozen North*. But even in Keaton's more site-specific comedies, chase trajectories typically unfold across new and sometimes startling environments, and romance plots, when favorably settled, often contrive to get the couple off and away to another place by the end.

This is the case in *The Scarecrow*, Keaton's fourth two-reel comedy, released in November 1920. The plot is a California slapstick staple: rivals flirt with a farmer's daughter, leading to physical combat and an elopement and vehicular chase. Like many of these films, the "rural" dimension to the farm is quickly, and in this instance immediately, qualified. The rustic simplicity evoked by a poetic opening title, "Slowly and majestically the sun steals gradually over the hilltops," is undercut when a special effect sun pops up over a generic barn and silo, with a sky matted in above, and nary a hillside in sight. And the residence the rivals share is, in the tradition of Keaton's trick houses, an elaborately mechanized cottage furnished with contemporary, convertible appliances and gadgets. The neighboring farmhouse where the daughter lives is cordoned off by a sculpted, arched hedge, behind which is planted a lushly bearded palm tree. The farmer (Joe Keaton) sports a straw boater and a wide-striped shirt; his daughter (Sybil Seeley), inspired by a magazine photo of Mlle. Danceabitski, fashions herself a haystack ballerina. From the outset, in short, cultural valences in *The Scarecrow* are complicated.

But what centrally concern me here are the two long chases that comprise most of the action of the film, both of a kind that Keaton favored. The first we might describe as *permutational*, with the chase occasioning a systematic exploration of the physical parameters of a single structure.[28] The second is *longitudinal*, linking dispersed and topographically varied settings through continuous action. The earliest example of Keaton's many permutational chases occurs at the end of *The High Sign* — the first short Keaton directed, although seventh in order of release — when a seaside Victorian home in which Buster has gained employment as a security guard is turned into a cutaway set with four quadrants, two rooms upstairs, two rooms down, through which he is pursued by his employer's assassins. Perhaps the most famous is the wake-up scene aboard the ocean liner in *The Navigator*, with Buster and Katherine McGuire in pursuit of one another through the ship's tiered deck, a lattice-work of walkways and ladders. Keaton's permutational chase in *The Scarecrow* commences with a flat, frontal shot of a decayed, brick building (Figure 10.1a). Buster and the "mad dog" (Roscoe Arbuckle's bull terrier, Luke) twice circle in and out of the windows, which are framed in rough symmetry to the right and left of the front door. We also get a view of the back of the building, on a diagonal, as Buster, then Luke, exits the rear door, and race in opposite directions around the perimeter of the house to meet again in the front. There are then two interior views, as Buster and Luke exchange looks before Buster's variant exit through a small hole low in the left-side wall, followed by an exterior view on the other side as the cycling of their movements is tightened: out the hole, pause, then a reversal back in. Meanwhile, the formal threshold of the house, the front door, is never crossed; it remains a permutation conspicuously avoided. With three of

(a)　　　　　　　　　　　　　(b)

(c)　　　　　　　　　　　　　(d)

Figure 10.1

The permutational chase in *The Scarecrow* (1920)

the walls and their apertures surveyed, the chase then moves vertically up to the next level with several bi-directional and variant cycles around the building's top rim (Figure 10.1b).

Much of the pleasure of a permutational chase resides in its quality of abstraction. The movement of the actors and shifting placement of the camera serve to foreground geometric patterns that are implicit in the structure and rendered explicit through movement measured on a human scale. There are social and material implications as well. However crude, the damaged, abandoned structure, aided by camera framing and choreography, retains an element of architectural design, a design we may find all the more compelling or poignant for the effects of time on structural materials and their function, which is to say, on the environmental, economic, or social histories of which it is a trace. What are we to make of this architectural oddity, an unlikely, untimely ruin? Where exactly do we *place* it? Observed from above in an aerial view during the second stage of the chase, the rectangular structure appears surrounded by vast countryside, but when Buster sits down and takes a breather (and a smoke), perspective shifts. The house, we discover, is fronted by a street, down which automobiles pass, and is lined with a windbreak of tall trees and telephone poles. In the distance the street intersects a perpendicular

181

road, with commercial billboards on display.[29] Then, again, at the close of the sequence, a bucolic tone is temporarily restored when the rear door frames a wholly rustic landscape, affording us a homeowner's picture window view, before the chase is resumed.

To a certain extent, diegetic coordinates for the location of the structure are established during the chase by a series of cutaways to Buster's suddenly skittish rival (Joe Roberts) as he purchases medical paraphernalia in anticipation of injury by the dog. No doubt inserted in part to cover discontinuities in a complicated chase involving an animal, the cutaways also have the effect of expanding our sense of fictive space and keeping the rivalry plot in play. Through continuity editing, the spatial adjacency of the abandoned one-room building and the mechanized one-room cottage is then confirmed when Buster races to the latter for cover (Figure 10.1c). Building on comedy action set up earlier in the gadget-rigged house, Buster employs a convertible bathtub/divan and garbage disposal/trapdoor to elude capture by the dog (Figure 10.1d). At the cottage the "in-and-out-the-windows" choreography of the chase is also briefly reprised. Viewed in succession, the first and second sections of the chase thus explore distinctly different shelters in a common way, with the second bringing to the first a more explicit treatment of the clever, mechanistic thinking that underpins permutational chases of this kind. At the same time, highlighted through juxtaposition are the differences between the abandoned shelter, roofless ruins exposed to the elements, and the highly engineered, modern-day cottage, whose breakfast tabletop converts into a placard posing a pointed question to its bachelor occupants: "What is Home Without a Mother?"

This stitching of the permutational chase across two diegetically proximate, and semantically comparable, locations anticipates the form and effect of the longitudinal chase that follows. Chases that move beyond a given structure to construct an imaginary geography also have an abstract dimension. Longitudinal chase trajectories can be linear and expansive (as is the case here), or looping (as in *The Paleface*), or variously lateral, perpendicular, and diagonal, constructing a kind of urban chessboard free of clearly defined borders (as in *Cops*). But the escape of the eloping couple in *The Scarecrow*, with both father and rival in pursuit, follows a trajectory that also juxtaposes different options for human commerce and habitation. Settings shift from cornfields to a harness shop, from the harness shop to a railroad yard. The couple escape on horseback, the pursuers by car; but when the father cranks the auto it rears up like a horse (Figures 10.2a–10.2b). Trading the horse for a motorcycle, the elopers embark on a still more elaborate route. Class contrasts are highlighted as Buster, sporting a floppy scarecrow hat, with his bride-to-be nestled in his sidecar, steers the motorbike under a train trestle and into a posh residential neighborhood where gently curving boulevards converge. Coinciden-

(a)　　　　　　　　　　　　　(b)

(c)　　　　　　　　　　　　　(d)

Figure 10.2

The longitudinal chase in *The Scarecrow* (1920)

tally, yet perhaps not surprisingly given the expectations cued by the cross-cut and the logic of genre convention, they collide with a minister, who has been conversing with well-dressed male companions at the edge of carefully manicured lawns. A mobile wedding ritual unfolds against a changing panorama of ceremonial palm trees, beyond which are well-appointed houses, then less fancy residences, then mainly open fields (Figure 10.2c). The trio next abruptly arrives at a less hospitable, sandy landscape, and the ending comes, as it often does in California slapstick, with all three figures in the water, a place where social divisions by convention are dissolved (Figure 10.2d).

Bengtson's research provides us with a guide to some of the locations where *The Scarecrow* was filmed.[30] A vacant lot adjacent to the Keaton studio provided space for the exterior of the jerry-rigged house. Side streets served as the location for early segments of the elopement chase, and for the cutaways to the fearful rival watching the first chase by the dog. When the rival hobbles down on a roadway, and is struck by a truck, the pan of the camera reveals a distant field of oil derricks, jutting out of the flat, rural landscape. The derricks mark the La Brea oil fields, between the Keaton studio and Culver City, a dense industrial complex that would two decades later give way to the mixed residential–commercial corridor of the Park La Brea district, north of Wilshire Boulevard, the pre-industrial history of which would be memorialized by the La Brea Tar Pits. The new, upscale development of Beverly Hills, west of Hollywood, was the location for the convergence of the motorbike and the minister, at the intersection of Beverly Drive, Canon Drive, and Lomitas Avenue, followed by a ride down the elegantly curved Beverly, part of a system of symmetrically interlaced roads through this newly planned community, not yet fully built out. As the motorcycle speeds down the long length of Beverly, agricultural lands, backed by the Hollywood hills, become visible behind an already planted row of stately palms. The chase then cuts to Balboa Island, roughly 50 miles to the southeast, the location selected for the story's baptismal-matrimonial finish. Out of these diverse and dispersed locations Keaton thus stitches together a comic chase that highlights topographical variety and the diversity of social spheres through which the eloping couple are propelled.

## rethinking california slapstick

The distinctiveness of any particular California slapstick chase resides in part in the way elements of the built and natural environment serve as the ground for comic action, and in part in the way discontinuous or fragmented elements are recombined. To specify the terms of a film's use of the formal conventions of chase comedy, we need to be attentive to this constructive − not just destructive − energy. Drawing on themes common to California slapstick, *The Scarecrow* scrambles distinctions between rural and urban settings for comic effect, but also explores settings systematically and draws comparisons among different culturally resonant sites. Both within and across the film's carefully choreographed chase sequences, the staging of comic action is informed by abstract and associative thinking, emphasizing patterns of spatial and social orientation and habitation. Starting with similar materials, other comic performers charted different but interconnected paths. Charlie Chaplin erected a three-story, working-class "T-street" set for his Lone Star−Mutual short, *Easy Street* (1917), based on his memories of a London slum, but evidenced less interest in the kind of architectonic permutations that Keaton would exploit in a comparable two-reeler, *Neighbors* (1920), which features a three-story tenement set that Keaton built at Chaplin's former studio site. But Chaplin clearly appreciated the merits of longitudinal comic trajectories, and incorporated into the central chase of *Easy Street* a brief, lateral side-trip through a ramshackle downtown area of old Chinatown, a location he favored in his early comedies, on through his first feature, *The Kid*, in 1921. In fact, *Easy Street* may have inspired Keaton's similar, if more elaborate, longitudinal chase in *Neighbors*, which at one point traverses nearby streets in the same déclassé downtown neighborhood, a setting more expansive than, but bearing social affinities with, Chaplin's "T-street" and Keaton's tenement studio set.[31] In his comedies of white-collar aspiration, Harold Lloyd frequently turned to the city's modern business district, and famously used camera angles and framing to enhance the sense of giddy disorientation and danger afforded by modern skyscrapers. But he also pushed to the extreme chase patterns of the kind that I have identified in *The Scarecrow*, demonstrating in *Safety Last* (1923) how a vertical, permutational chase could provide the scaffolding for a feature-length slapstick plot. At the close of *Girl Shy* (1924), he also orchestrated one of the most wildly variegated and extended longitudinal chases, or deadline races, to be found in California slapstick: a 20-minute race-to-the-altar sequence in which "Harold Meadows" commandeers a series of horses, wagons, and motor-driven vehicles to travel from the sleepy, country town of "Little Bend" to Los Angeles, by way of various rustic, residential, and commercial sectors, to arrive by horse at an exotically landscaped urban estate, from whence the closing elopement proceeds. The basic vocabulary of California slapstick over time thus proved highly supple and elastic, and was woven into stories of varying length and social implication.

Here, perhaps, we confront one of the limitations of Leyda's brief account of the formal and social history of California slapstick. By collapsing West Coast slapstick filmmaking into a single period, starting with Keystone in 1912 and continuing on through the late silent era, Leyda effaces key changes in slapstick forms and themes during these years, as chase comedy was folded into other genres, both comic and dramatic, and the violent and irrational strains of early slapstick yielded in some instances to more orderly forms, some conventional, others more intricate.[32] Comic actors, writers, and directors who migrated to Southern California in the 1910s and 1920s came with templates for staging motion picture action, including the basic principles of continuity, variety, disruption, and delay central to the comic chase. Our task as historians, in part, is to specify how slapstick forms evolved in different locales.[33] Toward that end, a history of California slapstick would gain greatly from a comparative study of geographic patterns in earlier comedies filmed in, say, New York City, Fort Lee, Philadelphia, Chicago, Sheffield, Paris, and Nice. It would gain much, as well, from tracking the social geography of slapstick in other regions *after* the broad impact of Keystone had been felt, and concurrent developments during the early 1910s in Jacksonville, Florida, which briefly staked a rival claim to that of Los Angeles as the ideal center for year-round filmmaking.

If Southern California in the 1910s and 1920s was a terrain upon which the effects of modernization were displayed in broad daylight, California slapstick heightened and brought into relief the incongruities and new continuities engendered by these social processes. The slender plots of many of these films replay one of the central tropes of modernity, the travel between country and city, finding comedy in the adjustments required of movement in either direction, and of instantaneous decision-making informed by recollections of past encounters and charged with new possibilities. With this in mind, we might say that California slapstick imagines for physical comedy the processes of becoming modern over and over again. To the extent that silent comedy is perceived as an altogether quaint form of cinema, contemporary viewers may miss both the potent currents of social antagonism that Leyda treats as a defining element of California slapstick and the capacity of film comedy to channel this kinetic energy into patterns of movement with a form and social logic of another order, proposing through the action of an agile and resilient comic figure alternative ways of responding to changes that were unfolding underfoot. The broad appeal of slapstick comedies made in Southern California, from this perspective, may have followed from the palpable form they gave to ways of thinking about the ability to move and act intentionally and find a fit in the modern world. Playing with and against narratives of technological progress and class mobility, the films made possible imaginative participation in the articulation and disarticulation of different social landscapes, a likely factor of their appeal in regions where modernization competed with deeply rooted provincialisms, in the United States and elsewhere. Affixing a made-in-California label to this comedy invites closer scrutiny of both the settings in which these slapstick chases flourished, and the ways in which, through various chase trajectories, the social geography of Southern California was comically re-mapped.

## notes

\* I wish to thank Edward Branigan, Rob King, and Tom Paulus for their comments on an earlier version of this chapter, and to all of the participants in "(Another) Slapstick Symposium" at the Cinémathèque Royale, Brussels, May 14–15, 2006.

1. Jay Leyda, "California Slapstick: A Definition," in Eileen Bowser, ed., *The Slapstick Symposium* (Brussels and New York: Fédération Internationale des Archives du Film, Museum of Modern Art, 1987), 2.

2. John Bengtson, *Silent Echoes: Discovering Early Hollywood through the Films of Buster Keaton* (Santa Monica: Santa Monica Press, 2000); *Silent Traces: Discovering Early Hollywood through the Films of Charlie Chaplin* (Santa Monica: Santa Monica Press, 2006). Some of Bengtson's discoveries initially appeared, and updates continue to appear, in *The Keaton Chronicle*, the newsletter of the Damfinos, the International Buster Keaton Society, www.busterkeaton.com.

3. Ron Magliozzi, "Report from the Slapstick Symposium Seminar," in Bowser, ed., *The Slapstick Symposium*, 95.

4. Reyner Banham, *Los Angeles: The Architecture of Four Ecologies* (Berkeley: University of California, 2001 [1971]), 232.

5. Bengtson, *Silent Traces*, 298.

6. This approach dates back at least as far as Gilbert Seldes' commentary on Keystone in *The Seven Lively Arts* (New York: A. S. Barnes, 1962, first published in 1924), 24–25, and perhaps receives its fullest elaboration by Walter Kerr in the preliminary chapters to *The Silent Clowns* (New York: Alfred A. Knopf, 1975), 2–48, although in neither case does the historical specificity of Southern California – as either a physical or an imagined place – play a part.

7. William Alexander McClung explores the interplay between these arcadian and utopian themes in twentieth-century California literature, architecture, photography, and painting in *Landscapes of Desire: Anglo Mythologies of Los Angeles* (Berkeley: University of California, 2000).

8. Before Essanay's western unit settled in Niles in 1912, locations for the company's rural slapstick comedies ranged widely over the state. Touring California in the winter of 1910–1911, G. M. Anderson filmed the last two entries in Essanay's nine-film "Hank and Lank" series, which similarly featured Carney and Postel, in Los Gatos, at the base of the Santa Cruz Mountains, south of San Francisco. The following spring Anderson directed the first "Alkali Ike" comedy, *"Alkali" Ike's Auto*, in Redlands, near the San Bernardino Mountains, at the easternmost extension of the Southern California's Pacific Electric Railway. He followed this up one month later with *The Infant of Snakeville* in the Santa Monica Canyon, along the coast. In the spring of 1912, Anderson directed four other comedies in the by then popular "Alkali Ike" series in Lakeside, east of San Diego. See David Kiehn, *Bronco Bill and the Essanay Film Company* (Berkeley: Farwell Books, 2003), 311–327.

9. Filmographies for the Louise Lester "Calamity Ann" and George Field "Heine" shorts and the Kolb and Dill features at the American Film Company are available at www.filmandmedia.ucsb.edu/flyinga/people/index.html, an excellent website developed by Dana Driskel, who kindly alerted me to the documentation concerning these films.

10. "Lillian Hamilton," *Moving Picture* World, June 12 (1915): 1764; Kalton C. Lahue, *World of Laughter: The Motion Picture Comedy Short, 1910–1930* (Norman: University of Oklahoma, 1966), 65–66; Anthony Slide, *The New Historical Dictionary of the American Film Industry* (Lanham: Scarecrow, 2001), 177.

11. Leyda, "California Slapstick: A Definition," 1.

12. Note, for example, the recent releases of multiple-disc video collections of silent comedy shorts under the title "American Slapstick" by David Kalat for All Day Entertainment in 2006 and 2008.

13. Vachel Lindsay, *The Art of the Moving Picture* (New York: Liveright, 1970 [1915]), 245–252.

14. Ibid., 246.

15. Ibid., 248.

16. Ibid., 249.

17. Ibid., 251–252.

18. Early accounts of filmmaking in California frequently employed extravagant analogies of this kind. Picturing California as an Elysium for moviemakers, for example, Terry Ramsaye recalled in 1926 that sessions conducted by D. W. Griffith "with his company about him on the grass under the pepper trees of California are reminiscent of the garden schools of the old Greeks." *A Million and One Nights: A History of the Motion Picture through 1925* (New York: Simon and Schuster, 1926), 644.

19. Eileen Bowser emphasized the relationship between Sennett and Griffith in her contribution to the first Slapstick Symposium program; see "Subverting the Conventions: Slapstick as Genre," in Bowser, ed., *The Slapstick Symposium*, 13–17. In his contribution in the same volume, Tom Gunning refers similarly to a symbiotic relation between silent comedy and melodrama, as evidenced in Sennett's reworking of Griffith, but he frames this within the wider context of the visual conventions of stage melodrama, with particular focus on Vitagraph's 1914 production, *Goodness Gracious*. See Gunning's "Take This Book and Eat It: Burlesque and the Comedy of Signs in Vitagraph's 'Goodness Gracious,'" in Bowser, ed., *The Slapstick Symposium*, 5–11.

20. This seems to me the central drawback of an otherwise suggestive and perceptive thematic reading of the tropes of anarchy, lawlessness, cardependency, and Hollywood glamour in silent comedies filmed in Southern California by Kristen Anderson, in which the author treats all Los Angeles-based silent comedy under the umbrella term of "Hollywood," with its attendant mythology, and concludes that "the history of Los Angeles development can be seen as a metaphorical byproduct of its cinematic fragmentation" (89), roughly the reverse of my argument here. See Kristen Anderson, "'Go West!': The Representation of Los Angeles in Silent Film Comedy," *Spectator* 21.1 (2001): 82–90.

21. See Carey McWilliams, *Southern California Country: An Island on the Land* (New York: Duell, Sloan & Pearce, 1946); Robert Fogelson, *The Fragmented Metropolis: Los Angeles, 1850–1930* (Berkeley: University of California Press, 1967); Banham, *Los Angeles: The Architecture of Four Ecologies*; Allen J. Scott and Edward W. Soja, eds., *The City: Los Angeles and Urban Theory at the End of the Twentieth Century* (Berkeley: University of California Press, 1996); Greg Hise, *Magnetic Los Angeles: Planning the Twentieth-Century Metropolis* (Baltimore: Johns Hopkins University Press, 1997); William Deverell, *Whitewashed Adobe: The Rise of Los Angeles and the Remaking of the Mexican Past* (Berkeley: University of California, 2004).

22. Fogelson, *The Fragmented Metropolis*, 1.

23. Ibid., 85–134.

24. Ibid., 92.

25. See, for example, Richard S. Weinstein, "The First American City," in Scott and Soja, *The City*, 22–46.

26. While Keaton was serving in the US Army in 1918–1919, Arbuckle's company also filmed *The Sheriff* (1918) at the Diando studio in Glendale and *Camping Out* (1919) on Catalina Island, off the shore of Long Beach. Comique's locations in and around Los Angeles are reported by Sam Gill in his Arbuckle filmography in Andy Edmonds, *Frame-Up: The Untold Story of Roscoe "Fatty" Arbuckle* (New York: William Morrow, 1991), 294–299. Also see Robert Young, Jr., *Roscoe "Fatty" Arbuckle: A Bio-Bibliography* (Westport: Greenwood Press, 1994), 176–186; and James L. Neibaur, *Arbuckle and Keaton: Their 14 Film Collaborations* (Jefferson: McFarland, 2007). Comique's period at Balboa in Long Beach is discussed in Jean-Jacques Jura and Rodney Norman Bardin II, *Balboa Films: A History and Filmography of the Silent Film Studio* (Jefferson: McFarland, 1999), 56–59, 75–76, 132–135.

27. The facility was known as the Lone Star studio during Chaplin's residency, a label that likely originated not with Chaplin's star status, as has sometimes been reported, but with the title of a major Climax production from 1915, *The Lone Star Rush*.

28. Jon Gartenberg employs a similar notion of permutational form in his analysis of vertical patterns of movement in Larry Semon's shorts for Vitagraph, in "Vitagraph Comedy Production," in Bowser, ed., *The Slapstick Symposium*, 45–47. For more on the use of tall buildings by Keaton, Harold Lloyd, and others, see Steven Jacobs' contribution to this volume.

29. Gabriella Oldham writes of the abandoned building: "This startling structure figuratively hangs, like in limbo, between the well-controlled house and the liberating elysian farmland." See Oldham's *Keaton's Silent Shorts: Beyond the Laughter* (Carbondale: Southern Illinois University, 1996), 49.

30. Bengtson, *Silent Echoes*, 30–35.

31. In *Easy Street*, when Chaplin is chased by Eric Campbell from Los Angeles Street onto Alameda Street, the performers are watched by a group of local residents from the porch of the old Olvera Adobe, located on the corner. The Adobe was razed one year later. Detailing the history of this intersection, John Bengtson also identifies its use in chase scenes in three other comedies: Keaton's *The Goat*, Lloyd's *From Hand to Mouth* (1920), and the Larry Semon–Stan Laurel short, *Frauds and Frenzies* (1918), from Hal Roach. See Bengtson, *Silent Traces*, 131–138. On the locations for the chase sequences in *Neighbors*, see Bengtson, *Silent Echoes*, 36–39.

32. A point of entry into this more historically sensitive understanding of California slapstick, for example, might start with the relationship between the changing urban spaces of Los Angeles and the key shifts that Rob King has identified in Keystone comedies during the years 1912–1917, as well as variations in the work of the many minor companies that emerged following Keystone's success. See King's chapter in this volume, as well as his incisive, deeply researched study, *The Fun Factory: The Keystone Film Company and the Emergence of Mass Culture* (Berkeley: University of California Press, 2009). Also see Doug Riblet, "Keystone Comedy and the Historiography of Early Slapstick," in Kristine Brunovska Karnick and Henry Jenkins, *Classical Hollywood Comedy* (New York: Routledge, 1995), 168–189.

33. Such an inquiry might test, for example, David Levy's argument in the first Slapstick Symposium that the comic chase after 1908 underwent a discernible change across three registers – the scale of the chase based on the number of settings and characters, the structure of the chase through the development of chain reaction gags, and the transformation of the victim of the chase from a pariah to a hero – and that these changes are attributable in part to the transformation of the motion picture industry in California. See "The Streetmob as Rube Goldberg Machine: A Note on the 'Chase' Film in the Slapstick Era," in Bowser, ed., *The Slapstick Symposium*, 81–87.

# bodies and performance

part three

# dancing on fire and

# water

## charlot and *l'esprit nouveau*

e l e v e n

a m y   s a r g e a n t

Élie Faure (doctor, essayist, art critic, collector, and historian) is probably now best known to film students for the inclusion in anthologies of his 1920 article, "Cinéplastique."[1] Chaplin, said Faure, was the first man to realize a purely cineplastic drama, where the action does not merely illustrate a sentimental fiction or a moral purpose. "Charlot," concluded Faure, "thinks cinematographically" – subsuming the separate subsidiary categories of poet, painter, architect, mime, and actor.[2] But in all Faure's activities, Chaplin was a touchstone and a guide: "After Montaigne, Cervantes and Dostoevsky, I have learnt most from Charlot," he claimed in 1920.[3] Academically, Faure approached Chaplin with the same seriousness accorded to Titian, Shakespeare (with whom he found much in common), and his friend, Picasso, while confessing that Velasquez, Goya, Assyrian rÉliefs, and Japanese prints had as often provoked laughter: "If one doesn't laugh at the Louvre, it's out of respect for things which are established."[4] Faure persistently renounced a hierarchy between fine and popular art and happily discussed the archaic alongside the modern; he credited Chaplin with equivalent or even supreme poetic dignity:

Charlot is the only modern poet who infallibly and conscientiously contemplates life from an heroic point of view. There is more style in the most apparently insignificant gesture of Charlot than in all the combined works of all the French Academies.[5]

During his service in the medical corps in World War I, Faure noted the healing properties of Chaplin's humor.[6] A true fan, Faure enthusiastically welcomed the release of each new movie (he had seen *The Gold Rush* (1925) five times by January 1926) and his daughter, Zizou, collected Chaplin souvenir figurines.[7] Faure encountered the man himself, at a distance, during Chaplin's 1921 visit to Paris, but confessed that he was unable to approach him.[8] He contributed to the intellectual and cultural program of the League of Nations and, in the 1930s, optimistically suggested that Chaplin alone had contributed more toward international peace and understanding than the League's 50 conferences.[9] In 1931 Chaplin was rewarded by being made a member of the Légion d'honneur. Chaplin returned the compliment: in his preface to a 1953 collection of essays, he acknowledged Faure's prescient recognition not just of his own artistry but of cinema as art, of which, Faure maintained, Chaplin served as exemplar and endorsement. In a typical piece of late Chaplin pomposity, the comedian said that he judged people by whether they had read Robert Burton's 1621 *Anatomy of Melancholy* and Faure.[10]

In this chapter I shall attempt to restore Faure's essays of the 1920s to their original context, in terms of their publication and of Faure's broader interests. The chapter is especially concerned with two publications. First, Faure's 1920 *Danse sur le feu et l'eau* – described by Faure as the exposition of a concept of history both moral and aesthetic, and covering such various topics as civilization, tragedy as mother of the arts, morality in art, and the immorality of justice. Second, his article "Charlot," which appeared in the March 1921 issue of *L'Esprit nouveau*, a journal founded by the painter Amedée Ozenfant and the architect/painter best known as Le Corbusier, for whom Faure's younger son worked on the Algerian Garden City project. The journal's declared agenda (an international illustrated review covering contemporary activity in arts, letters, science, and sociology) corresponded with the range of Faure's own preoccupations. Modern artists, musicians and poets, circus and cinema, are discussed alongside Aristophanes, Boileau, El Greco, Poussin, and Ingres. Provocatively, the journal launched a questionnaire: "Should the Louvre be burnt down?"[11] But in both instances, the past and the present, there is an urge toward the discovery of functional and aesthetic principles – and Faure defined art as a biological necessity – underlying the various themes under discussion, rather than a cumulative eclecticism for its own sake. The journal sought to establish connections

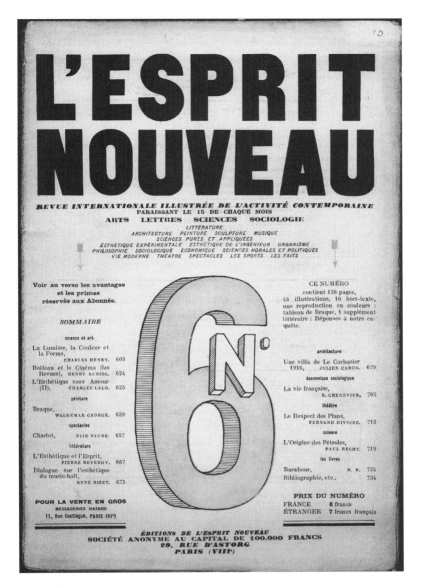

Figure 11.1

The March 1921 issue of *L'Esprit nouveau*, including Élie Faure's essay "Charlot"

195

between different disciplines and to stimulate a discussion between elites in their respective fields. Proclaiming progress in all realms of activity in modern art and ideas (and that art could not be separated from the realm of ideas), *L'Esprit nouveau* dedicated itself to a rigorous purge of elements from the past, which no longer had reason to survive in the present. It was important to discriminate, said the editors, between what was alive and valuable and what was moribund and redundant. Chaplin, while lauded for his originality, was appropriated to this pretext. Furthermore, for both Faure and *L'Esprit nouveau*, dance was regarded as something of a progenitor of the other arts — and I am primarily interested here in Chaplin as a dancer.

## rhythm

"Since the end of the nineteenth century, above all since the beginning of this century", declared Jean d'Udine in 1921 in *Qu'est-ce que la danse?*, "there has been much and constant talk of rhythm, in relation to all matters and often to matters to which it is irrelevant":

> One knows vaguely what it may be, one feels it yet more vaguely and more still the idea which remains for us nebulous, the more so because it seems to be sustained by a respect combined with fetishism. *Rhythm, Eurhythmy* are certainly fine-sounding words.... We have seen every critic, in any field whatsoever, increasingly invoking "rhythm" in the verse or prose, in the painting or sculpture, in the music or the architecture of our own times and of other times; sometimes it is identified in precisely the least rhythmic works of all.[12]

*L'Esprit nouveau* advertised courses in eurhythmics based on the method of the Swiss educationalist Emile Jaques-Dalcroze, a system of rhythmic gymnastics vaunted for its ability to develop natural powers of expression. The journal also reviewed performances of Sergei Diaghilev's Russian Ballet (with costumes and decors supplied by Picasso) and of the Swedish Ballet's production of *The Skating Rink*, where Fernand Léger integrated the dancers into his design — a single, plastic entity, he said.[13] Le Corbusier's brother, Albert Jeanneret, in a number of articles in *L'Esprit nouveau* devoted to dance, advised that "the study of rhythm underlies all modern education; rhythm being the root of all arts as it is of life."[14] D'Udine, meanwhile, held little truck with modern dance (to which he generally ascribed a "frightful aridity"), and excepted gymnastics and sport from qualification as dance while accepting that these activities could prove useful to a dancer.[15] Similarly, dance, for D'Udine, was more than pantomime, because it represented "the exaltation of man's spontaneous movements, the exaltation in duration, exaltation in amplitude, exaltation in intensity of his natural gestures."[16] D'Udine (like *L'Esprit nouveau*'s René Bizet) was impressed by the elegance and suppleness of music hall performers, applied to a particular purpose to affect an audience. Like dancers, they employed artificial and purely decorative elements, methodically and emphatically repeated:

Whether our movements have a purely dynamic origin
and seek to please in themselves or whether they trans-
late more or less faithfully our sentiments and our
thoughts with an intensity more or less affecting, they
needs must be subject to certain requirements and reg-
ulated in order that they attain that certain degree of
style required to aspire to the dignity of art.[17]

"Rhythm" may well have been a catchphrase, a common currency of
artistic discourse in the 1920s, but its exact meaning was nonetheless contested – in dance as elsewhere. Nor was it sufficient to appeal to its ability
to capture "rhythm" to secure for cinema any aspiration to artistic status.
Cinema was simultaneously theorized as an autonomous art while also
being appreciated as the synthesis of plastic arts (architecture, painting,
and sculpture) and rhythmic arts (music, poetry, and dance). As Faure
remarked, while dance was a neglected art, cinema was an embryonic art;
as Laurent Guido has subsequently observed, dance had previously
undergone a similar process of comparison, distinction, definition, and
stylistic evaluation.[18]

## routine

In his 1927 edition of tributes to Chaplin, Robert Florey noted the comedian's apprenticeship on stage with the dancing troupe, The Lancashire
Lads. It was also known that Chaplin's mother, in her better days, had
been a dancer and had taught her sons to dance. Florey praised especially
"The Dance of the Bread Rolls" in *The Gold Rush*.[19] Louis Delluc, filmmaker, critic, and sometime contributor to *L'Esprit nouveau*, identified the
balletic qualities in Chaplin, aligning him with Isadora Duncan, Anna
Pavlova, Loie Fuller, and, above all, Vaslav Nijinsky.[20] Chaplin was flat-
tered by the comparison and was pleased to receive Nijinsky as his guest
in Los Angeles, while the "Greek" dancing in *Sunnyside* in 1919 (a dreamlike
flight of fantasy from which, as in the later *The Kid* in 1921, Chaplin is
rudely awakened) seems to owe as much to Dalcrozian "plastic expression" as to Duncan and her many less gifted but well-meaning imitators
and disciples.[21] Duncan and Nijinsky were also drawn by Marc Chagall for
his mural at the Paris Opéra, the fluidity and force of their movements
here translated to another medium.

The connection between Faure and Chaplin was thus more than personal. Amidst a general renewal of interest in the 1920s, Faure noted that
dance (an art which, he suggested, preceded that of music and architecture) and cinema (a new art) were both little known. "However," he
enthused, "it seems to me that cinema and dance may teach us the
hidden relationship of all the plastic arts with space, of which geometric

figures serve as both measure and symbol": "Dance, of any epoch, like the cinema of tomorrow, is charged to combine plasticity with music, vividly conjuring a rhythm which is both visible and audible, enabling entry into the dimension of space through time."[22] But Chaplin's technique, while capable of expressing a grace comparable to that of Duncan, could also extend to its antithesis. "All humanity," suggested Faure, "shudders at the sharp, angular contortions of this strangely mechanized, puppet silhouette."[23] The British painter, poet, and critic Percy Wyndham Lewis endorsed the assessment, if only to use it as ammunition in his tirade against the public's star worship of Chaplin (as pathetic and sentimental as its object, he determined) and as an example of a depraved infant cult. He despised Chaplin's "irresponsible epileptic shuffle" and his "puny" tininess.[24] The sense of Charlot as puppet was enhanced by his diminutive, narrow-shouldered physique, further defined by his typical tight waistcoat and tailcoat worn over baggy trousers – the vestiges of a disintegrating gentility.[25] Everything about Charlot, observed Florey, was miniature.[26] Chaplin's stature was exaggerated by the casting of Marie Dressler, "built like a battleship," as his foil in *Tillie's Punctured Romance* (1914), by the "David and Goliath" pairing of hedgehog assistant and propmaster in *Behind the Screen* (1916), and by the bulk and weight of his cabin-mate "Big Jim" in *The Gold Rush.* Faure's Chaplin is an artist even at his most ungainly; for Faure, what kills art is "the cult of beauty."[27]

Often humor derives from a contradictory juxtaposition of gawky, abrupt angularity or small, awkward, fussy movements with fluidity of expression in Chaplin's own body; nervous agitation is set against expansive self-assurance. A Chaplin gag is generally, noted Eisenstein, individually alogical.[28] Delivery is one aspect of this alogicality. Chaplin's "mechanism" in performance was celebrated in Purist Paris as much as his manufacture of a commercial type and trademark, alongside Marinetti's "La Danse Futuriste" (Danse de l'Aviateur; Danse du Shrapnel; Danse du Mitrailleuse) as detailed in *L'Esprit nouveau.*[29] In *Dough and Dynamite* (1914), Charlot is pitted against bread dough (the most plastic of materials), failing to extricate himself from its sticky surface and succeeding only in tying himself in knots; he becomes the subject, rather than the master, of his adversary. In *Modern Times* (1936), Chaplin unsuccessfully competes with – then mockingly produces fluid dance gestures in response to – the relentless, steady pace of a factory conveyor belt. He rebels, it may be said, against the mechanization of modern life. "Science may be progress," said Faure, "but it is only one sort of progress"; the programme of *L'Esprit nouveau* resolved to determine what products of mechanization were useful and what not.[30]

Léger, frequent apologist for the machine aesthetic, produced numerous starkly monochromatic, graphic, and angular images of Charlot:

static or animated, the individual fragments present Charlot as an infinitely re-constitutable assembly of individually identifiable parts.

> I can take a subject from anywhere. I like the forms necessitated by modern industry and I use them: a smelting furnace will have thousands of colored reflections both more subtle and more solid than a supposedly classical subject. I consider that a machine gun or the breach of a 75 is more worth painting than four apples on a table or a Saint Cloud landscape.
>
> My objective is to try and establish the following: no more cataloguing of beauty into hierarchies — that is the most clumsy mistake possible. Beauty is everywhere, in the arrangement of saucepans on the white wall of your kitchen, perhaps more than in your eighteenth-century salon or in official museums.[31]

Illustrations to Ivan Goll's 1920 *Chapliniade*, similarly depicting Chaplin as an assemblage of geometrically stylized and solid components, were reproduced in another international journal — the Berlin-based *Veshch' Gegenstand Objet*.[32] However, in "Le ballet-spectacle, l'objet-spectacle," Léger observed that the strength of Chaplin lay in his "unmistakable instinct," an organic, pre-logical capacity.[33] For the Purists in general (repeatedly citing *Matter and Memory* and *Creative Evolution*) and for Faure in particular, who had studied with Henri Bergson in Paris, this mechanism of the body — or its converse in response to mechanization — was an essential constituent of Chaplin's humor and humanity. In his 1899 essay, *Laughter*, Bergson commented:

> What society now has to dread is that each one of us, content with paying attention to what affects the essentials of life, will, so far as the rest is concerned, give way to the easy automatism of acquired habits.[34]

Echoing Bergson, Faure concluded: "Mechanism serves to expose the universe of mechanical objects to man's gaze, and to restore it to a space where, having re-ordered it in accord with his own heart and spirit, duration forcefully encroaches."[35]

## repetition

The British critic, Caroline Lejeune, paired Chaplin with the dancer Alla Nazimova (possibly best remembered for her dancing in the 1923 film *Salome*) for their graphic qualities and the "restless rhythm in her bones." "These two," commented Lejeune, "shared in a kinship of quality. Both pantomimists, both masks, they developed, each round a single pre-determined figure, a saga of film fortune and adventure."[36] Lejeune later aligned Chaplin, as a dancer, with Fred Astaire:

> Watching him, you are suddenly aware that the lower half of the cinema screen has been wasted all these years.... I know of no screen stars except Chaplin and Fred Astaire, who have really learnt to act volubly from the knees down.[37]

Indeed, in Walter Ruttmann's *Berlin: Die Sinfonie der Grosstadt* (1927) a cropped frame of dilapidated boots shuffling through snow and the bottom of a cane is sufficient to identify a sequence from *The Gold Rush*. "Un chapeau melon et une badine et voilà – Charlie," observed Henry Michaux in 1924.[38]

Lejeune, amongst many other critics, drew an analogy between Chaplin and the masked tradition of *commedia dell'arte*, while Edouard Ramond compared him to the Pierrot figure in English pantomime.[39] Marc Chagall's frontispiece to René Schwob's *Une Mélodie silencieuse* (1929) showed the Charlot "mask" and idiosyncratic boot displaced from Chaplin's face and body – in the manner of a cut-out souvenir "Movy Doll." Roland Barthes was later to comment on "the flour-white complexion of Charlie Chaplin, the dark vegetation of his eyes, his totem-like countenance," thinking especially, perhaps, of Chaplin's mug shot wearing convict's stripes in *The Pilgrim* (1922), while André Bazin commented on the moustache as the defining, metonymic Chaplin symbol.[40] "Chaplin is more popular than all the other 'greats' of today," said Tokine in "The Aesthetics of Cinema" in the first issue of *L'Esprit nouveau*. "Why? Because he expresses ideas with the type which he has created."[41] This "type" is characterized as much by his idiosyncratic gait – the birdlike waddle intimated by Chagall – as it is by physiognomy.

In France, Chaplin's early comedies were pre-determined as standardized products in their very titles. Jean Epstein's 1921 *Bonjour Cinéma* reproduces a poster for Chaplin alongside one for Nazimova. Charlot is headlined as main attraction with his roles as vagabond, fireman, soldier, and violinist subtitled.[42] *The Rink* (1916) became *Charlot patine*, *The Champion* (1915) became *Charlot boxeur*, and *Dough and Dynamite*, *Charlot mitron*. *Tillie's Punctured Romance* was re-titled *Le Roman comique de Charlot et Lolotte*, and *A Woman* (1915) became *Mamzelle Chaplin* (in which Chaplin appeared clean-shaven). In homage, Epstein (who also contributed to *L'Esprit nouveau*) titled a chapter in *Esprit de cinéma* (1955) "Charlot débiteur," while admitting that the legacy of stardom inaugurated by the confused coupling of Charlot–Chaplin had subsequently constituted a form of tyranny.[43] However, in the 1920s, the figure of Charlot and his recurrent gestures and sequences (*City Lights*, for instance, repeats wholesale from *The Champion*) were celebrated as a serially produced commodity. In this they were akin to the industrially manufactured goods – especially the products of

American industrialization (grain silos, pre-fabricated building parts, Ford cars, as advertised in *L'Esprit nouveau*), British sanitary ware, Omega watches, Hermès luggage, Ripolin paint, etc. – celebrated by Le Corbusier in *L'Esprit nouveau*, *L'Art decoratif d'aujourd'hui* (1925), and *Vers une architecture* (1923). Faure was similarly generous in his selection of examples demonstrating the quality he intended by "cinéplastique" (functional and aesthetic stylization). Such celebration was perhaps paradoxical, as Chaplin was simultaneously upheld as an artist or "auteur" in the romantic sense, with his increasing command of the work in which he appeared, produced, and directed: he was more than just an adept "cinémime," as Epstein observed, "from gesture to gesture/precise and sure."[44] Henri Poulaille commented: "An admirable mime, Chaplin knows the value of the smallest gesture. It is not repetition which counts, it is a matter of knowing what gesture is useful where."[45] Chaplin thus answered *L'Esprit nouveau*'s first law of economy, which it defined as the perfect adaptation of means to ends.[46]

For some of us, Chaplin's dance turns provide, to adopt Roger Manvell's phrase, some of the most "delicious fragments" of the films.[47] Sometimes they offset the slapstick while also retaining an element of humor in themselves, because they come as such an incongruous surprise. The skating scenes in *The Rink* and *Modern Times* are breathtaking for their virtuosic balletic grace, even assuming recognizable motifs and poses – an easy pirouette here, a controlled arabesque there – but this impression is enhanced by an anticipation of imminent catastrophe, which is, however, withheld. In a deserted department store in *Modern Times*, Chaplin, on roller skates, boasts that he "can do it blindfolded": blithely, obliviously, he glides backwards, using his outstretched arms and his cane to balance himself while teetering perilously close to the edge of a mezzanine; when his alarmed gamine partner interrupts his reverie he nervously scampers backwards on his skates. *The Gold Rush* finds him unevenly, lumpen-footedly, executing a waltz with his own golden girl, Georgia. Meanwhile, he hitches up his trousers – fortuitously he finds a piece of string, only for this to be shown to be tied to a dog, which then chases a cat. In Chaplin's 1915 version of *Carmen* (a response to DeMille's very respectful adaptation), dance contributes to the burlesque, with Chaplin crazily kicking and bottom-bumping on the tavern's table tops. In *The Great Dictator* (1940), Chaplin's nimble but self-indulgent dance with a vast inflated globe proves prophetic – the balloon bursts.

Elsewhere, in *Carmen*, *The Rink*, and *The Champion*, potential violence is diffused by action so astutely choreographed that it approaches dance[48] – and much was made, by contemporary industry commentators, of the pains taken by Chaplin in the rehearsal and execution of these "set pieces," or "delicious fragments." Charlot, again a little the worse for drink, suspends disbÉlief and elegantly retains his balance when a tipsy stumble beckons; "he boxes," noted Faure, "but when a policeman unexpectedly makes an appearance, he dances."[49] Fisticuffs with a toreador degenerate into a game of patacake; Charlot shadow fences (with a bent or broken blade) or shadow boxes; he twirls under his unwitting opponent's sword as if partnering him in a staged routine. Sometimes dances are performed with less likely objects (indeed, any everyday object that comes to hand can generate a dance, a gag, or both). In *The Champion* he coquettishly bobs and weaves, "floats like a butterfly," to evade his adversaries' punches, then "stings like a bee" – by fair means or foul (secreting a horseshoe into his glove). Chaplin's dance with bread rolls in *The Gold Rush* (pathetically substituting for a partner who has connivingly failed to appear) matches the surrealism of a famous 1952 Robert Doisneau photo-portrait of Picasso, with bread rolls wittily substituting for the artist's fingers, splayed on the table at which he sits. Indeed, in an earlier essay devoted to Picasso's drawings, Faure explicitly stated that it is Charlot – and Goya – of whom he was most reminded.[50] Chaplin, Faure reported to his American translator in 1920, apropos of *Danse sur le feu et l'eau*, "was creating a furore in Paris, especially amongst the painters."[51] In *The Gold Rush*, in the absence of Georgia, Chaplin delicately executes a tour de force solo performance, assiduously and coquettishly directing his eyes and eyebrows to observe his "pointes" and po-facing forwards for a plié and the splits. For once, as Bazin observed, "inanimate objects," with which Chaplin is so often at odds – and one might think, here, of his Tati-esque altercation with swing doors in *The Rink* – readily become accomplices in the action.[52] Pierre Leprohon, writing in 1935, dated the confrontational significance of objects in Chaplin's performances back to his first Essanay film, *His New Job* (1915), sometimes according them a "striking magic" in opposition to which people are reduced to mere puppets. *His New Job*, argued Leprohon, already marked a typically stylized, purely plastic delivery, culminating in a carefully choreographed, dramatized, and orchestrated crescendo: "An exposition, several routines knowingly combined, then a musical composition with an accelerating rhythm, rising to a ballet finale score accompanying the end of battle."[53] Chaplin's happier appropriation and partnering of objects in routines such as "The Dance of the Bread Rolls" again seems to direct our attention forwards to Fred Astaire and Gene Kelly.[54]

202

## reverie and rapture

Dance was, claimed d'Udine, the most universal of arts and the least understood by aestheticians. Faure noted that even the youngest children dance. Dance, I suggest, marks Chaplin's "infantilism" as much as his naïve visual gags, his personae, and his asociality. For Faure, universal, primordial "infantilism" is a positive quality, distinct from the puerile "infantilism" and primitivism of which Chaplin's films were accused elsewhere. "If dance is close to God," concluded Faure exultantly,

> I imagine that, by way of the most immediate gesture and insuppressible instinct, it symbolizes for us the giddy heights of thoughts which cannot find rest other than in the dangerous state of perpetual motion; beyond the unstable state which these thoughts occupy, it urges us to seek rest in the drama of movement.[55]

Chaplin's religious significance for Faure was rooted in more than his sublime prowess in dance. Writing as a Jew, in a series of articles distinguishing different styles of comedy, Faure found Chaplin's tragi-comic fatalism exemplarily Jewish – as did the critic René Schwob, even before hearing that Chaplin claimed Jewish ancestry and long before Chaplin cast himself as "a Jewish barber" in *The Great Dictator*.[56] The Jewish émigré, Chagall, in his drawing for Schwob's *Une Mélodie Silencieuse* (dedicated to Daniel Halévy), depicts Chaplin as an angelic, grotesque variant of a familiar Chagall figure, the Wandering Jew, with which Chagall himself identified.[57] The boot and the cane are recurrent motifs. Interviewed by Jacques Guenne for *L'Art vivant* in December 1927, Chagall affirmed that: "Chaplin seeks to do in film what I am trying to do in my painting. He is perhaps the only artist today I could get along with without having to say a single word."[58] The image is doubly, and familiarly in Chagall's work, an anthropomorphized animal and a zoomorphized human. Chaplin appears as a chicken in Big Jim's hunger-fueled hallucination in *The Gold Rush* and as an angel in *The Kid*. But this figure also responds directly to Schwob's text: "Charlot is two-sided. Animal and angel. He makes us laugh at our automatism but at the same moment draws our attention to our decay."[59] Chaplin's international appeal was asserted in the range of contributors included in Michaux's 1924 anthology, *Charlot*: the British art historian, John Middleton Murray, of the *Adelphi* magazine no less, sits alongside the Spanish critic, Ramon Gomez de la Sema writing on "Charlotisme," and Faure, whose *L'Esprit nouveau* article is here reproduced.

Many commentators in the 1920s presumed for Chaplin an international appeal and employed this as an expedient validation of cinema's newfound status. Faure's writing on Chaplin, it seems to me, fitted the agenda of the international journal *L'Esprit nouveau* where it spoke for a biologically determined universalism and a concomitant social optimism. Charlot as a commodity and type matched the journal's enthusiasm for serial production as an elevated form of selection and stylization. Faure evaluated the inheritance of the past using modern criteria, even when, as d'Udine dared to suggest, these were far from clearly formulated. Submitting to rhythm, paying rhythm its due obeisance, declared Faure, "inspires that lyrical exaltation which permits man to attain the most elevated morality, raising his spirits to the vertiginous heights at which enlightenment and the desire for liberty can be found."[60] While grounding the origins of dance in animal life and childhood, he reaches out towards infinity. Faure's aspirations for art, and especially for dance, verge on the metaphysical even while *L'Esprit nouveau*'s modernism declared war on the old metaphysics. Both the critic and the journal were engaged in an act of faith. Furthermore, if, for Faure, art is born of dance (spontaneity) and tragedy (an outcome governed by fate), then Chaplin embodies that spirit. As Faure advises in his epigraph to *Danse sur le feu et l'eau*, "treat everything as a tragedy – and take nothing seriously." As Charlot's posters promised, "Mourir de rire."

## notes

1. See, for instance, Daniel Talbot, ed., *Film: An Anthology* (New York: Simon and Schuster, 1959), 3–14.
2. Élie Faure, "Charlot," *L'Esprit nouveau* 6 (1921): 659, from Élie Faure, *Cinéplastique* (Paris: Nouvelles Éditions Séguier, 1995 [1920]), 19.
3. Élie Faure, *La Danse sur le feu et l'eau* (Paris: Éditions Georges Crès, 1920), 16; Henry Poulaille, *Charles Chaplin* (Paris: Grasset, 1927), 80. Faure's book had previously been serialized in the June–September issues of the journal *L'Europe nouvelle* in 1919.
4. Élie Faure, *Formes et forces* (Paris: H. Floury, 1907), 108–109.
5. Faure, *La Danse sur le feu et l'eau*, 16.
6. Ibid., 16–17. For details of Faure's war service and the trauma he suffered, see Martine Courtois and Jean Paul Morel, *Élie Faure: biographie* (Paris: Seguier, 1989).
7. Letters to Walter Pach, October 27, 1921 and January 19, 1926, from *Oeuvres complètes d'élie Faure*, vol. 3 (Paris: Jean-Jacques Pauvert, 1964), 1032, 1058.
8. Ibid., 1032.
9. Ibid., 420.
10. Chaplin's preface in Élie Faure, *Fonction du cinéma: de la cinéplastique a son destin social* (Paris: Librairie Plon, 1953), 67.
11. *L'Esprit nouveau* 2 (1920): 9; for the results of the questionnaire, see issue 6 (1921).
12. Jean d'Udine, *Qu'est-ce que la danse?* (Paris: Henri Laurens, 1921), 54–55.
13. *L'Esprit nouveau* 17 (1922); see also "Popular Dancing" from *Bulletin de l'Effort Moderne* (1925) in F. Léger, *Léger and Purist Paris* (London: Tate Gallery, 1970), 93–94; Tag Gronberg, *Designs on Modernity* (Manchester: Manchester University Press, 1998), 94.
14. Albert Jeanneret, "Le Rythmique," *L'Esprit nouveau* 2 (1920): 183–189; *L'Esprit nouveau* 3 (1920): 331–337; *L'Esprit nouveau* 4. Douglas Fairbanks was praised by *L'Esprit nouveau* critics as the supreme example of the benefits of sport and eurhythmics.
15. d'Udine, *Qu'est-ce que la danse?* 6, 14, and 27.
16. Ibid., 1 and 19.
17. Ibid., 38; see also A. Bizet, *L'Esprit nouveau* 3 (1920), 353–354; *L'Esprit nouveau* 6 (1921), 675–678.

18. Faure, "La Danse et le Cinéma" (1927), in *Fonction du cinéma*, 16; Laurent Guido, "Entre performance rythmée et modèle stylistique," in Enrico Biasin, Giulio Bursi, and Leonardo Quaresima, eds., *Film Style* (Udine: Forum, 2007), 500.

19. Robert Florey, *Charlie Chaplin* (Paris: Jean-Pascal, 1927), 39.

20. Louis Delluc, *Charlie Chaplin*, trans. Hamish Miles (London: The Bodley Head, 1922), 15.

21. John McCabe, *Charlie Chaplin* (London: Robson Books, 1978), 106; Charles Chaplin, *My Autobiography* (New York: Simon and Schuster, 1964), 190–193.

22. Faure, "La Danse et le Cinéma," 15.

23. Faure, "Charlot," 664.

24. Percy Wyndham Lewis, *Time and Western Man* (New York: Harcourt, Brace and Co., 1928), 62, 66–68. J. M. Barrie had hoped to persuade Chaplin to appear as Peter Pan.

25. See Bernard Rémy, "L'Invention du corps céleste," *Beaux Arts Magazine*, Chaplin issue (2005). 15; Chaplin secured rights to his outfit to deter imitators – see Sam Stourdzé, "Character," *Chaplin in Pictures* (Paris: NBC Editions, 2005); Charles J. Maland, *Chaplin and American Culture* (Princeton: Princeton University Press, 1989), 10.

26. Florey, *Charlie Chaplin*, 54.

27. Faure, "Danse sur le feu et l'eau," in *Oeuvres complètes*, vol. 3, 200.

28. S. M. Eisenstein, "Montazh kinoattraktsionov" (1924) in Richard Taylor, ed., *The Eisenstein Reader* (London: BFI, 1998), 37.

29. Marinetti, "La Danse Futuriste," *L'Esprit nouveau* 3 (1920): 303–307.

30. Faure, "Danse sur le feu et l'eau," *Oeuvres complètes*, vol. 3, 185; "Ce que nous avons fait: ce que nous ferons," *L'Esprit nouveau* 11/12 (1921): 1211–1214.

31. Léger, "Correspondance" (1922), *Bulletin de l'Esprit nouveau* 4 (1924); "The Machine Aesthetic/The Manufactured Object/The Artist and the Artisan," *Bulletin de l'Effort Moderne* (1924) in *Léger and Purist Paris*, 85, 87–88.

32. *Veshch' Gegenstand Objet*, facsimile edition (Berlin: Lars Müller, 1994).

33. Fernand Léger, "Le Ballet-spectacle, l'objet-spectacle" (1923), in Sylvie Forestier, ed., *Fonctions de la peinture* (Paris: Gallimard, 1997), 70–71. See also "À propos du cinéma" (1930–1931), ibid., 166.

34. Henri Bergson, *Laughter*, trans. Cloudesley Brereton and Fred Rothwell (London: Macmillan, 1911), 19.

35. Faure, "Esthétique du machinisme" (1921), in *Oeuvres complètes*, vol. 3, 302.

36. C. A. Lejeune, "Nazimova," in *Cinema* (London: Alexander Maclehose and Co., 1931), 82; see also Robert Florey, "Comment on a tourné *Salomé*," *Cinémagazine*, March 14 (1924): 441–442; "Nazimova – Salome," *Mon Ciné*, November 9 (1922): 12–13.

37. Review of *Top Hat*, in Anthony Lejeune, ed., *The C. A. Lejeune Film Reader* (Manchester: Carcanet, 1991).

38. Henry Michaux, "Notre frère Charlie," in Henry Michaux, ed., *Charlot* (Paris: Le Disque Vert, 1924), 18.

39. See Lejeune, *Cinema*, 28 and 191; Edouard Ramond, *La Passion de Charlie Chaplin* (Paris: Librairie Baudinière, 1927), 135; Delluc, *Charlie Chaplin*, 28–29.

40. Roland Barthes, "The Face of Garbo," *Mythologies* (London: Vintage, 1993), 56; André Bazin, "Introduction à une symbolique de Charlot," *Qu'est-ce que le Cinéma?* vol. 1 (Paris: Éditions du Cerf, 1958), 97.

41. Boris Tokine, "L'Esthétique du Cinéma," *L'Esprit nouveau* 1 (1920): 85.

42. Jean Epstein, *Bonjour cinéma* (Paris: Editions de la Sirenne, 1921), 61.

43. Jean Epstein, *Esprit de cinéma* (Paris: Editions Jeheber, 1955), 166.

44. Epstein, *Bonjour cinéma*, 83.

45. Poulaille, *Charles Chaplin*, 42.

46. Faure, "Ce que nous avons fait," 1212.

47. See Roger Manvell, *Chaplin* (London: Hutchinson, 1975), 90.

48. Delluc, *Charlie Chaplin*, 40 and Manvell, *Chaplin*, 81–82, 108 quote Max Linder to this effect. Linder admired Chaplin as much as Chaplin admired Linder.

49. Faure, "Charlot," 663.

50. Faure, "Dessins de Picasso," in *Oeuvres complètes*, vol. 3. For Picasso's 1922 portrait of Faure, see Courtois and Morel, *Élie Faure*, 168.

51. Faure to Pach, January 11, 1920, in *Oeuvres complètes*, vol. 3, 1025.

52. Bazin, "Introduction à une symbolique de Charlot," 98.

53. Pierre Leprohon, *Charlot ou la Naissance d'un Mythe* (Paris: Editions Corymbe, 1935), 50; see also the 1936 correspondence between Faure and Leprohon in *Oeuvres complètes*.

54. See Gilles Deleuze, *L'Image-temps* (Paris: Les Editions de Minuit, 1985), 83–85 on Astaire and Kelly.

55. Faure, "Charlot," 666. On "infantilism" as an aspect of Chaplin's humor; see also S. M. Eisenstein, "Charlie the Kid," in Jay Leyda, ed., *Film Essays* (London: Dennis Dobson, 1968), 110. From his student days, Faure was a self-conscious disciple of Lamarck.

56. René Schwob, *Une Mélodie silencieuse* (Paris: Bernard Grasset, 1929), 53.

57. Benjamin Harshav, ed., *Marc Chagall on Art and Culture* (Stanford: Stanford University Press, 2003), xi.

58. Benjamin Harshav, quoting Chagall, *Marc Chagall and His Times: A Documentary Narrative* (Stanford: Stanford University Press, 2004), 323–324. Sidney Alexander, *Marc Chagall: A Biography* (London: Cassell, 1979), 37, comments that Chagall's "clowning is like Chaplin's, tragicomic, compassionate and mocking at once." The first monograph devoted to Chagall, published in Russia in 1918, carried Chagall's *A Man with his Head Reversed* on its cover, a precedent for the frontispiece drawn for Schwob.

59. Schwob, *Une Mélodie silencieuse*, 46.

60. Faure, "Danse sur le feu et l'eau," in *Oeuvres complètes*, vol. 3, 200.

# splashes of fun and

# beauty*

mack sennett's bathing

beauties

t w e l v e

h i l d e  d ' h a e y e r e

*Shall I get wet, or shall I not?*

(*Mack Sennett Weekly* 1917[1])

This chapter deals with Mack Sennett's so-called "Bathing Beauties," a bevy of beautiful babes in bathing suits on a beach appearing in Sennett's slapstick comedy shorts between 1915 and 1929. By examining the depiction of the girls and their bathing attire, as well as by analyzing the timing and frequency of their appearances in movies and promotional materials, it links the shifting status of the Bathing Beauties to changing studio publicity policies and slapstick spectatorship.

Even before Mack Sennett and his brand-new Keystone Company arrived in Evendale, California, the attraction of beaches and piers on the waterfront was apparent in his movies. In the company's first split-reeler, *The Water Nymph*, directed by Mack Sennett and released in 1912, a girl in a bathing suit frolics on a beach in New Jersey and dives into the ocean. This girl is the former illustrator's and photographer's model Mabel Normand, who became the attractive and athletic mold for all future

Bathing Beauties. After that first iconic moment, countless girls in bathing suits trotted in and out of an undefined number of Keystone and Sennett movies set in the sunny outdoors. When they performed indoors, the girls sported dress variations such as pajamas, nightgowns, or harem attire. In *The Beach Club* (1928), however, they prefer bathing suits even when playing billiards in a hotel lobby.

The Sennett Bathing Girls began their cinematic career in the Triangle–Keystone comedies of 1915. They briefly disappeared from movie screens in 1922 before staging a remarkable comeback in the late 1920s.[2] Today a surprising number of publicity shots survive in film archives and on the internet, but assembling an actual list of films in which the girls appeared is quite hard. In some cases, the Bathing Girls were part of the publicity materials without featuring in the actual films. It appears that Mack Sennett's promotional strategies were not always so tightly linked to the slapstick movies they were supposed to illustrate.

## bbs and kks

Sennett's girls were alternately referred to as the *Bathing Beauties*, the *Sennett Bathing Girls*, the *Sennett Belles*, the *Bathing Cuties*, the *Rosebuds*, the *Splash Me Girls*, or the *Little Dippers*. The Beauties were selected to look like a multiplication of a single type of actress: a young, white, lively, and athletic girl, with a pleasant face, an attractive smile, and a beautifully curved, short body. Physically, the girls had to have the "necessary qualifications," which were specified in 1927 by Sennett's publicity department in answering a request by the organizers of a beauty contest in Phoenix, Arizona:

> For the judging and measurements of your perfect models: ... a girl 5ft tall, must weigh approximately 100 pounds, 5 pounds are added for each additional inch over 5 ft; features must be attractive, teeth regular, limbs shapely, skin clear; a good carriage and bearing are most requisite.[3]

In publicity shots, the girls appeared in large numbers. They were arranged in orderly line-ups and rows, like twin sisters in a family picture or dance hall girls in a chorus line. In the publicity pictures of 1916–1918, the Bathing Girls even wore very similar bathing suits to emphasize and exploit their identical morphology (Figures 12.1 and 12.3). It's interesting to compare the collective body of the Bathing Girls to that of the Keystone Kops, that other famous Sennett trademark that achieved stardom *en masse*. The Kops, of course, give a completely different spectacle since they were played by male actors of very different shapes and sizes. While nearly every Bathing Girl in the Keystone Company was extremely

Figure 12.1

Bathing Beauties and Keystone Kops, production stills, 1916. From Daniel Blum, ed., *A Pictorial History of the Silent Screen* (London: Hamlyn Publishing Group Ltd, 1962), 109

attractive, few of the men could be called handsome. Nicknames described their physical marks: "Fatty" Arbuckle, "Slim" Summerville, or "Shorty" Hamilton. Their faces were dressed up with mustaches, whiskers, funny hairdos, and heavy make-up. At rest they were easily recognizable characters with distinct screen personas. During their fast-paced, destructive chases, however, the Kops became interchangeable bodies littering the frame: their misfit police uniforms and hats blending their very different faces, bodies, and movements. Publicity shots tended to emphasize their disarray, spreading the bodies chaotically throughout the image and accentuating their explosive energy.

Both the collection of "one-mold girls" and the accumulation of different-shaped Kops wearing the same uniform facilitated the strategic interchangeability of the actors. True to the saying, "start with Sennett — get rich somewhere else," Sennett saw a huge turnover of actors over the

209

years, but this drop-out rate was never problematic since every newcomer on the Keystone lot could easily don a uniform to play a Keystone Kop. And even in the late 1920s, Andy Clyde (or Will Rogers of the Hal Roach studios) could still be made up to spoof Ford Sterling, the original chief of the Kops, by wearing the goatee hair piece essential to the latter's "Dutch" make-up. Similarly, no studio information was initially released to help audiences identify the anonymous and underpaid girls. A typical caption for a production still or publicity shot in 1915–1916 simply read "Bathing Beauties in a Keystone comedy." Hence the confusing credits for the Beauties in both movies and photographs, although some of the girls, such as Juanita Hansen or Phyllis Haver actually achieved stardom in the 1920s.

## a splash of fun and beauty

In the legendary 1928 interview with novelist Theodore Dreiser for *Photoplay* magazine, Mack Sennett stated: "Besides, in the kind of burlesque comedy I was doing, there had to be a relief in the form of beauty of some sort."[4] Convinced that pretty girls could not be laughed at, Sennett considered the Bathing Beauties primarily as a "beautiful break" and decided that their physical activities did not necessarily have to be fast and funny. Indeed, the girls were generally portrayed as beautiful, healthy, young bodies in motion, diving into the ocean or playing a ballgame at the beach. They were "splashes of fun and beauty," light-hearted playmates who countered the wildly aggressive comics with serene beauty.[5] The Beauties were presented as counterpoints to the violent slapstick, not as participants in it. "They were neither simpering, nor blatant in manner. They simply existed, delightful, not quite bright, ideal foils for the cavorting grotesques around them," as Richard Schickel puts it.[6] The slapstick part of the action was reserved for the Kops and the male and female comedians, who resorted to similar strategies for comic effect based on crazy body language and dressing down with funny hairdos and make-up.

The Bathing Girls usually appeared in the second part of the two-reel shorts. Maybe the main character wants to escape his nagging wife by inviting his sweetheart to the beach, or maybe the girl prefers a game of softball with her female friends to hanging out with her flirtatious fiancé. In all cases, the leading characters end up at a seashore, swimming pool, or beach resort, where a troupe of Bathing Beauties happens to hang out. Suddenly the frantic slapstick action comes to a stop. The pace slows down: the action is gentle, the setting peaceful, the frame stable, and the editing unobtrusive. The change of tempo is startling, like stepping into a different genre or taking a commercial break. Hal Roach pointed to this show-stopping quality of the Bathing Beauties, and felt it was a mistake:

"When you put the Bathing Beauties in a movie ... people stop laughing and you have to start your comedy all over again."[7] In so doing, however, the Bathing Beauties' sequences contributed to the stop–start rhythm that commentators such as Tom Gunning, Donald Crafton, and Henry Jenkins find characteristic of slapstick comedy.[8]

## beach culture

Inevitably, these depictions of beach life have a certain documentary quality. Cameraman Eddie Cline claimed that the whole idea for the Beauties started with some casual but eye-catching action of girls frolicking in the background of a beach shot taken in Santa Monica in 1915.[9] Films featuring the Bathing Beauties perfectly conveyed the new popularity of the beach as a top spot for tourism and leisure. The separate bathing areas for men and women of the previous decades were abandoned for mixed-sex beaches, providing a new stage for informal movement and the study of human anatomy. Summer entertainment on the beach allowed for an uncovering of the body, the semi-nudity motivated by the place, the activities, and the weather conditions. The seashore became the prime location for the family man as voyeur, who takes visual pleasure in this public display.[10] Remarkably, popular seaside resorts, such as Santa Monica beach in 1907, featured a "beach camera obscura," which offered voyeuristic views of what went on at the seashore by projecting

Figure 12.2
Frame enlargement from *Those Bitter Sweets* (1915)

images in the dark interior of a beach hut.[11] Around the turn of the century, beach life (i.e., human behavior on a beach) also became a recurrent motif in painting, photography, and the movies. As Nancy Mowll Mathews notes, "[p]hysical activity on the beach usually consisted of informal games or dances, but it was novel and endlessly fascinating to painters and filmmakers alike, as well as to their audiences."[12] A lot of these pictures show the loose physical behavior and the informal beach attire in stories about surprising (illicit) lovers in the act or females (un)dressing. Beautiful and famous examples are the series of snapshot photographs made with a candid box camera by Paul Martin in 1892 on the beach in Yarmouth (UK), the Edison comedy short *Getting Evidence* (1906), and the numerous Keystone productions following *The Water Nymph* (1912).

In the Keystone movies of 1915–1916, girls strutting around under the approving gaze of male bystanders are occasionally captured in an actual point-of-view shot. In the one-reeler *Those Bitter Sweets* (1915), three girls skillfully perform fancy dives, cheered on by their boyfriends. In a series of close shots, each girl is isolated in a circular mask, which contributes to the voyeuristic mood of the scene (Figure 12.2). The alternation between shots of the applauding spectators and shots of the performing girls confirms the subjective viewpoint of the latter. A recurrent shot with a similar tension is a peek at someone changing from street-wear to swimwear, framed in a mask as if seen through the keyhole of a changing cubicle (e.g., in *The Surf Girl*, 1916). Clearly, any anthropological interest in public behavior at the beach is superseded in these movies by the spectacle of the girls showing off their graceful bodies and demonstrating their athletic skills. Before long, they will also be modeling their bathing suits.

## (in)decent dresses

Before 1910 women didn't swim and beachwear was designed almost exclusively for strolling on the beach. The only permissible water activity for women involved jumping through the surf while holding on to a rope, an activity not made any easier or any more elegant by the uncomfortable Victorian-style bathing costumes. To protect the wearer against indecent exposure, weights were sewn into the hem of the black, knee-length, woolen dresses with a sailor collar for the nautical look. To support and mold the body underneath, a swimming corset was worn over combination underwear. The beach attire further consisted of bloomers trimmed with ribbons, long black wool stockings, lace-up bathing slippers, and a fancy cap or hat prescribed by the rule of etiquette that stated that at all times headwear should be worn when outside. All this added up to nine items of clothing, weighing up to 20 lb when wet. Needless to say, these bathing dresses impeded any kind of swimming.

The Australian swimming and diving champion Annette Kellerman decided to go against the current. Stating that she "could not swim in more clothes than you hang on a clothesline," she exposed herself in a self-made bathing suit much like a skintight body stocking, which left arms and sometimes the lower part of the legs uncovered. In the summer of 1907, she was arrested for public indecency at Revere Beach near Boston. However, in 1913, the Jantzen Knitting Mill of Portland, Oregon, started manufacturing these Kellerman suits and launched the publicity slogan, "the suit that changes bathing into swimming." During World War I the public attitude toward women doing physical activities gradually changed. Consequently, the overdressed affair of bathing turned into the physically conscious act of swimming.[13] Swimming became fashionable, not only as an athletic activity good for health and hygiene, but also as an opportunity for the display and judging of female pulchritude. When women's swimming became accepted as an Olympic sport in 1912, local beauty contests started to include a public parade in bathing suits. Beauty contests had been popular for decades, but were mainly concerned with facial beauty and based their judging on a submitted "photographic likeness" rather than an actual live performance, let alone one in bathing attire.[14] In 1921, however, 16-year-old Margaret Gorman of Washington, DC, bearing a striking resemblance to Mary Pickford, won the first official Miss America pageant in Atlantic City, dressed in a modest costume with dark stockings. Fittingly, during those days the Atlantic City police dressed like Keystone Kops, leading a critic of the event to complain that "[t]hey set up Mack Sennett as a standard of customs and manners."[15] Because of Mack Sennett's reputation as a beauty expert, he was frequently invited to be a judge at these beauty pageants. Sometimes he even recruited the winning girls for his bathing troupe.[16] Of course, the titillating novelty of a beauty contest in bathing costumes also became a motif in Sennett's movies – particularly in *Picking Peaches* (1924), Harry Langdon's first movie for Sennett Comedies. By that time, bathing suits were no longer meant only for swimming. The outfit, originally a cumbersome wrap allowing women to exercise their body without showing it and later a means to display female beauty, rapidly turned into an object of beauty itself.

## diving girls

The suits of the Bathing Beauties differed from contemporary bathing attire in several ways. For a 1916 publicity picture, the Bathing Girls wore variations on the Jantzen–Kellerman dark, skintight, one-piece bathing suit "for daring swimmers" (Figure 12.1). Just three out of the thirteen girls have suits cut above the knee; the others wear body stockings that cover the legs, feet included. One girl in a lighter-colored suit is hiding on the extreme left of the image, possibly because light-colored fabrics are more likely to be see-through when wet.

In another 1916 promotional picture with Chester Conklin (Figure 12.3), the girls wore suits that could never have been displayed on a public beach since they were designed to show the legs and came with a hoop skirt that drew attention to the underwear. Swimming attire of the first decades of the twentieth century was designed *not to show* certain parts of the body, to hide contours and naked flesh. These suits, of course, were not bathing attire but stage costumes, probably rented from one of the costume stores in Hollywood or on loan from a theatrical company. The costumes have an old-fashioned "French cancan" ring for comic effect. In addition, they show far more of the bare legs, arms, and chest than was customary on beaches in 1916. The burlesque, vaudeville, and Broadway costumes in the closed theaters of the first decades of the twentieth century were far more revealing in terms of nudity and transparency than swimsuits seen and allowed on the beach at that time.

A comparison of Figures 12.1, 12.2, and 12.3 with mail order catalogs and department store advertising of the same period is telling. The spring and summer collections of 1915 at B. Altman & Co. on Fifth Avenue in New York show bathing dresses rather than swimming suits. Under "Women's, Misses' and Children's Bathing Suits, Etc." on page 11, we find non-clinging, knee-length, dark dresses with contrasting collars and trimmings (Figure 12.4). Sleeves are shorter than in earlier versions,

Figure 12.3

Bathing Beauties with Chester Conklin (*c.*1916). Courtesy of the Ciné-mathèque Française

Figure 12.4

"Women's, Misses' and Children's Bathing Suits, Etc.," 1915 Spring and Summer Catalog, B. Altman & Co, New York

almost disappearing entirely. The waist is loosely marked by a sash. The dress is no longer worn over bloomers, but the legs are still covered by black stockings. The purchase of matching rubberized bathing slippers or high-cut boots and a satin or rubber bathing cap was recommended. Available colors were black, navy, or Yale blue for the suits, and red, green, or purple for a cap "finished with a bunch of berries of rubber."

Again, it's clear that the costumes of the Bathing Beauties were not primarily intended to reflect the fashion of the day. Rather, the girls' dark, skintight maillots were a cinematic means to provide contrast with the sandy or watery setting in which they appeared. In the black-and-white movies, the suits reduce the Bathing Girls to dark silhouettes. In *The Surf Girl*, their silhouetted outlines allow the viewer to admire the girls' skillful dives and athletic moves even when performed in the background of extreme long shots. Clearly, as Rob King notes, photographing profile views of these streamlined bodies also accentuates the curves of breasts and buttocks.[17] This outline makes for an easily recognizable logo, already used in the promotional campaign for *The Water Nymph*, for which Mabel Normand posed. Diving champion and actress Annette Kellerman used a similarly stylized representation of her shapely diving body when advertising *The Body Beautiful*, her book on the virtues of good health and a perfect figure in 1917. The outline is very similar also to the logo that Jantzen Knitting Mills started using in 1920 to promote their line of bathing products. The "Red Diving Girl" presented a side-view of a girl clad in a red bathing suit with beanie and socks, gracefully diving with outstretched arms. In an attempt to popularize swimming and bathing attire, Jantzen's "Red Diving Girl" was even made available as an enamel ornament to mount on the windshield and hood of a Model T Ford, the preferred vehicle of the Keystone Kops (and millions of American families). All these side-view diving cutouts hint at the ideal American qualities – youth, health, physical beauty, and athletic prowess – embodied by the Bathing Beauties.

## pin-ups

In 1917, as the United States joined the Allied Forces on the European front, the publicity department of the Mack Sennett Comedies (now released by Paramount and no longer part of the Triangle Film Corporation) started putting out pictures with a different scope. A new "cheesecake" quality is apparent in both the publicity stills and the movies of the period 1917–1921. The stills are framed a lot closer than the group shots earlier in the decade. Whereas earlier promotional photographs mainly depict larger groups of girls, publicity shots from the 1917 season onward show the Beauties either individually or paired up. The girls strike playful and teasing poses, uncovering their bare legs (Figure 12.5). In the Bathing Beauties sequence of *Hearts and Flowers* (1919), the pin-up approach shines through the *mise-en-scène*: the largely high-angled shots peep right into the cleavage of the smiling girls (Figure 12.6). In both the movies and the promotional pictures, the physical *nearness* is almost tangible. For the first time you can actually see just how beautiful these girls were. They face the camera with bright eyes and ravishing smiles. These are not the faces of the female slapstick comedians, heavily made up with greasepaint and dark lipstick, but real girls looking squarely in the eye of the male filmgoer or reader of sports magazines like the *Police Gazette* or *Red Head Weekly*.

Figure 12.5
Phyllis Haver on a French picture postcard

No wonder these pin-up shots circulated widely as picture postcards during the war years in Europe.

In the production stills some of the girls still wear versions of the skin-tight one-piece bathing suit, albeit with shrinking shoulder straps and cut higher on the thighs. The dark suits are brightened up with decorations and accessories: contrasting trimmings on the hem around the legs

Figure 12.6

Frame enlargement of Phyllis Haver in *Hearts and Flowers* (1919)

and/or the neckline, striped socks, lace-up shoes, and a patterned scarf around the head. Two-piece suits, with a top covering the hips, worn over shorts, now appear in lighter shades than the earlier available black, marine, or brown. Most of the Bathing Girls, however, wear very different cotton or silk dresses in elaborate designs and rich prints. Bows on shoulder-straps, collars in contrasting prints, floppy hats, ribbons and lace: the skintight diving suits have become parading dresses designed for the beach rather than the ocean. From now on, only rarely would the suits of these Beauties actually get wet.

In announcing the triumph of the Keystone Beauties in the Great Bathing Parade at Venice Beach, the *Mack Sennett Weekly* of June 25, 1917 stated: "Incidentally, it may interest some of the women readers to know what the girls wore."[18] The article describes the costume of second-prize winner Juanita Hansen:

> [she] graced a dazzling costume of gold cloth and gold lace, finished off with a green flop hat and shoes and hosiery to match. It was fashioned in the new Chemise style, narrow shoulder straps and hanging in loose folds not quite halfway to the knees.[19]

In conjuring up the dizzying supply of colors and forms, the article uses fashion jargon ("the new Chemise style") and denotes the attire as a combination, designed "to match." Although some of the girls, notably

Juanita Hansen, supposedly made their own bathing costumes, the article also mentions the assistance of designers at costume companies (like the Schlank Costume Company of Los Angeles) and suits furnished by bathing suit stores (like the Venice Bathing Suit Store or the Bernal Dyas Company of Los Angeles). Such publicized appeals to the professional aid of costume companies and clothes manufacturers perfectly tallies with the history of film costume design. In the early 1910s, the movie industry did not generally boast of having wardrobe departments or employing professional costume designers. It has become part of early Hollywood lore, for instance, that the costumes for *Birth of a Nation* (1915) were home-made by Lillian Gish's mother. Similarly, Norma Talmadge went on record to state that during her first years in motion pictures she designed and sewed a great number of her dresses herself. In a 1922 press release, however, the Mack Sennett Studio credited a Mrs. George Unholz, professionally known as Mme. Violet[20] with

> creating the styles disported by the Mack Sennett comediennes for the past six years. With a competent corps of assistants, Mme. Violet designed and personally supervised the making of the entire wardrobe for every Sennett short length picture and feature production.[21]

This announcement made, notably, in the year that the girls were withdrawn from movie screens, added a new dimension to the promotional potential of the Bathing Beauties. It also marked a shift of attention away from the Bathing Girls' bodies and athletic skills to their suits and their fashion-consciousness. A new world of potential commercial tie-ins by manufacturers of bathing suits and accessories, hats, hosiery, furs, and toilette preparations opened up. In other words, when the Bathing Girls ceased to appear in the slapstick movies, the range of their commercial advantages widened. From playful pin-ups on card games, candy boxes and tobacco cards, they were repositioned as professional advisors in the world of cosmetics and fashion. Meanwhile, Mack Sennett guaranteed continued attention for his ex-Bathing Girls by providing press agencies with nostalgic and amply illustrated stories, as in the article "When They were Bathing Girls," in the September issue of *Photoplay Magazine* in 1923. Furthermore, he also made sure merchandising dealers were supplied with stock pictures of Bathing Beauties to cement existing contracts.[22]

## a fashionable comeback

Less than two years after their disappearance from the screen, the return of a new collection of Bathing Girls became a tantalizing promise in Sennett's press releases from February 1924 onwards.[23] Once actually realized, however, Sennett only hesitantly developed a promotional strategy for them. Trying out a series of different approaches, he seems to have been unsure how to position his Beauties. In several shorts from 1924, Sennett first tried teaming up the girls with his latest discovery, the comedian Harry Langdon. For the "Beauty and Fashion Contest" in *Picking Peaches*, several Bathing Girls give solo performances in bathing suits and essay fancy dives. In *His New Mamma* (1924), they appear merely as a group of girls playing and dancing at the beach. In 1926 Sennett finally decided to fully revive his Beauties by putting a whole new series of shorts into production under the working titles "Sennett Bathing Girl Story Number xxx." These shorts were to foreground the Bathing Beauties as their main attraction and to exploit the girls in their promotion. Between 1927 and 1929 only seven shorts were released in this series. Meanwhile the Beauties kept turning up in other films, in the "Taxi Driver" series or the "Smith Family" series, appearing both in the films' narratives and in the promotional stills.[24]

At the same time Sennett was working on another strategy, as shown by the correspondence between the New York office and the Los Angeles-based publicity department from January to April 1927. Sennett's publicity department was put to work to *dispose* of the bathing pictures and ordered to look for photo syndicates interested in buying the exclusive distribution rights to Mack Sennett Bathing Girl photographs, "stills that usually publicize little nobodies whom we may not use once a month in our comedies."[25] The same letter also states quite bluntly that Sennett is "not very keen about bathing girl publicity any longer – says he is tired of being called a beauty expert – wants more dignified publicity."[26] In addition, Sennett was preparing to make a feature-length production on the rise to fame of a Bathing Beauty, "a human and real story," showing "the metamorphosis in slow motion, detail by detail."[27] The story line of this movie underwent considerable changes and was eventually released as *The Good-Bye Kiss* in 1928. In the *Mack Sennett Pathé Studio Review* issue of December 1927, *The Good-Bye Kiss* was announced as "a well balanced blend of comedy and romance," attractive to all movie fans because "it is human" and "it is clean!"[28] "Clean pictures" and "dignified publicity" clearly indicate the new direction Sennett was considering to revive declining interest in his movies. At one point it looked as if the Bathing Beauties were going to be retired for good, but eventually Sennett decided on a more pragmatic strategy.[29] In October 1927, the Sennett Studio launched its first *Mack Sennett Pathé Studio Review*. The cover page of the first edition of this lavishly illustrated publication promised to continue "as long as the supply of Mack Sennett bathing girls holds out."[30] The Bathing Beauties were the magazine's main (if not only) asset. The photography promised to be "a sample of what we can turn out in the way of art,"[31] and the still camera was handled by Edwin Bower Hesser – a pho-

Figure 12.7

"Mack Sennett Bathing Beauty chorus, in the latest in beach costumes for spring. Left to right: Della Peterson, Dolores Mendez, Julia Duncan, Betty Byrd, Carol Wines and Evelyn Francisco." This text is typed on a label on the reverse of this publicity still by George F. Cannons. Courtesy of the Academy of Motion Picture Arts and Sciences

tographer known both for his glamorous portraits of movie actresses and stage stars and for his magazine, *The Arts Monthly Pictorial*, filled with scantily clad, artistically backlit female bodies, sold "to an anonymous readership of 'art students.' "[32] Again it is clear that Sennett wanted it both ways, publicity both "clean" and "titillating." This he hoped to achieve by signing an exclusive long-term contract with Hesser as house photographer of the girls, a deal turned sour when the pictorialist was arrested in 1928 under suspicion of narcotics peddling and for impersonating a police officer in connection with the death of a starlet.[33] Most of the promotional stills of 1928 and 1929 were made by George F. Cannons.

The design of the suits worn by the girls in the 1927–1929 period inspired rather salacious commentary in the press, noting that these were "such abbreviated costumes that they had to be glued on to insure their staying in place."[34] Of course, Sennett's own publicity department was responsible for most of these notices and the information was lazily copied in contemporary newspapers. A closer look confirms that these accolades were indeed mere publicity talk; in the films the Bathing Beauties sport highly fashionable, tasteful, and elegant suits designed for perfect models rather than more scanty variations for added pep. We

221

should also note that the measurements of the girls had changed over the years: 1928 bathing girls like Carole Lombard and Sally Eilers were definitely taller and slimmer than their counterparts from 1915. Both publicity shots and movies from 1927 to 1929 show the girls in outfits with striking designs: contrasting zigzags, bold stripes, and checkered patterns (Figures 12.7 and 12.8). The beach is cluttered with items matching the blatant prints and tints of the bathing suits: the parasols, hats, bags, belts, socks, shoes, and cardigans of supporting actors feature graphic patterns similar to the Beauties' bathing suits and caps.

The year 1928 also saw the introduction of a technical novelty in the two-reel comedies. To keep up with the new swimwear now available in fabrics of brighter and more varied color (orange, red, turquoise, sapphire, jade, scarlet, or yellow), some of the Bathing Beauties sequences were filmed in two-color Technicolor. Color inserts promoting the latest developments in color film technology were not uncommon in feature films of the mid-1920s.[35] Typically these sequences were of beauty pageants and fashion shows. In *The American Venus* (1926), for instance, only the beauty pageant scenes are in color; they feature contestants of the Atlantic City Miss America Pageant, including Miss America of 1925, Fay Lanphier. Fashion parade sequences were filmed in two-color Technicolor for the feature film *Irene* (1926), with flapper Colleen Moore as a dressmaker's model, and for *Fig Leaves* (1926), directed by Howard Hawks

Figure 12.8

Frame enlargement from *The Campus Vamp* (1928), originally in two-color Technicolor and starring former Bathing Beauty Phyllis Haver. In 1928, Dr. Herbert Kalmus launched the two-color Technicolor process #3 (with a dye imbibition projection print replacing the double-cemented print of process #2). This improved color technique was tried out in the Bathing Beauties sequences of several "Sennett Bathing Girl Stories" of 1928. A press release of Sennett's publicity department claimed that "[t]he combination of Technicolor film and unique lighting effects will give the films an artistic touch never before known in two-reel comedies."[36] Nevertheless, as soon as these sequences end, the films abruptly switch back to black-and-white for a few concluding shots, as in *The Campus Vamp* (aka *Sennett Bathing Girl Story #304*) (1928).

Not just the new color process distinguishes the Bathing Beauties sequences from the rest of these movies, but also the use of slow motion effects realized through over-cranking the camera; prolonging the seaside cavorting of the Beauties gives them an unreal, dreamlike presence. The Keystone Kops films, by contrast, tended to be under-cranked to speed up the action to a frantic pace. In *Crazy to Act* (1927), the title card introducing the slow motion sequence with the Bathing Beauties provides an ironic commentary on the new style. It reads: "With a thrilling burst of speed, the heroine's girl friends dash madly to her rescue" – as if introducing a madcap chase by the Kops.

## new women

Mack Sennett was first and foremost a shrewd businessman. He recognized the declining popularity of his knockabout style and sensed the changing taste of the audience. He also became aware of the economic significance of female filmgoers. Realizing that his violent and loud slapstick did not appeal to women, Sennett was looking for new ways to please the moviegoing majority of the late 1920s. He found that the female consumer, the New Woman of the Jazz Age, looked to movies and fashion magazines to find out what she was supposed to wear and how she was supposed to cut her hair. By reviving his Bathing Beauties as models for fashion and beauty as well as pictorial art, Sennett tried to tap into this new mass of filmgoers and readers of weekly magazines, without alienating the male part of the audience.

For publicity stills of the late 1920s, the Bathing Beauties modeled the latest swimwear fashions and posed as expert users in a testimonial type of advertising for furs, bandanas, knitwear, hosiery, toiletry, beauty parlors, etc. By the end of the 1920s, Sennett's commercial strategies had been adopted by the other studios, which even had their "serious" dramatic actresses such as Janet Gaynor, Myrna Loy, or Joan Crawford pose for magazines in the newest bathing suits. From the 1930s onwards, so-called "leg art" in sun-wear creations was taken of every actress who signed up with a major studio. Bathing suit manufacturers started using movie stars like Ginger Rogers, Gene Tierney, or Betty Grable for testimonial type advertisements in the trade press. By the 1940s, finally, swimsuit designers had teamed up with Hollywood's top costume designers, like Edith Head, Milo Anderson, Vera West, and Travis Banton, to bring a new generation of well-designed suits to both movie star and moviegoer.

## notes

\*  This chapter draws heavily from material in the Mack Sennett Collection at the Margaret Herrick Library of the Academy of Motion Picture Arts and Sciences, Los Angeles. I would like to thank Barbara Hall, Faye Thompson, and Warren M. Sherk for their invaluable assistance in making it available.

1. *Mack Sennett Weekly*, April 9 (1917): 4.

2. "Bathing Beauties Are No More," *Motion Picture Magazine*, June (1922): 20–21, 98–99. Mack Sennett claims in this article: "I always make it a rule to get tired of everything first, before the public does."

3. Letter dated September 22, 1927, Publicity Department Correspondence Files, Mack Sennett Collection, Academy of Motion Picture Arts and Sciences, Los Angeles (hereafter MSC).

4. Theodore Dreiser, "The Best Motion Picture Interview Ever Written," in George C. Pratt, ed., *Spellbound in Darkness: A History of the Silent Film* (Greenwich, CT: New York Graphic Society, 1973), 192.

5. "The Great Big Splashes of Fun and Beauty" is the headline of a trade press advertisement for Mack Sennett's Keystone Comedies in 1917, reprinted in Daniel Blum, *A Pictorial History of the Silent Screen* (London: Hamlyn Publishing Group, 1981), 132.

6. Richard Schickel, "Mack Sennett," in Stuart Byron and Elisabeth Weis, eds., *The National Society of Film Critics on Movie Comedy* (New York: Grossman Publishers, 1977), 6.

7. Simon Louvish, *Keystone: The Life and Clowns of Mack Sennett* (New York: Faber & Faber, 2003), 234.

8. Tom Gunning, "The Cinema of Attraction: Early Film, its Spectator and the Avant-Garde," *Wide Angle* 8.3–4 (1986): 63–70; Donald Crafton, "Pie and Chase: Gag, Spectacle and Narrative in Slapstick Comedy," in Kristine Brunovska Karnick and Henry Jenkins, eds., *Classical Hollywood Comedy* (London and New York: Routledge, 1995), 106–119; Henry Jenkins, *What Made Pistacchio Nuts? Early Sound Comedy and the Vaudeville Aesthetic* (New York: Columbia University Press, 1992).

9. Louvish, *Keystone*, 234.

10. Peter D. Osborne, *Travelling Light: Photography, Travel and Visual Culture* (Manchester: Manchester University Press, 2000), 92–106.

11. Brian Coe, *The History of Movie Photography* (Westfield, NJ: Eastview Editions, 1981), 23. See also the website of Jack and Beverly Wilgus, "The Magic Mirror of Life: An Appreciation of the Camera Obscura," at http://brightbytes.com/cosite/santamont.html.

12. Nancy Mowll Mathews, "The Body in Motion," in Nancy Mowll Mathews, ed., *Moving Pictures: American Art and Film 1880–1910* (Manchester, VT: Hudson Hills Press, 2005), 92–93.

13. See Patricia Campbell Warner, *When the Girls Came Out to Play: The Birth of American Sportswear* (Amherst and Boston: University of Massachusetts Press, 2006).

14. See Lois W. Banner, *American Beauty: A Social History through Two Centuries of the American Idea, Ideal, and Image of the Beautiful Woman* (New York: Albert A. Knopf, 1983), and Jeanne Houck at www.pbs.org/wgbh/amex/missamerica.

15. Banner, *American Beauty*, 397.

16. "Mack Sennett to be Judge at Atlantic City Beauty Pageant," *Mack Sennett News Bulletin*, February 23 (1924): 1; and "Sennett Finds New Beauty," *Mack Sennett News Bulletin*, November 15 (1924), MSC.

17. Rob King, *The Fun Factory: The Keystone Film Company and the Emergence of Mass Culture* (Berkeley: University of California Press, 2008), 304 n. 33.

18. *Mack Sennett Weekly*, June 25 (1917): 2, MSC.

19. Ibid.

20. As noted in Banner, *American Beauty*, 46–47: "All the fashionable dressmakers in the United States seemed to be French.... No dressmaker was considered 'orthodox' if she did not have the prefix of 'Madame' or call herself a 'modiste.' "

21. Press Release, 1922, MSC.

22. Correspondence between the Sennett Publicity Department and the Max B. Sheffer Card Company of Chicago (1922–1925), MSC.

23. *Mack Sennett News Bulletin*, February 10 (1924): 2; *Mack Sennett News Bulletin*, February 23 (1924): 1, MSC.

24. For an excellent overview of the films in specific series, see "Appendix D: Working Titles" in Warren M. Sherk, *The Films of Mack Sennett: Credit Documentation from the Mack Sennett Collection at the Margaret Herrick Library* (Lanham: The Scarecrow Press, 1998), 257–287.

25. Letter dated April 29, 1927, Publicity Department Correspondence, MSC.

26. Ibid.

27. Letter dated January 3, 1927, Publicity Department Correspondence, MSC.

28. *Mack Sennett Pathé Studio Review* 1.3 (1927).

29. It remains unclear why the offer of the International News, the Hearst syndicate, was not accepted. The correspondence files mention a proposition of 60–40 on the returns from the sale of the stills, the 40 percent share being for the Sennett Studio. Possibly Sennett decided that this offer was not profitable enough.

30. *Mack Sennett Pathé Studio Review* 1.1 (1927): cover page.

31. Ibid.

32. See David S. Shields in "Broadway Photographs: Art Photography and the American Stage, 1900–1930," at http://broadway.cas.sc.edu/index.php?action=showPhotographer&id=54.

33. Ibid.

34. *The Calgary Herald*, October 4 (1927), as quoted in Louvish, *Keystone*, 236.

35. See Fred E. Basten, *Glorious Technicolor: The Movies' Magic Rainbow* (Camarillo: Technicolor Inc., 2005), 15–33.

36. Unidentified clipping, 1928, Press Clippings, MSC.

# back to the "slap"

slapstick's hyperbolic gesture

and the rhetoric of violence

thirteen

muriel andrin

The life of slapstick bodies is far from peaceful. Faces are hit by pies, bodies suffer slaps and blows, they tumble, fall, collapse, are dropped, ejected, or thrown from cars or trains at full speed, are run over by buses and knocked down by fists, bricks, frying pans, or mallets. Already in the opening scene of *The Fatal Mallet* (1914), an aggressive Charlie Chaplin throws a brick at Mabel Normand and Mack Sennett, playing a pretty girl and her suitor, then gets it thrown back at him; in *Laughing Gas* (1914), Chaplin pretends to be a dentist though he is only the janitor at the dentist's office; when a patient can't stop laughing because of the anesthetic gas, Charlie knocks him out with a club. In *One Week* (1920), while struggling with a build-it-yourself house kit he received as a wedding gift, Buster Keaton gets crushed by a piano (twice), falls from a high window and then from a rafter that he saws off while sitting on it, and is finally ejected from his portable home when it starts spinning during a storm.

I have always been amazed and somehow frightened by what human bodies have to endure in slapstick comedy. Some theorists, like Petr Kral or Raymond Benayoun, see poetry or surrealism in these destructive and violent acts and situations. Ado Kyrou finds in these moments of "humour fou" a liberating principle that provides an anarchic answer to the question of why "we should accept the laws that dog us like hard collars, why logic must always keep us away from our dearest needs."[1] Yet these views on slapstick films seem to me an easy way to forget about (or conveniently put aside) the extreme violence they display, the darker side of an apparently joyful genre. Even Petr Kral finally admits that the wildness of slapstick alienates (fascinates) as much as it liberates: "The most poetic violence on screen carries inevitably an obscure part that only the spectator can finally reject."[2]

My own attempt to come to terms with what Donald Crafton has called "the violent aural effect of the 'slap,' "[3] seemed quite timely after the Centre Georges Pompidou's 2004 slapstick retrospective opened under the title "L'Horreur Comique." In that retrospective the curators brought to light the mainsprings of burlesque comedy: "Why are comedy's traditional themes usually taken from the register of violence and cruelty — hunger, ugliness, stupidity or destruction? Why does one say 'roar with laughter' or 'to kill oneself laughing'? Why this conjunction of euphoria and horror?"[4] Horrifying and violent effects on the spectators' bodies are at the core of slapstick's peculiar type of laughter, as idioms in many languages testify: in French, for instance, you have "mourir de rire," "crever de rire," "éclater de rire," "se plier de rire," "rire à se rouler par terre," while in English you get "to roar with laughter," "to hold one's sides with laughter," or "to kill oneself laughing." In a paradoxical twist, pain seems as implicated as joy in the process of laughter.

What follows in this chapter, then, should be considered a personal investigation into the physical violence conveyed by the bodies, gestures, and actions of slapstick comedy that sometimes exceeds its intended comical effect. Indeed, it seems that to laugh at such violent acts calls into question our relationship to others and reveals our repressed desire to humiliate other human beings.

Violence, cruelty, ugliness, and destruction appeared in slapstick as the breeding ground for a new type of comedy. As Eileen Bowser explains, in the cinema of the 1910s and 1920s, "all things that the moral melodrama was meant to suppress appeared again in slapstick comedy: anarchy, amorality, eroticism, vulgarity, fantasy, cruelty, the total disrespect for the forces of organized society."[5] Yet slapstick also shares with melodrama one of its constitutive rhetorical figures, the expression or representation of actions, characters, and gestures in excessive or exaggerated ways. We take our lead from Baudelaire who, in an essay on comedy and laughter in the arts written after attending an English pantomime show, came to the following conclusion: "It seemed to me that the distinctive sign of this type of comedy was violence.... It was the hyperbole's vertigo."[6]

As Dominique Nasta explains in her essay on European melodrama of the 1910s, hyperbole is a rhetorical figure finding its roots in the Greek word *hyperballein* (to exceed), containing *hyper* (over) and *ballein* (to throw).[7] In hyperbole, exaggeration is used for emphasis or effect, as in "It will never happen *in a million years*" or "I'm so hungry I could *eat a horse.*" It is a figure

> which heightens or diminishes things with excess and presents them in a way beyond or below what they really are, not to betray them, but in order to reveal the truth and to fix by the incredible what should really be believed.[8]

If words are the first conveyor of this rhetorical device, the latter can also be conveyed by visual representations based on excess. The use of hyperbolic exaggeration in slapstick and melodrama seems strangely similar, even if the effect it helps create is quite different (an emotional impact in the case of melodrama, laughter in slapstick). As in melodrama, in which hyperbole plays a constant and essential part in order to trigger excessive emotional states, hyperbole in slapstick can be conveyed through the representation of specific elements like bodies, gestures, and objects in order to induce laughter. The hyperbole can typically be found in exaggerated versions of everyday tools (the giant-sized kitchen props in Keaton's *The Navigator* (1924)), unusual uses of objects (pies as fighting props), or the accumulative effect of what Petr Kral describes as "*the frenzy of the material*" in which there is a visual overloading of things, "mixing bodies, objects and all sorts of material," in order to "make us feel the strength, the weight and the texture of things."[9] But if objects perfectly convey the visual hyperbole, bodies also have an essential function in the process; hyperbole can be seen in the violent and excessive gesture, but also in its effect, or even in the repetition of both gesture and effect.

A short example can illustrate. In Mack Sennett's *Tillie's Punctured Romance* (1914), a city slicker (Chaplin) comes to the country looking for an easy living and meets Tillie (Marie Dressler). She is playing fetch with her dog, using a heavy brick as a toy, and accidentally hits Chaplin who keels over twice from the shock. (One extant version of the film accentuates the violent charge of the meeting with a punning title: "Tillie sees that she has made an unexpected *hit.*") Their violent introduction continues as Tillie wants to take her new friend home: again by accident she hits him in the face then steps on his foot, her oversized body preventing him from moving. After meeting her father, they go out again and end up dallying next to a rose bush. When he proposes to escape to the city together, Tillie nudges him with her hip and Charlie falls down again. She then throws a rose as a sign of her budding love, but he gets it straight in the face and drops again. Laughing, he in turn hits her with the brick she had used in the fetch game. She replies in kind, throws the brick back at Charlie but, when he ducks, hits her father instead. If the gestures themselves are not necessarily hyperbolic, the effect (the over-explicit physical reaction of the body) is. The accidental repetition of the action and the change of objects used (from a rose to a brick) also introduce a hyperbolic dimension that is stressed even more when considered in the narrative context of a courtship. As the example shows, the effect of the hyperbolic gesture is modulated by time and rhythm. The extreme rapidity and mechanical repetition both of the violent gesture and the reaction it provokes turns characters into jack-in-the-boxes. The quick pace leaves no room for emotion or empathic response, confirming Henri Bergson's insight in his famous essay "Le Rire," (1900) that laughter has no greater enemy than emotion.[10] Slapstick laughter plays on the spectator's insensitivity by allowing no time for healing or commiserating, submitting the character to a deliberately excessive and constant assault.

Of course, this first example only shows a modest application of the principle of repetition. The same principle can be applied on a much larger scale since, as Bergson established, exaggeration produces a comical effect when it is extended and especially when it is systematic.[11] The same gesture can be repeated over and over again, playing on a logic of accumulation and becoming increasingly more violent as movement becomes heightened, as in two Chaplin comedies from 1916, *Behind the Screen* and *The Rink*, in which Charlie either accidentally or deliberately causes several or even entire groups of characters to fall down. In *Behind the Screen*, he plays an assistant on a movie set whose job it is to manage heavy props, like the oversized column he tries to balance but instead ends up crushing several members of the crew. In *The Rink*, he is the unexpected guest at a skating party where he systematically causes the skaters to lose their equilibrium, first one after the other, then as a group, escaping both their wrath and the police only through swift arabesques. In these examples hyperbolic composition relies to an important degree on setting – extreme environments or dangerous situations logically increase the threat to the characters. Even mundane settings like the park can turn into dangerous playgrounds, but boxing rings (Keaton's *Battling Butler* (1926)), skating rinks (Chaplin's *The Rink*), skyscrapers (Lloyd's *Never Weaken* (1921)), balloons (Keaton's *The Paleface* (1922)), etc., carry a more intrinsic threat (or promise) of blows, spills, or even death.

Excess is produced through gesture, but also applies to the bodies themselves. Chaplin, for instance, presents us with a markedly *visceral* character, perpetually shaken by a series of short visual shocks, physical and hyperbolic fits that bring to mind the body's convulsions in cases of epilepsy or even hysteria. Nineteenth-century neurologist Jean-Martin Charcot's listing of the physical manifestations of hysteria sounds quite familiar in this context: "shakes, quivers, cramps, jumps, and jolts" can easily describe both Chaplin's slapstick body and those of hysterical patients.[12]

Slapstick bodies play an essential part in the action, yet they do not operate as human organisms with predictable physical reactions; they quite literally *are* the *slap-stick* – the instrument that gave its name to the genre, a club-like object composed of two wooden slats that produce a loud smacking noise when struck together. Much more than pies, sticks, bricks, bombs, frying pans, or other objects, these dry, cold, yet elastic bodies are instrumentalized, used as props or tools to induce laughter through their exposure to and actual confrontation with cruelty and physical threat; they *embody* the emphatic and violent gesture. They deliver violence but are also its ideal target or victim, the intensified effects of the original blow coming back at its owner like a boomerang. Like the accumulating violent gestures, slapstick bodies can be multiplied, piled up until violence and chaos are exponentially increased; see, for instance, Mack Sennett's collectives of Keystone Kops and Bathing Beauties, or Buster Keaton's mobile group choreographies in *Cops* (1922) and the amazing *Seven Chances* (1925), in which Buster is chased not by the usual army of policemen but by a myriad of brides. In the Keaton examples it is the sheer strength in numbers, the power engendered by their vision as a group that produces violence – in *Cops* a weary Buster lets himself be engulfed in a stream of policemen when he is snubbed by the woman he loves.

Laughter is, of course, the direct effect and first objective of these displays of violence. But when you look at the historical context of the slapstick era, more seems to be at stake. For the curators of "L'Horreur Comique," as for Bergson, the burlesque character, soiled, disfigured, deprived of its physical and moral integrity, embodies the disintegration of the self and questions the value of individuation in a mechanical society; as products of the industrial age, slapstick bodies are machine-like, forever reproducing the same unemotional gestures, like the "jerky rhythm" of the film projector itself.[13] I agree with this interpretation, even though I think that some bodies – like Keaton's – are more plastic than mechanical, and that this view is, once again, too poetic. The Keaton examples show indeed that each slapstick body has its own specific way of dealing with hyperbolic violence: if Chaplin's signifies a forward thrust, a cruel and forceful violence imposed on a bourgeois society, Keaton's body – perfectly integrated in the composition of the shot – expresses a more geometrical violence, stripped of all humanity. Keaton's films almost systematically demonstrate that the individual body, abstracted from the rest of the world, is the first instrument of violence against itself; in most of his films, Keaton's character willingly puts himself in danger.

By now it should be clear that hyperbole and its associations of exaggeration, repetition, and excess can help us understand the humorous effect produced by the display of violence – we laugh at violence when violence is so extreme that it assures the comic purpose of exaggeration. Moreover, we are more likely to laugh if we don't actually see the effect of violence on the body. Mark Sufrin is right to point out that in slapstick bodies are paradoxically "all beaten up but unharmed," and that

> finally, the slapstick fairytale dimension prevails. Despite the violence, chases, slaps, malformations, gunshots and all the improbable violations of natural laws, no one is hurt, no one suffers, no one is hungry, no one cries and no one ever dies. They teach us a lesson without pain or suffering.[14]

The near total absence of injury on the slapstick body is indeed quite striking; burlesque characters do not bruise, bleed, or die. Pain and suffering exist, yet they are portrayed in an excessive, unrealistic manner. Similarly, although there are some comedians who cry – but then in an obsessive and stylized manner, like Stan Laurel – most do not, offering the spectator a blank face (like Keaton's "Great Stone Face"). Their resistance or immunity becomes even more striking when seen next to minor characters who do suffer – as in *Laughing Gas*, in which the dentist's patients all perfectly act their toothache while waiting to be handled by the doctor. While injuries were everyday fare on a knockabout set (as Buster Keaton testifies in his autobiography), wounds or broken limbs are nowhere to be seen on screen; whatever the shocks perpetuated, temporary dizziness seems the only apparent effect on these bodies under attack.[15]

These are "bodies without organs," immune to fragmentation or, when they do suffer fragmentation, insensitive to trauma. They remain whole no matter what the threat, displaying not a permanent *moral* integrity like melodramatic characters, but a lasting *physical* integrity. The remarkable absence of injury and/or any other effect on the body brings us back once again to the "slap-stick" itself, known to produce a great big noise but very little damage. The slapstick world is a perfect place for instant healing. In this sense, and even if the slapstick universe is far from early melodrama's "dream world," both genres seem to share a link with the world of children's dreams, where actions can be performed outside the realm of social conventions. What Eric Bentley establishes for melodrama is also true for slapstick: "Its exploitation of a childhood condition when thoughts seem omnipotent, when the distinction between *I want* and *I can* is not clearly made," sets in place a world according to the old dream of unrestricted action which doesn't have to bear the restrictions of real life.[16] Despite its human and more or less realistic appearance, the slapstick body constantly defies gravity and matter, seems invulnerable, conveying a vital power that no shock can actually diminish. There is hidden in this kind of representation of the violent gesture without consequence the wish of totally controlling one's body, but also the childish refusal to die or to surrender to the laws of logic and nature. This desire already came to the fore in the earliest days of cinematographic illusion; many "primitive" films display visual trickery involving dismembered bodies, fragmented body parts magically floating through the air, etc. In *Le Barbier fin de siècle* (1896), for instance, beheading becomes funny because the terrible act is reversible and no blood is shed. Body parts scattered on the street and "magically" put back together again in Cecil Hepworth's *How to Stop a Motor Car* (1902), or death by car accident followed by the resurrection of the victim in William Paul's *Extraordinary Cab Accident* (1903), are just a few more examples in a very long list of similar yet always inventive productions. Slapstick comedies of the 1910s proposed variations on these physical transformations, sometimes in even more poetic ways (think of Max Linder varying his height and metamorphosing his body in the manner of Méliès in his 1912 *Max Veut Grandir*).

But the slapstick body only takes on its full "slap" dimension after 1914; the visualization of repetitive violent acts in accelerated and excessive rhythms belongs mainly to the end of the 1910s and to the 1920s, reflecting contemporary and very real preoccupations – the discovery of the intrinsic violence of hysterical bodies photographed by Charcot and, to a far greater extent, the frightening images of battlefields covered with burned and scattered bodies testifying to the impact of the first generation of weapons of mass destruction. Slapstick reflects this historical moment in a rather complex way: fully exposing its subversive intentions, it bombards us with violent images that the body politic would rather have repressed; yet the slapstick body remains unaffected by the kind of violence that, in reality, would cause death and suffering. In the latter (idealist) function slapstick fulfills the desire to make those terrifying war images disappear from the collective unconscious and (quite impossibly) regain a lost state of innocence. In *Shoulder Arms* (1918), Chaplin's doughboy goes to war in the trenches, but nobody gets hurt, as if reality were still too painful for cinema to try its illusionary or magical tricks on. As Leonid Karassev points out, laughter, time, and death (or violence) are intricately linked: excessive movement, the acceleration of time, causes death which is in turn denied by laughter, a laughter caused by repetition, acceleration, accumulation, and the slapstick body's final escape from death.[17]

The films of Buster Keaton uphold the idea of slapstick as the realm of invincible bodies, but at the same time offer a meaningful variation. Trained from a very early age to be used as a prop in his father's shows, Keaton learned to deal with pain in his own films. As he told John Spotton quite without irony in 1966, he must have broken every single bone in his body during shooting, from his leg (while filming *One Week*) up to his neck (during production of *Sherlock Jr.* (1924)). These perilous shooting experiences are of course directly linked to the films' narratives, in which Keaton's body is systematically submitted to very harsh treatment. But in Keaton's films violence is not limited to the punctual harassment of bodies, it also extends to an obsession with the threat of death – from capital punishment and execution (*Convict 13* (1920)), to suicide (*Hard Luck* (1921)); *The Electric House* (1922)), murder (*The Frozen North* (1922)), or fatal accident (*The Love Nest* (1923)). Yet again, as Jean-Pierre Coursodon notices,

> the comedy hero cannot die, these deaths have to remain in the realm of fantasy and their reality is denied by a narrative twist: suicides are narrowly averted, hanging fails because of an elastic rope, murders and accidental deaths turn out to have been only dreams.[18]

We find another striking instance of the same principle in *The Paleface*, in which Buster is set on fire but survives by grace of an asbestos suit worn underneath his clothes. The irony comes from his final gesture, exemplifying K. W. Sweeney's idea of the "over-adaptation" of the slapstick hero: having survived the fire, Buster lights himself a well-deserved cigarette.[19]

Even so, Keaton's fascination with death, manifest also in the suggestion of his hero's final demise – as in the closing shot of a tombstone from which hangs Keaton's trademark pork-pie hat in *Cops* (there's a similar coda in *College* (1927)) – is quite unique. In *The General* (1927) Keaton definitively crossed the line by showing – contra Chaplin – that war actually *kills* people. During the extended battlefield sequence, Buster tries to manipulate a sword and accidentally throws it in the back of an enemy, who dies. Critics vividly reproached him for this act of transgression of the genre's conventions: "When the actor gets lost on a real battlefield, the illusion is immediately shattered."[20] The filmic illusion of a perfect dream world – where the body is repeatedly saved from harm until the next attack – fails and the hero is exposed as human again.

Keaton's subversive portrayal of slapstick death looked ahead to changing times. After the 1920s the violence imposed on slapstick bodies reappeared in multiplied and more diverse forms.[21] As Alex Clayton notes in his recent book, *The Body in Hollywood Slapstick*, films by The Three Stooges, Jerry Lewis, and others have continued the slapstick tradition by going back to a more brutal side of comedy; yet, contrary to our examples from the 1910s and 1920s, these comedians seem to derive laughter less from the display of violence itself than from the pain and suffering caused by violence.[22] Clayton points out that in *There's Something About Mary* (1998), the by-now-infamous scene in which Ben Stiller gets his manhood stuck in his zipper delights the audience *because of* the character's pain:

Very few comedies go so far as to expose the potential for malice in an audience's response to human suffering, a potential unleashed here by the ordinary circumstances out of which that suffering arises, and by the prolonged way it mushrooms absurdly with the gathering crowd and the final dash to the ambulance.[23]

Even if hyperbolic gestures and the rhetoric of violence still play a significant part in this new type of slapstick, another kind of spectacle is at stake for the spectator, now torn between sharing the pain and, more cruelly than before, laughing at it.

## notes

1. Ado Kyrou, *Le Surréalisme au cinéma* (Paris: Ramsay, 1985 [1963]), 93 (my translation).
2. Petr Kral, *Le Burlesque ou la morale de la tarte à la crème* (Paris: Stock, 1984), 218 (my translation).
3. Donald Crafton, "Pie and Chase: Gag, Spectacle and Narrative in Slapstick Comedy," in Kristin Brunowska Karnick and Henry Jenkins, eds., *Classical Hollywood Comedy* (New York: Routledge, 1995), 106–120.
4. Philippe-Alain Michaud and Isabelle Ribadeau Dumas, eds., *L'Horreur comique: esthétique du slapstick* (Paris: Editions du Centre Pompidou, 2004), preface, n.p.
5. Ibid.
6. Charles Baudelaire, "De l'essence du rire et généralement du comique dans les arts plastiques," in Michaud and Dumas, eds., *L'Horreur comique*, 104 (my translation).
7. Dominique Nasta, "L'Hyperbole dans le cinéma européen des années 10," in Elena Dagrada, ed., *Il Melodramma* (Roma: Bulzoni, 2007), 221–230 (my translation).
8. C. Du Marsais and P. Fontannier, *Les Tropes* (Paris/Genève: Slatkin reprints, 1984) quoted in Nasta, "L'Hyperbole," 225.
9. Petr Kral, *Le Burlesque*, 169 (my translation).
10. Henri Bergson, *Le Rire: essai sur la signification du comique* (1900) (Paris: Presses Universitaires de France, 1959 [1924]).
11. Ibid., 10.
12. See Georges Didi-Huberman, who quotes Charcot's description of hysterical cases in *Invention de l'hystérie: Charcot et l'iconographie photographique de la Salpétrière* (Paris: Macula, 1982), 122.
13. Daniel Royot, "Flashes sur l'humour *made in* Hollywood," in Daniel Royot, ed., *Humoresque: humour et cinema* (Paris: Presses Universitaires de Vincennes, 1995), 9.
14. Mark Sufrin, "The Silent World of Slapstick," *Film Culture* 2.4 (1956): 21–22.
15. See Buster Keaton's autobiography, with Charles Samuels, *My Wonderful World of Slapstick* (New York: Da Capo, 1960), but also Emma Lindsay Squier's article, "The Sad Business of Being Funny," *Motion Picture Magazine*, April 1919, reprinted in Michaud and Dumas, eds., *L'Horreur comique*, 107–113.
16. Quoted by Peter Brooks in *The Melodramatic Imagination: Balzac, Henry James, Melodrama and the Mode of Excess* (New Haven: Yale University Press, 1995), 35.

17. Leonid Karassev, "Le Rire et le temps," in Royot, ed., *Humoresque*, 18.

18. Jean-Pierre Coursodon, *Buster Keaton* (Paris: Seghers, 1973), 26.

19. Sweeney considers Keaton's gags to be based on three main stages: first, the confrontation with a social norm with which the hero does not conform, then, progressive attempts to master the norm with various but still unsatisfying (or dramatic) results, and finally mastering the norm physically and intellectually, an "over-adaptation" that goes beyond expectations. K. W. Sweeney, "The Dream of Disruption: Melodrama and Gag Structure in Keaton's *Sherlock Junior*," *Wide Angle* 13.1 (January 1991): 104–120.

20. Penelope Houston, quoted in Robert Benayoun, *Le Regard de Buster Keaton* (Paris: Ramsay/Editions Herscher, 1982), 21.

21. Cartoons convey the same kind of violent aggression, especially Tex Avery's explosive shorts from the 1940s. Tremendously funny yet almost unbearably horrific mutilations of characters are proposed and joyfully received by audiences — to cite just one example, I'll bring to mind Avery's Big Bad Wolf Adolf being shot a dozen times, big holes all over his body, yet still standing in *Blitz Wolf* from 1942.

22. Alex Clayton, *The Body in Hollywood Slapstick* (Jefferson: McFarland & Co., 2007), especially the chapter "Body and Pain: Brutality and Suffering in the Slapstick Tradition," 168–182.

23. Ibid., 170.

# the art of imitation*

the originality of charlie

chaplin and other moving-

image myths

f o u r t e e n

j e n n i f e r   m .   b e a n

> *Incessant and spontaneous change: in Chaplin, this is the*
> *utopia of an existence that would be free of the burden of*
> *being-one's-self.*
>
> (Theodor Adorno, *"Chaplin Times Two"*[1])

There is a scene in *City Lights* (1931) where Charlie Chaplin's little tramp, des-
perately seeking funds for the sake of the blind flower girl he adores,
arranges to spar at a boxing match; that is, he arranges to lose, and split the
winner's pot with his so-called opponent. The stage is set, yet the play
cannot proceed as planned, given that the tramp's partner in crime receives
a missive, alerting him that the police are hot on his trail, at which point
said partner promptly scampers out of town. Left to his own devices, and
facing an aggressively professional opponent, the tramp quivers in the dressing room, rubbing the foot of a presumably lucky rabbit against his face
before hefting up a much larger (perhaps luckier?) horseshoe in one hand.

I begin with this description not in order to recapitulate the details of
the scene, but rather to recount my experience of watching it recently –

and the two are rather comically incommensurate. Let me explain that at the moment the horseshoe came into view I chuckled, due in part to Charlie's marvelously funny squirming as he eyes his massive opponent practicing a few punches on the other side of the room. But I also chuckled in anticipation of the joke to come, my smirk a delighted response to the slip of meaning that takes place when the – at once wily and bumbling – tramp slips the horseshoe into his glove, thus opting for a pragmatic application of the horseshoe's mythical lucky status. Charlie's horseshoe is lucky, that is, because it is in the wrong place, the glove, which then gives him the upper hand. This peculiar twist of fortune fits the tramp neatly, fitting not in the manner of a hand in a glove, but appropriately (for the tramp, on whom nothing fits neatly) that of a shoe in a glove. Quite frankly, the scene affords even more wordplay than this, insofar as the joke builds (as most jokes do) to the punchline: rendered quite literally here when Charlie *punches* his opponent with the slaphappy force of a shoe-heavy right hook.

While such a scene is fun to talk about, ultimately the joke is on me. The tramp never does put the horseshoe in his glove. Rather, he enters the ring empty-handed, depending instead on his feet, in a marvelous dance pantomime that dazzles his opponent, who waltzes opposite him in dreamy cadence. I should hasten to add that the joke I have detailed to such degree is not wholly a fabrication on my part, but more simply a mistake: a gag misplaced, misremembered. It is not Chaplin's 1931 *City Lights*, but his 1915 Essanay comedy, *The Champion*, where the little tramp spars with a husky opponent and winds up for an iron-shoe-packed punch.

What interests me about this mistake is that it corresponds, in turn, to a seemingly endless recycling of gags and scenarios – even whole story treatments – that define the first three-and-a-half decades of American film comedy. The dance with which Chaplin dazzles his opponent in *City Lights*, for instance, is itself a variation of the boxing-waltz performed at the end of *The Champion*. But anyone interested in comic transformations of fight to dance might also look to a Keystone production, *Lover's Lost Control* (1915), set in a shoe store turned impromptu boxing ring, where a comedian named Chaplin squares off with a testy clerk turned rival. Dashing back and forth, preparing to fight, the two men suddenly raise their hands above their heads and mirror each other in a series of failed pirouettes. It's a wonderful moment, and a little-known film, partially because this Chaplin's first name is not Charles, but Sydney, Charles' half-brother who worked at Keystone before leaving the screen to manage his increasingly famous sibling's affairs in 1916. Speaking of the Keystone screen, however, it is worth noting that *The Champion* recycles in the most general and obvious way the scenario of Keystone's 1914 release, *The Knockout*, in which Charlie plays the referee, and Roscoe "Fatty" Arbuckle the boxing tramp, albeit a chubbier one. There are neither horseshoes nor dances in *The Knockout*, but there is the celebrated moment of Fatty's preparation for the fight, when he begins to unbutton his trousers and gestures to the camera, directing the frame to tilt upward and thus modestly place his disrobing off screen. In *The Champion* it is not a costume change but a kiss that motivates Charlie to nod at the camera, gesticulate briefly, then raise his beer can to hide the intimate exchange with Edna that follows.

These accumulating examples indicate the degree to which any assessment of American film slapstick catalyzes us to rethink our histories of cinema's silent past in terms other than those of evolution – of progress and development, of maturation and growth. Rather than history written as a teleological drive toward ever-greater efficiency and textual autonomy, slapstick demands a perspective capable of entertaining the textual intricacies of recursion and repetition, a sort of genealogical gestalt through which the very possibility of determining an origin, or site of originality, disappears. Although I cannot account for every exigency that writing such a history might entail, it means taking seriously, as this volume reveals, the many minor or lesser-known comic performers and studios, as well as revising our understanding of those categorically hailed as "great." Put differently, it means taking seriously Don Crafton's astute observation: "Slapstick cinema seems to be ruled by the principles of accretion ... as though the modernist emphasis on originality and the unique text was unheard of."[2]

By framing my thoughts in these terms it might seem that I am arguing for an approach that would eclipse Chaplin's prominence in our histories as an individual artistic genius, a figure of unique originality. Baldly put, this is true. But what animates my efforts is an interest in dismantling the tired distinctions between "originality" or "authenticity" and its putative other, "imitation" or "copy," a binary that has for too long taken hold of our thinking. I want, then, to investigate this wobble by entertaining a set of related questions that emerge from the historical phenomenon of Chaplin's star status, a tale that begins in 1914 when film-goers detected amid the Keystone ballyhoo a particular performer of whom they wanted to see and know more. The story that follows is familiar, telling as it does of the clown's startling success, proceeding with increasingly unprecedented salary hikes through sequential contracts with Essanay, Mutual, and First National, before marching onward to the formation of United Artists in 1919, each accompanied by an ever-greater, ever-more global, celebrity status.

If such statistics mount the inescapable fact that Chaplin was unique and hence original, different from the rest, then I will argue that Chaplin's uniqueness is, however ironically or paradoxically, founded on its opposite. To wit, what he excels at is the art of imitation, the mimicking of an always-absent original thing or self. In turn, it may be that what made him the original comic star *sine qua non* is the simple fact that Chaplin's performance style is endlessly imitable, prone to repetition and recycling. In both cases, the capacity to wander out of an authentic self, to be something *other* than one's self, raises issues central to theories of identity directly tied to the formation of modern culture, to the status of the work of art in the age of mechanical reproducibility, and ultimately to the physiological effects, the very aesthetic experience, of laughter.

## "to be chaplinesque"

To say that Chaplin excels at imitation is hardly news. One immediately calls to mind a scene in *The Limelight* (1952), where Chaplin's aging "tramp comedian," Calvero, informs his ailing houseguest, the young dancer Terry: "I can imitate anything," and then proceeds to perform in the manner of a Japanese tree. In the 1910s Chaplin famously imitated a much larger tree in *Shoulder Arms* (1918), a scene to which we will later turn, but what he may have imitated best was walking – the walk in particular of a man named Rummy Binks. At least this is how Chaplin tells the story to reporter Helen Druey in an April 1917 issue of *Woman's Home Companion*. The interview begins with Chaplin reminiscing on his childhood playground – or "stamping ground" as he called it – in London, in the vicinity of the Old Queen's Head in Lambeth:

> The Queen's Head was a "pub." There was a cab stand near by and an old character they called "Rummy" Binks was one of the landmarks. He had a bulbous nose, a crippled, rheumatic body, a swollen and distorted pair of feet, and the most extraordinary trousers I ever saw. He must have got them from a giant, and he was a little man.
>
> When I saw Rummy shuffle his way across the pavement to hold a cabman's horse for a penny tip, I was fascinated. The walk was so funny to me that I imitated it. When I showed my mother how Rummy walked, she begged me to stop because it was cruel to imitate a misfortune like that. Then she went into the pantry and giggled for ten minutes.[3]

Insofar as this anecdote reveals that Chaplin's famous duck-like waddle is not entirely his own but more properly an imitation, and that his mother's initial apprehension dissolves into laughter, then it mimics (or imitates) the rhetorical aim of the essay more generally, which opens with the claim that Chaplin provides "a safety valve for children's crude sense of humor. They imitate his funny walk with the little swinging cane, and the stiff hat topping sober face. He is a kind of clown-hero."[4]

To be sure, many decried the clown's impact on viewers as something other than safe. On April 13, 1916, the Illinois Congress of Mothers convened in Chicago where "[p]ie, licorice, snakes, Charlie Chaplin, and the lard dinner pail were classified as among the evils to which childhood is heir."[5] Although these mothers restrained from describing the "atrocities committed by Mr. Chaplin's cane," even a cursory glance at the 13 Essanay films released the previous year reveal the cane's artful capacity to lift up ladies' skirts, to initiate a teasing flirtation, and to swipe, hook, crank, probe, or trip any object that enters its orbit. A lithe extension of the clown's body, the cane's multi-directional arc proved dangerous in imitators' hands, allegedly triggering a juridical case in 1917 when a "Finnish sailor on shore leave was hailed before a magistrate for knocking a young woman down in Battery Park, New York, while pulling off Chaplin stunts." Whether or not the woman experienced injury is a moot point for this writer, who instead recalls the sailor's unique mode of defense: "He demonstrated before the magistrate by kicking his left foot in the air and manipulating a pencil like a cane. The magistrate laughed and ordered the culprit's release."[6] Less laughable perhaps were the "Charlie Chaplin Bandits" who robbed a saloon in West Chicago in late January 1916 while sporting as disguise "the lip adornment of the great and only." These mustachioed muggers snatched the proprietor's revolver, robbed the sole customer present at the time, gleaned monies from the till, and "executed a one-footed shuffle around the corner for a getaway."[7]

Regardless of how one evaluates the propriety of such behavior, there can be little doubt that the sudden profusion of Chaplin imitators marks a phenomenal surge in the ideation of mass culture. In 1917, when one writer for *Illustrated World* proclaimed "Charlie Chaplin has countless impersonators in real life," he emphasized the "countless," a mass body defying the logic of statistic enumeration.[8] That the penchant for imitating Chaplin likewise defied the distinctions imposed by nation, age, gender, and class provoked a lyrical tribute from Lupino Lane, who sang "That Charlie Chaplin Walk" for the revue *Watch Your Step* in 1915:

> It doesn't matter anywhere you go
> Watch 'em coming out of any cinema show,
> Shuffling along, they're acting like a rabbit,
> When you see Charlie Chaplin you can't help but get
>     the habit.
> First they stumble over both their feet,
> Swing their sticks then look up and down the street,
> Fathers, mothers, sisters, brothers,
> All your wife's relations and a half dozen others,
> In London, Paris or New York,
> Ev'rybody does that Charlie Chaplin Walk![9]

Seen as a transnational phenomenon (something "ev'rybody" does), the penchant for imitating Chaplin's screen antics noisily foregrounds the democratizing principle underlying mass culture, which always favors a vision of the many rather than the one. But what are we to make of the implications "That Charlie Chaplin Walk" raises for unmitigated homogeneity, for the leveling of difference among viewers of sundry sorts in "London, Paris, or New York," each of whom apparently succumbs to a phenomenological "habit," an action one "can't help" but imitate?

Our response is limited in part since the historical record leaves little to explore in terms of Lane's stage performance, which most likely incorporated a variation on the "shuffling" antics of which he sings. Nor is it a stretch to speculate that his audience may have stumbled about elsewhere that year to the tune of a popular foxtrot, also titled "That Charlie Chaplin Walk," if not to a broader array of musical numbers in the United States, such as "The Charlie Chaplin Glide" and "Charlie Chaplin – March Grotesque" (or, alternatively, to the "Charlot One Step" in France).[10] Whether shuffling, gliding, marching, stepping, or trotting, these verbs hint at a diversified physiological register, a multi-faceted cultural response to Chaplin's iconic status, and hence one that counters any simple assessment of Lane's lyrical tribute as a commentary on the transformation of film viewers into "shuffling" things, into automatons (or "rabbits"), habituated by an unconscious and involuntary reflex.

Of course the concept of imitative behavior as pathology has become a standard of cultural histories in recent years, animated in part by an interest in hysteria as the paradigmatic malady of the European *fin de siècle*. As Mark Micale observes, the spectacular parade of Jean-Martin Charcot's hysterical patients at the Salpétrière Hospital during the 1870s and 1880s, and the concurrent work of French clinicians, such as Pierre Janet and Alfred Binet among others, generated a "diverse pool of psychological ideas, theories, and vocabularies" that were readily "available for cultural appropriation."[11] Preeminent among these ranks the concept of the "corporeal unconscious," which psychologists, sociologists, and social commentators in the late nineteenth century understood as a merger of animal instinct (because of the nature of the instinct, associated with the lower, bodily faculties) and the mechanical (because the instincts surge up in an unconscious, automatic manner). "Nowhere is this fusion seen more clearly than in somnambulism and hysterical gesture," writes Rae Beth Gordon, who also posits a direct lineage between hysterical modes of unconscious imitation, like those studied in Charcot's "living theater of pathology" at the Salpétrière Hospital, and popular comic traditions in late nineteenth- and early twentieth-century France. In Gordon's analysis, the hysteric's body manifests awkward gaits, nervous tics, convulsions, and grimaces similar to the many clowns, contortionists, and cabaret performers that attracted, amused, and contagiously infected *fin-de-siècle* audiences. When this mass body convulses in turn with laughter, or responds in a state of shock with nervous twitches and spine-tingling sensations, it irresistibly submits to the lower faculties, a popularized incarnation of the "corporeal unconscious."[12]

Although I am convinced that the phenomenon one writer termed "Chaplinitis" in 1915 heralds an alternative model of imitative behavior and a concurrent theory of selfhood that I will shortly explore, Gordon's study illuminates a genealogy that the craze for all things Chaplin inevitably invokes.[13] Indeed, as my reader may immediately surmise, the very term, "Chaplinitis," suggests something of an involuntary condition, the dangerous implications of which generated any number of creative commentaries. A particularly playful tongue-in-cheek report – noisily titled "It'll Get *You* Next!" – appeared as a June 1915 entry in *Puck* magazine. Structured as a conversation between a "desperate" businessman, John, and his wife, on the morning "after his worst attack," the piece opens as the wife cautiously raises the subject of his antics the previous night (when he pitched his daughter out of the window and walked on her before striking his son with a baseball bat). When she hesitantly queries how often he "indulges," John fiercely responds: "I'm ashamed to tell you. Four or five times a night – as long as any places are open; and I run out in the daytime every two hours or so." Carefully scripted to defer the question of what, precisely, John's "habit" entails, the rhetorical structure of the piece plays a game of misdirection, hinting at a tradition of male brutishness and addiction associated with alcoholism before revealing in the final lines that John is nothing more, and nothing less, than "a dreadful victim of the Charlie Chaplin habit."[14] Insofar as the male inebriate, like the female hysteric, demonstrates "an enormous development of the tendency to imitation," "the growth of mental suggestibility," and the propensity to develop dissociated (multiple) personalities, this entry from *Puck* could function as a key intertext linking Chaplinitis with a tradition of imitative pathologies.[15] The stress in the previous sentence, however, should be placed on the term "intertext," since it is only by virtue of Chaplin's ubiquitous iconic presence and notoriety as an endlessly imitated figure that *Puck*'s punchline can work.

I put the matter this way in order to invoke something of the dense referential web that Chaplinitis fueled in the 1910s, in which the attempt to locate any singular meaning or phenomenological effect is bound for derision. The "shuffling" filmgoers envisioned in Lupino Lane's song, for instance, who "can't help" but replicate that "Charlie Chaplin Walk," cannot but remind us of Chaplin's childhood memory of the London cabman who also "shuffled." ("That walk was so funny to me I imitated it," as he explained.) That he provided such an explanation *after* Lane performed in the well-known revue suggests that Chaplin, too, may have got the habit – the habit of adding to and drawing from a spiraling vernacular gestalt in which shuffling and waddling, mustaches and canes, baggy trousers and derby hats all reverberated with unprecedented semiotic energy.

It is hardly surprising that any number of the film industry's media offshoots capitalized on that energy by selling products geared to aid the imitative instincts. In late 1915, for instance, the Nuidea Company advertised their "Charlie Chaplin outfit" – a mail-order packet including a mustache, a gold tooth, and a medallion coin with a "life-like" image of Charlie on it – which lucky fans could purchase for the cost of a mere dime (plus 2¢ postage).[16] Florenz Ziegfield, Jr. also profited when his "girls" performed "Those Charlie Chaplin Feet" in a lavish Follies production on Broadway, allegedly "marring their beauty with mustaches, derby hats, big shoes and baggy trousers."[17] The state of the girls' beauty, however, is less interesting than the radical difference between the chorus girls' extravagant replay of Chaplin's "feet" and the brutish behavior of "John," that "victim of the Charlie Chaplin habit." Other notable differences prevail in commentaries that highlight the more subtle inflections and gestures of Chaplin's many imitators. Consider, for instance, the descriptive observations of Charles J. McQuirk, the writer who coined the term, "Chaplinitis." He wrote:

> Among the happy youths of the slums, or the dandies
> of clubdom and college, an imitation of a Chaplin flirt
> [sic] of the coat, or the funny waddle of the comedian,
> is considered the last word in humor. To be Chaplin-
> esque is to be funny; to waddle a few steps and then
> look naively at your audience.[18]

The intrusion of that quirky adjective, "Chaplinesque," into the vernacular we are tracing bears attention before moving on. Insofar as an adjective is a word whose main syntactic role is to modify a noun or a pronoun, then this adjective paradoxically incorporates a proper name – "Chaplin" – into its modifying gesture. To be "Chaplinesque," then, technically means to be like *Chaplin*, although such a state of being is difficult to pinpoint with any precision. It is also difficult to sustain, even for Chaplin himself, who appeared to reporter Emma Squier as "rather un-Chaplinesque" when she tracked him down behind the set of *Sunnyside* (1919) and discovered the comedian "had changed from his dusty clothes, had removed the make-up and the little mustache, and was wearing, in addition to his civilian's togs, a philosophical expression."[19] Rather than linger over the oft-quoted commentaries from the period that laboriously distinguish between the elusive person (Charles Spencer Chaplin) and his well-known screen persona ("Charlie" or "the tramp"), it is possible to extrapolate from Squier's comments a peculiar twist on the nature of early film stardom. As Richard deCordova famously argued, stardom emerges in part through a multi-media discourse that enhances an individual's unique "personality," a concept understood as the essence of a living soul or being, and links it with the mannerisms and gestures of the character on the screen.[20] Chaplin's exceptional stardom rudely interrupts that pattern. Touted as quiet, dignified, and altogether serious, Chaplin's personality sharply contrasts with that of his iconic screen character.[21] The point I am making is this: To be "Chaplinesque" means to adopt a "persona" — a Latinate derivative meaning "mask" or "character" — which is not a proper identity at all, but rather a performance. Hence the tramp's persona travels; its semiotic power is transitive.

### charlie-the-tree

What's fun about all this wordplay is that the tramp's persona is predicated on traveling, precisely because he is a tramp, a little fellow lacking a home, and thus lacking ties to common indicators of identity such as regional location or cultural tradition. Of course other indicators of identity appear on the body's surface, and the temptation to derive a meaningful essence of the tramp's character from his iconic costume — to claim the mustache a "pert sign of vanity," or the cane "a symbol of attempted dignity," and the whole ensemble a personification of "the fallen aristocrat at grips with poverty" — is admittedly seductive.[22] It is also misguided. Such an interpretive gesture can hardly account for Charlie's many costume changes, whether his transformation from mashing tramp to seductive female in *A Woman* (1915), from soup-kitchen idler to busy policeman in *Easy Street* (1917), or from escaped convict to wealthy yachtsman in *The Adventurer* (1917). In films like *One A.M.* (1916) and *The Cure* (1917), Charlie appears not as a tramp at all, but as a wealthy (albeit drunken) gentleman, replete with top hat and tails. In fact, for anyone who read the comedian's interview with reporter Kitty Kelly immediately following his contract deal with the Mutual Company, such alterations in the tramp's iconic costume were anticipated: "I'll keep the moustache, but won't stick so closely to the other clothes," he explained. "It'll depend on what the circumstances demand. And it doesn't matter what one is funny in so [long as] one is funny."[23]

To be funny is never simple, in part because humor often emerges from the incongruous clash of otherwise normative or accepted meanings. The point attains clarity if we turn to Noel Carroll's taxonomy of silent-era "sight gags," all of which celebrate the "ambiguity of appearances" and "presuppose the possibility of visually interpreting the image in two (or more) ways."[24] What Carroll calls "mimed metaphors," for instance, use pantomime to visually draw an analogy between dissimilar things, as when Charlie transforms an old shoe into a gourmet meal in *The Gold Rush* (1925). We see the shoe — but we also see the meal, the alternative thing conjured through the tramp's gestures and mannerisms. In similar fashion we see a clock that a patron brings in for assessment in *The Pawnshop* (1917), which Charlie transforms to a beating heart (by holding a stethoscope to its center), a can of sardines (by screwing open its top and smelling inside), and a swarm of insects (by beating the small mechanisms with a hammer and squirting them with an oil can, the latter of which then looks like insecticide). The magisterial clock scene is justly famous, as Bryony Dixon discusses elsewhere in this volume, but it bears mentioning that Charlie's capacity for metaphoric play dominates even seemingly minor moments. Earlier in *The Pawnshop*, for instance, Charlie busies himself with the business of sweeping the shop, an action interrupted by a long twine that gets tangled in the broom and which he inadvertently pulls across the floor. Spying the mishap, he spontaneously turns and, holding the broom across his chest like a balancing baton, teeters across what we see as a string – and which also, suddenly, resembles a tightrope.

Is it also possible that we see Charlie as a menial employee at the pawnshop in this scene, and yet also as a circus performer, a tightrope debonair? I put the matter this way in order to suggest that Charlie's well-known capacity for altering the meaning of things through pantomime holds true for the tramp's identity per se, which is always ambiguous, never stable, and decidedly prone to mimetic transformation. Carroll's taxonomy once again proves useful, insofar as the category of sight gags that he terms the "switch image" implicitly brings us closer to assessing the tramp's characteristic mode of metamorphosis. *The Pawnshop* remains illustrative: when the tramp fights with his office mate the boss walks in and Charlie alters the punching movement to resemble scrubbing movements, just as he "switches" from a boxing movement to a waltzing glide outside when a cop arrives on the scene. These "switch images," Carroll says, "derail one line of thought and send it in another direction," thus retrospectively rendering the meaning of any one activity or movement ambiguous, open to alteration.[25]

They also derail any attempt to pinpoint the tramp's identity once we grasp the fact that the tramp switches constantly, imitating the action that any given situation invites him to imagine. Little motivation in the plot is necessary for the tramp to transform from bumbling employee to heroic rescuer at the end of *The Pawnshop*, for instance, or from a jauntily uncoordinated waiter in the opening sequences of *The Rink* to the most graceful of gliding skaters. He may be a criminal on the lam in *The Pilgrim* (1923), but can perform as a pastor and deliver a well-received sermon; he may be an impoverished émigré on a sea-rocked ship in *The Immigrant* (1917), but will also be an ace gambler with a knack for rolling dice. Occasionally, to be sure, the plot will explain a change in behavior, nowhere more ironically than in the climactic scene of *Easy Street*, when Charlie, a homeless itinerant turned policeman, inadvertently sits on a syringe full of dope and thus defeats his massive foes in a drug-induced delirium. The ironic twist whereby illegal opiates enable social peace is, admittedly, a funny bit of incongruity. It is also perfectly congruous with the incongruities that define the tramp's persona: stoned on drugs, the policeman becomes something other than himself, and hence emblematic of the tramp's capacity to mock what we usually mean when we speak of a "character" as the fictional reflection of a singular, unified self.

Perhaps nowhere is this penchant for becoming "other" more remarkable than in *Shoulder Arms* (1918), Chaplin's spoof of the Great War, where Charlie disguises himself as a tree by donning a wood and canvas contraption painted with bark and leaves. On a mission behind enemy lines, and suddenly aware of an approaching band of German soldiers, Charlie bolts upright into a motionless position: arms held out like branches; legs pinioned like roots; eyes barely visible through a slit in the tree suit. "One of the funniest things in the comedy is Charlie's camouflage as a tree trunk," commented the *Los Angeles Times*, "a trunk that can swat the Huns with its limbs and take to its heels in case of too much danger. A Hun tries to chop him down for firewood – and of course the Hun himself is felled." The *New York Times* critic resolutely agreed, adding with pleasure that Charlie's "baggy, black trousers" were gone, and that "the limber little stick [cane] which had begun to lose its comic character through overuse, does not appear. Instead Chaplin, camouflaged as a tree trunk, plays destructively with one of the tree's branches."[26]

Such praise, however positive, engenders a bit of a paradox. If "camouflage" refers to the concealment or disguise of any object or person, then Charlie's performance as a tree, reiterated in these reviews as the high point of the film, is decidedly visible.

Or is it? We might consider the scenario more properly as a game of hide and seek, if not a marvelous sleight of hand ("Now you see it, now you don't!"). The game begins when Charlie gambols across the open field in a tree-and-bark costume that shrieks of artifice. When the German soldiers march into view and Charlie strikes his tree pose, however, he does indeed look remarkably like a tree, a rather "unreasonable facsimile." This is a phrase derived from Hillel Schwartz's erudite study of replications, doppelgangers and twins in the modern age, in which the facsimile appears "unreasonable" precisely because it undermines fundamental epistemological and subjective precepts, an uneasiness exacerbated by the reproductive powers of technologies that challenge our ability to distinguish between the real and the copy, the authentic and the inauthentic, the natural and the mechanical.[27] But Chaplin, who notoriously resisted artificial tricks (unlike his former supervisor Mack Sennett), and who resisted even the visual mobility available through tracking shots, changing angles, and rapid editing, labored to distance his performances from all things mechanical. The "unreasonable facsimile" in *Shoulder*

*Arms* emerges instead from the physical performance, which is another way of saying that Charlie simulates appearances with the uncanny degree of likeness usually reserved for machines.

Importantly, this performance neither resembles nor recalls Henri Bergson's oft-cited proclamation that the "attitudes, gestures, and movements of the human body are laughable in exact proportion as that body reminds us of a mere machine." For Bergson, physical humor emerges when the routinized, automatized behavior of mechanical objects seeps into, or appears "encrusted on," an otherwise living, thinking, spontaneous human subject.[28] It is imperative to note, then, that Charlie can *be* almost anyone or anything, as we have seen, but with one exception: he cannot behave like a machine. He is incapable of accommodating repetitive routines. Gerald Mast illuminates this point when he discusses the opening sequences of *Shoulder Arms*, where Charlie, inducted as a new recruit in the army, fails at learning even the simplest of basic training drills: march forward, step backward, fall in line, etc. As Mast puts it, "The soldier is asked to perform like a machine, and Charlie, the natural man, is the opposite of a machine … he is adept only at accomplishing a task in his own personal, unexpected way."[29] The impasse restricting Mast's analysis, however, stems from his reflexive recourse to a binary logic, one that opposes the "natural man" to the "machine," and then lauds Charlie's "personal" way of "accomplishing a task," which ultimately amounts to assigning Charlie a unique identity and definable personality.

The most ambitious attempt to undermine these binaries comes, not surprisingly, from André Bazin, who emphasizes the temporal dimensions of the tramp's performance style. As he puts it, Charlie inhabits a time "suited to one instant," and one instant only. "That is what is meant by 'repetition,'" he explains, which is rather different from routinization.[30] By severing time from biographical and social frameworks – in which the depths of a weighty past enhance an accumulating future; wherein actions, decisions, and potentialities can be weighed in relation to political, cultural, or individual histories – Charlie's incapacity to act in any way other than what the "instant" allows warps what we usually mean when we speak of an individual's sense of continuity. It also warps the well-oiled tyranny of the assembly line or the rationalizing imperatives of industrial capitalism, in which the repetitive cadence of the machine produces endless configurations of the same. By contrast, Charlie's penchant for inhabiting the moment both mimics and ingenuously mocks the larger machinery of modernity insofar as it endlessly produces difference, an effect illuminated for Bazin in the scene from *Shoulder Arms*. "The sudden vegetable-like immobility of Charlie-the-tree is like an insect playing dead," he observes, signaling a double movement of mimicry and mockery: Charlie is like a tree, which means he is also "like an insect."

Moreover, that insect is mimicking death. If a good imitation of death means that the subject has become wholly an object, a material thing lacking reason and will, then it is Chaplin's dynamic capacity to spontaneously reverse those terms that fascinates Bazin: "What distinguishes Charlie from the insect is the speed with which he returns from his condition of spatial dissolution into the cosmos, to a state of instant readiness for action."[31]

The ironic ontology attending this state of "instant readiness" means that Charlie is ready to become not his self but something (or someone) else yet again, a penchant for imitating that defines the tramp's very essence. Walter Kerr came close to articulating as much when he observed that

> [t]he secret of Chaplin, as a character, is that he can be anyone.... That is his problem. The secret is a devastating one. For the man who can, with a flick of a finger, or the blink of an eyelash, instantly transform himself into absolutely anyone is a man who must, in his heart, remain no one.

No one, that is, and yet everyone, since the paradox that Kerr plays with resides in his sense that "the tramp is the residue of all the bricklayers and householders and *bon vivants* and women and fiddlers and floorwalkers and drunks and ministers Chaplin played so well, too well. The tramp was all that was left."[32] The nigh tragic dimensions that Kerr assigns to the tramp's lack of selfhood, however, are countered by his significance as a cultural figure prone to endless imitation, a reverse phenomenological effect in which bricklayers and women, drunks and ministers – as well as students, dandies, soldiers, and Ziegfield Follies' girls – copied and regenerated the object life of the tramp. These imitations alert us in turn to alternative ways of thinking about the shifting significance of selfhood in an age of mechanical reproducibility, especially when we consider the increasingly professional, and incrementally clever, array of imitative tramps.

### the laws of imitation

Whether marketplace law means that supply generates demand or demand generates supply may be a chicken-and-egg question for those who sought to be Chaplinesque. The number of imitators escalated in cadence with the mounting of organized impersonator-performance venues, as well as with Chaplin's soaring celebrity status. In the summer of 1915 the *Cleveland Plain Dealer* announced that Cleveland "has been getting so full of imitators of Charlie Chaplin that the management of Luna Park decided to offer a prize to the best imitator and out they flocked," competing among themselves, if not with the 30 theaters in

New York City that, according to the *New York World*, were sponsoring Chaplin amateur nights.[33] Sheer quantity can astonish, but so too does quality. One young man by the name of Leslie T. Hope (later Bob) earned the grand prize for his turn as the tramp in Cleveland, while vaudeville player Stan Jefferson (later Laurel) garnered applause for his 12-minute stage sketch of Charlie. On the screen, comedians like Harold Lloyd, Billie Ritchie, and Billy West, among others, launched successful careers performing variations on the tramp persona, while vaudeville player Minerva Courtney wrote, directed, and starred in three films in which she, too, mimicked Chaplin. The only extant film of this trilogy, *Miss Minerva Courtney in Her Impersonation of Charlie Chaplin* (1915), begins by introducing the young woman playing herself, one of many hopeful actresses looking for work at the "May Be" film studio.[34] When refused, she asks if she can show the company executives her impersonation of Charlie Chaplin. After a dressing-room scene in which she has some problem affixing the mustache, thus lingering over and revealing the mechanics of the transformation from "Minerva" to "Charlie," Courtney embarks on one of the most remarkable extant impersonations of the tramp persona, enacted through a shot-by-shot copy of *The Champion* (up to the point of the actual boxing match) which Chaplin had released four months earlier.

Although I can only touch on the fascinating cultural relation between female comics and the performance of mimicry, Courtney's decision to include the dressing-room scene recalls the stage strategy of Gertrude Hoffman, one of the "army of mimics" that descended on the American stage in the early twentieth century. Hoffman, to my knowledge, never impersonated Chaplin, nor did other headlining mimics like Elsie Janis, Cecilia Loftus, or Juliet Delf, whose careers peaked prior to Chaplin's rise to fame. But as theater historian Susan Glenn details in a remarkable study, these women's impersonations of various well-known celebrities, including one another, played a key role in shifting debates about the significance of imitative behavior.[35] The fact that these comics were women cannot be underestimated, since the view of human imitation as abnormal pathology, popularized by French clinicians Jean-Martin Charcot, Pierre Janet, and Jean Binet, among others, understood women as primary candidates for such disorders, "seen as diffuse, changeable, lacking any core of individuality and permanent identity."[36] In turn, as Glenn reveals, the ingenuity and imaginative talent associated with female mimics' capacity to *purposefully* look and behave like someone else intersected with an emergent and eventually predominant model in American social science which viewed imitation as a universal human faculty, key not only to the development of a healthy or normal selfhood, but also to a harmonious, well-functioning social order.

Formative for this perspective is the work of William James, whose account of the social origins of the self radically undermined Emersonian ideals, thus anticipating Gabriel Tarde's 1890 publication, *The Laws of Imitation*. A French sociologist and sometime magistrate, Tarde argued that "society may ... be defined as a group of beings who are apt to imitate one another." Imitation, moreover, was "key to the social mystery," its fundamental principle.[37] Tarde's treatise "was greeted as 'brilliant,' 'fascinating,' and 'a work of genius' by his contemporaries in the United States," writes historian Ruth Leys, and thus provided a point of departure for a new generation of Progressive-era social scientists and psychologists such as Franz Boas, Charles Horton Cooley, Franklin H. Giddings, George Herbert Mead, and Mary Whiton Calkings (the latter two also former students of James).[38] In 1903 Elsie Clews Parsons published an English translation of Tarde's study, although James Mark Baldwin's 1894 study of child psychology, *Mental Development: The Child and the Race*, exhibits an even earlier influence. Like Tarde, Baldwin loudly rejected the notion that imitation was the province of nonvolitional or pathological behavior, arguing instead: "imitation represents the general fact that normal *suggestibility* ... [is] the very soul of our social relationships with one another." The "self," he insisted, "is realized in taking in 'copies' from the world."[39] In short, what Baldwin suggests here is that the individual self is not unique or individual at all, but rather social, produced through imitative behavior.

That his argument draws on metaphors associated with mechanical reproducibility (a process of "taking in 'copies'") assumes paramount importance in the present context, especially since such metaphors were hardly idiosyncratic to Baldwin. George Herbert Mead, for instance, referred to the inner life's "mechanism of introspection" when he explained identity as a process of mediation between the self and other in which "the individual experiences himself as such, not directly, but only indirectly" by first becoming "an object to himself ... by taking the attitudes of other individuals."[40] The metaphoric resonance rings even louder in Tarde's formative work when he defined imitation as "every impression of an inter-psychical photography," a process consisting of "the quasi-photographic reproduction of a cerebral image upon the sensitive plate of another brain."[41] It is relatively easy to speculate that the invocation of a mechanical metaphor lent credence to those who championed imitative behaviors by virtue of the machine's association with perfect control. Equally important is an inverse resonance linking mechanical perfection with human ingenuity and imagination, with traits usually reserved for the traditional arts. The "plate" of the brain that Tarde describes is noticeably "sensitive," while Mead's "mechanism of introspection" is also an "inner stage," a place where role-playing allows one to mimetically represent another's ideas "with his intonations and gestures and even perhaps with his facial expression."[42]

Insofar as these theories of imitative behavior undermine any essential, a priori distinction between mechanistic and artistic behavior, between what it means to behave like an object and what it means to be a subject, they provide an intriguing template for reflecting on the tramp's "identity" as something other than an overt critique of modern times. The discourse we have been tracing also explains a cultural fascination with the tramp's most talented imitators, exemplified by Betty Fleet's exclamation to readers of *Motion Picture Magazine* in April 1918 that

> like his fame, Charlie's mustache continues to grow —
> not on Mr. Chaplin's upper lip, but on those of his imi-
> tators. Billie West, chief among these, is so very clever,
> in his own way, that some cannot even tell the
> difference.[43]

Although simply rendered, the rhetorical twist draws attention to the curious paradox underlying models of human imitation inaugurated by Tarde. If the best imitations, as Fleet says of West's performance, are evaluated on the basis of apparently exact replication, of an almost mechanical reproduction (so that "some cannot even tell the difference"), then it is also true that West succeeds because of his unique talent — because "he is so very clever, in his own way." One cannot help but hear in this passage a dim echo of Charles Horton Cooley, who argued in 1902 that Baldwin was correct in his qualification that the process of "taking in copies from the world" was far from being, as he phrased it, "*absolutely* mechanical," adding: "A man cannot act without putting something of his idiosyncrasy into it — neither is there any invention that is not imitative in the sense that it is made up of elements suggested by observation and experience."[44]

I do not mean to suppose that the theories propagated by American pragmatism and related social scientists can answer all the questions raised by Charlie's phenomenal status as a mass cultural icon, not least given the localization of such theories in the United States — a limitation hardly imposed on the tramp. I do suppose that this discourse crosses the Atlantic and anticipates theories of mimesis as a mode of aesthetic behavior, most prominently those of the philosophers associated with the Frankfurt School. But before turning on our heel (with a slight hop) to consider that provocative overlap, the translation of Tarde's "laws of imitation" to US legal discourse in the 1925 case that granted Chaplin rights to the "originality" of the tramp persona commands attention as testimony to the far-reaching cultural shift from Cartesian ideals of a wholly autonomous self to modernity's more peripatetic constructions of the authentic and unique.

The trial was long in coming. Although many films in the 1910s starring Chaplinesque tramps paid tribute to the comedian — as implied, for instance, by a title like *Miss Minerva Courtney in Her Impersonation of Charlie Chaplin* — others were more impertinent, verging on insidious. As Charles

Maland reminds us, a mere two weeks after Chaplin released *Work* (1915), Billie Ritchie cavorted in a series of near identical routines in a film titled *The Curse of Work*, one of many L-KO shorts in which Ritchie performed a popular variation on the tramp persona.[45] Although Chaplin did not pursue Ritchie in the courts, such exploitation may have precipitated the legal measures the Mutual Company took in 1916 to ensure the 12 films slotted for production against "film pirates."[46] By the time Chaplin built his new studio following the contract with First National, he practiced a cautious form of advance advertisement. Following a tantalizing description of the forthcoming *A Dog's Life* (1918), *Motography* informed exhibitors: "To prevent imitators from stealing a march upon him the complete narrative of the adventures that befall this knight of the road and his dog will be kept secret until the picture is released."[47]

Notwithstanding such policies, the proliferation of clever and competitive Chaplin imitators ultimately led the comedian to seek legal "rights" to the "originality" of the tramp character. The defendant in the suit was Charles Amador, a Mexican actor who changed his name to Charles Aplin in 1920, successfully imitating Chaplin's routines in short reel comedies released through the Western Feature Film Company. Although initially scheduled for February 1922, the trial was delayed until 1925, at which point Chaplin took the witness stand and announced: "I got my walk from an old London cab driver," adding for emphasis that "[a] part of the character was inspired by Fred Kitchen, an old fellow-trouper of mine in vaudeville. He had flat feet." The peculiar twist through which Chaplin mounted a position that would confer "original" rights for the tramp costume and character overtly avoided traditional claims for authenticity, those predicated on an artist's capacity for inward reflection. He opted instead to intermingle a studied process of "copying" with more spontaneous bouts of whimsy. "The one-foot glide was an inspiration of the moment," he mused. The cross-examination by the defendant's counsel tossed a few hard questions: "Where did you get that hat?" "Oh, I don't know," Chaplin responded, "I just conceived the idea of using it." And then the lawyer quickly fired again: "Did you ever see any one wear pants such as you wear?" Chaplin's response – "Sure, the whole world wears pants" – reveals a logic deeply contingent on a cultural understanding of mimesis as a double register, at once spontaneous, inventive and creative, as well as ubiquitously reproducible.

The upshot of the trial, however, emerged from Chaplin's capacity to argue for his role as something less than an artist, and more like an assembler of the tramp's disparate parts. His final line of defense – "Nobody ever wore the combination that I adopted until I put them on" – settled the matter.[48] The court ruled in favor of Charles Spencer Chaplin, prohibiting others from dressing as "Charlie," his screen persona, which is another way of saying that "Charlie" assumed a new life as a legalized fiction, an artificial persona invested with presence and protected by rights. The proclamation of rights enabling Chaplin's monopoly on the tramp's outfit, or what the court called his "ensemble," however, was taken as a challenge by certain members of the public. In late 1925, Jacob Grossman, a small-town salesman from Pennsylvania, submitted a letter along with several photographs of himself to the *Los Angeles Times*, boasting that he could be Chaplinesque without "dressing the same."[49] A bit of bodily inflection, a twinkle in the eye, a knock-kneed stance: Grossman implicitly proposed a physiological mode of mimesis, much like laughter.

## the art of laughter

The laughter experienced by viewers in the 1910s was reportedly far stranger than Grossman's proposed impersonation. One 1917 essay in *Illustrated World*, conspicuously titled "Strange Effects of Photoplays on Spectators," trumpeted laughter's peculiar phenomenological effects by relaying the story of a woman "who explained that a comedy made her laugh so much that her [false] teeth dropped out unbeknown to her," while a soldier rendered deaf and dumb from "fighting for the British 'somewhere in France'" laughed so hard at Chaplin's antics that he recovered his speech.[50] That the intensity of these experiences defies reason is precisely this writer's point, and a playful one at that; other writers felt stymied, even upset. Following Essanay's release of *A Woman* (1915), for instance, one writer loudly complained: "It outrages the decency of decent people, for its vulgarity is of such an insidiousness that frequently it compels laughter, even while the laugher is angry at himself."[51] To be *beside* oneself with laughter, to wander away from the self – to forget one's teeth, if not one's sense of propriety – hints at the power of Chaplin's comedy to generate a kind of physical ecstasy, much like the "excess" of sensation that Linda Williams charts in other popular "body genres" such as melodrama, pornography, and horror. But as Williams aptly observes, the viewer's almost "involuntary mimicry of the emotion or sensation of the [female] body on the screen" in the three genres she considers differs from "physical clown comedy" precisely

> because the reaction of the audience does not mimic the sensations experienced by the central clown. Indeed, it is almost a rule that the audience's physical reaction of laughter does not coincide with the often dead-pan reactions of the clown.[52]

What, then, might the experience of laughter mean in relation to Charlie's activities on the screen?

Typical responses to this question regularly invoke the most well-known theory of laughter and the comic in modernity, specifically Henri Bergson's 1900 study, *Le Rire* ("Laughter"), which emphasizes the distance between a laughable object and a laughing subject, with the stress on object–subject binaries firmly in place. As noted earlier, Bergson writes that "[t]he attitudes, gestures and movements of the human body are laughable in exact proportion as that body reminds us of a mere machine." In so doing, he implicitly underlines the "mere," the lesser quality of a laughable object whose capacity for "constant alert attention" slips into unwilled "absentmindedness."[53] He submits that we laugh at mechanically repeated motions as a way of establishing our difference from such objects; a formulation that bears the imprint of his larger "vitalist" project wherein spontaneity, intuition, and inward intensities – in short, everything the mechanical is not – take priority as the apex of subjectivity. In this way laughter "exercises a high Aristotelian function," to follow Vincent Sherry's apt summation of what Bergson is getting at here: "It identifies the fool, rebukes the automaton, and purges the non-person, the thing, from proper society."[54]

Although Bergson's study draws from a tradition of stage clowns, rather than the screen, his perception of what constitutes the comic bears some affinity with the most well-known critique of the culture industry's ideological effects, specifically the perspective offered by Max Horkheimer and Theodor Adorno in *Dialectic of Enlightenment*. "What receives its comic comeuppance in [popular film comedy]," writes John MacKay in a remarkably pithy paraphrase of Adorno's perspective, "is anything opposed to or unassimilable by the status quo; mirth produces a false sense of liberation masking blind conformity to a cruel social order."[55] Noticeably, Adorno's grave condemnation of laughter openly challenges Bergson's belief that the experience of laughter positions the viewing subject as *different* from the unassimilable comic other, precisely because laughter reflects those qualities of inward intensity and spontaneous vitality that Bergson considers paramount for proper subjectivity. For Adorno, the reverse is true: "Such a laughing audience is a parody of humanity," he glumly observes in *Dialectic of Enlightenment*. "Its members are monads."[56] While Adorno's censure could hardly be clearer, it is equally clear that if the monadic self is a "parody of humanity," then the human self in its most perfect state is divisible, multiple, and perhaps permanently *open* to the other – qualities Adorno would later align with the mimetic.

Mimetic behavior in particular forms the basis of Adorno's brief but pointed homage to Chaplin on the occasion of the clown's seventy-fifth birthday. Published under the title "In Malibu," Adorno's exegesis claims the personal privilege of having been imitated by Chaplin at a social event in a villa in Malibu in the late 1940s. This experience prompts him to reflect:

It is as though he, using mimetic behavior, caused purposeful, grown-up life to recede, and indeed the principle of reason itself, thereby placating it.... Incessant
and spontaneous change: in Chaplin, this is the utopia
of an existence that would be free of the burden of
being-one's-self.[57]

By alleviating the burden of selfhood, one gets at the freedom and purity
of mimetic behavior, or simply mimesis, a term Adorno obsessively reiter-
ates in his later works to refer loosely to a non-conceptual mode of assim-
ilating oneself to an other (rather than subduing the other). I say
"loosely" because I agree with Frederic Jameson that Adorno's conception
of mimesis is at once "indispensable and indefinable," so that it permeates
the philosopher's late works as a "foundational concept never defined
nor argued but always alluded to, by name, as though it had
preexisted."[58]

It is also true that the very nature of mimesis for Adorno is precisely
an aspect of human behavior that is foundational and pre-existent, but
impossible to recover through language. Indeed, Jameson might well find
his conundrum articulated in Adorno's exegesis on Chaplin, where he
likens clowns to children, and observes:

More information about the clown is to be found
among children who, as mysteriously as they do with
animals, communicate with his image and with the
meaning of his activity, which in fact negates meaning.
Only one capable in language common to the clown
and to children, a language distanced from sense,
would understand the clown himself.... Nature, so
pitilessly suppressed in the process of becoming an
adult, is, like that language, irrecoverable by adults.[59]

The pronouncement is at once instructive in the present context and
apparently pessimistic. The emphasis on the "irrecoverability" of the
clown's language, as well as a vertiginous openness to others "pitilessly
suppressed" in the process of becoming an adult, lends itself to a by now
familiar image of Adorno as morose. But Adorno understands mimetic
behavior to have survived the transition to civilized adulthood in trans-
muted form; in the form, that is, of aesthetic behavior. As he writes in
*Aesthetic Theory*, aesthetic behavior is "neither mimesis pure and simple nor
the repression of mimesis" but rather a "process set in motion by mimesis,
a process also in which mimesis itself survives through adaptation."[60] The
aesthetic experience of laughter generated by Chaplin's physical clown
comedy, however, hardly achieves even this degree of theoretical rigor in
Adorno's Malibu memoir. The piece remains an oxymoron in many

ways, given the rarity, perhaps even hesitancy, with which Adorno lauds Chaplin in 1964, as well as the philosopher's ongoing refusal to consider the culture industry more generally as a viable site for the production of aesthetic experiences, mimetic or otherwise.

It is interesting in this light to consider Adorno's homage to Chaplin as an *apologia* of sorts to his late friend Walter Benjamin, whose celebration of the utopic possibilities of mass culture – emblematized by an "eccentric" figure like Chaplin – were resolutely chastised by Adorno in the 1930s. The mimetic/aesthetic theory he elaborates in his later works certainly hints at Benjamin's conception of children's play as an alternative form of cognition that subverted stilted forms of bourgeois socialization by replacing mental and rule-bound cues with a tactile knowing, one linked to physiological action. Benjamin's position remains firmly distinguished, however, by virtue of the priority he grants to the cinema as a medium capable of inciting the mimetic faculties, of "innervating" a collective body of viewers. As Miriam Hansen elaborates in a shrewd reading of Benjamin's position, "innervation" is the notion of a physiologically "contagious" or "infectious" movement that triggers emotional effects in the viewer, a form of mimetic identification based in the phenomenon known as the Carpenter effect.[61] Named after William Carpenter, a nineteenth-century British physiologist who claimed that we tend unconsciously to mimic the movement of another person whom we are observing, the Carpenter effect proved instrumental to the theories of biomechanics assumed by a Soviet avant-garde, notably pronounced in the theories of Eisenstein and Meyerhold, whose thinking was equally influenced, as Alma Law and Mel Gordon have argued, by the work of William James, and his student, Mary Whiton Calkings.[62]

If the interrelation of American social scientists and the Frankfurt school has been, in my mind, too often overlooked, the surprising overlap I am suggesting may be eclipsed by a second, specifically by the crucial interrelation of Benjamin and Freud regarding the "innervatory" effects of laughter. Of course, Freud's investment has little to do with the cultural and political implications of modernity, but it is misleading to reduce Freud's "joke book" to its apprehension of wit's relation to the unconscious, to the joke-work's commensurate relation to dream-work, and hence humor's capacity to alleviate censoring mechanisms and set loose hostile and or lustful instincts. More than any other text, *Jokes and their Relation to the Unconscious* (1905) clarifies the concept of mimesis underlying and competing with Freud's psychosexual theories of development, precisely because, in Freud's estimation, physical comedy and the physical response it generates lie outside the gambit of what he understood to be the unconscious.

In chapter seven of his study, "Jokes and the Species of the Comic," Freud elaborates a theory of how the affective interface between psychical and corporeal acts arises. Designed to explain how the perception of comic movement – the clown's ungainly leap, the waggling of ears – makes us laugh, the chapter claims that perceptions of space and motion come about "imitatively."[63] The imitative performance of movements sets a standard of "innervatory sensation," which the body remembers even in the absence of an actually performed movement. To cite Freud's most prevalent example, our conventional ideas of largeness and smallness reveal traces of our physically mimetic relations to objects and spaces. In other words, cognitive or rational processes, the "idea," and physiological or imitative processes, "mimetics," are inseparable. "The way is pointed out by physiology," Freud writes, "for it teaches us that even during the process of ideation innervations run out to the muscles." Hence, if one is describing "a high mountain" he might raise his hand over his head. Likewise, attempts to describe "a little dwarf" may be accompanied by a gesture that lowers the hand to the ground.[64] (More subtle versions of this ideational mimetics emerge when a speaker opens his eyes wide when speaking of largeness and squeezes them more tightly in the case of smallness.)

Freud's theory of the comic proposes that unusual or "incongruous" external perceptions catalyze the body into laughter's convulsions. Important here is the term "incongruous," since Freud's theories turn on the subject's internalization of a normative relation to space, movement, and objects. Hence, when we see another expending excessive, incongruous, or strange amounts of energy to perform an action (like the shuffling walk of a clown, or that of Rummy Binks), the attempt to understand the difference necessitates a mode akin to role-playing, of momentarily becoming the other:

> In "trying to understand," therefore, in apperceiving this movement, I make a certain expenditure, and in this portion of the mental process I behave exactly as though I were *putting myself in the place of the person I am observing*.[65]

But rather than merge entirely with the other, this "ideational mimesis" simultaneously brings with it a memory of earlier experiences that "enable me to estimate the scale of expenditure [usually] required for reaching that aim." Suspended in this instant, the "same moment" of acting like the other and remembering the norms of the self, the energy generated for mimetic play is recognized as unnecessary, or "superfluous," and "free for use elsewhere."[66] The elsewhere, that is, of laughter.

\*    This chapter is dedicated to John Thomas O'Neal, whose imitation of John Belushi, imitating Joe Cocker, makes me laugh. "I get by with a little help from my friends."

1.   Theodor Adorno, "Chaplin Times Two," trans. John MacKay, *Yale Journal of Criticism* 9.1 (1996): 60.

2.   Don Crafton, "Pie and Chase: Gag, Spectacle and Narrative in Slapstick Comedy," in Kristine Brunovska Karnick and Henry Jenkins, eds., *Classical Hollywood Comedy* (New York: Routledge, 1995), 107.

3.   Helen Duey, "Why Do We Like Them? The Three Most Popular Comedians of the Screen," *Woman's Home Companion*, April (1917): 26.

4.   Ibid.

5.   "Point to Perils Children Face," *Chicago Daily Tribune*, April 14 (1916): 12.

6.   Ernest A. Dench, "Strange Effects of Photo-Plays on Spectators," *Illustrated World* 27 (1917): 788.

7.   " 'Charlie Chaplin' Bandits Do One-Footed Shuffle," *Chicago Daily Tribune*, January 30 (1916): 7.

8.   Dench, "Strange Effects", 788.

9.   Lupino Lane's song is quoted in David Robinson, *Chaplin: His Life and Art* (New York: McGraw-Hill, 1985), 153.

10.  See Robinson, ibid.

11.  Mark S. Micale, "The Modernist Mind: A Map," in Mark S. Micale, ed., *The Mind of Modernism: Medicine, Psychology, and the Cultural Arts in Europe and America, 1880–1940* (Stanford, CA: Stanford University Press, 2004), 10.

12.  See Rae Beth Gordon, *Why The French Love Jerry Lewis: From Cabaret to Early Cinema* (Palo Alto: Stanford University Press, 2001), especially chapter one, "From Charcot to Charlot." The title of this chapter is especially interesting insofar as it suggests a lineage that leads directly from Jean-Martin Charcot's hysterics to the Chaplin phenomenon ("Charlot" is the French name for "Charlie"). More interesting still, given the thrust of my argument, is that Gordon's book only mentions Chaplin briefly in passing, and only then by way of quoting Jean Epstein's assessment of the comedian's performance style as akin to that of a nervous person, which he termed "photogenic neurasthenia." This reference appears on page 20, and again on page 173, of Gordon's study.

13.  The first use of the term "Chaplinitis" appears in a two-part spread, conspicuously titled "Chaplinitis," that Charles J. McQuirk wrote in the summer of 1915 for *Motion Picture Magazine*, July (1915): 85–89 and August (1915): 121–124.

14.  "It'll Get *You* Next!" *Puck*, June 26 (1915): 6.

15.  The quoted phrases come from James Mark Baldwin, *Mental Development: The Child and the Race* (New York: Macmillan, 1894), 404–406, and represent commonly held perceptions of hysteria, popularized by the work of Charcot and Janet, in the late nineteenth century.

16.  The Nuidea Company's outfit was advertised in *Motion Picture Magazine*, December (1915): 158.

17.  A rather bemused Chaplin described the Ziegfeld Follies girls' performance of "Chaplin numbers" in this way. See Charles Chaplin, *My Autobiography* (New York: Simon and Schuster, 1964), 173.

18.  The quoted phrase comes from part one of McQuirk's essay, "Chaplinitis," 87.

19. Emma Lindsay Squier, "The Sad Business of Being Funny," *Motion Picture Magazine*, April (1919): 45–46.

20. Richard de Cordova, *Picture Personalities: The Emergence of the Star System in America* (Urbana and Chicago: University of Illinois Press, 1990). See especially chapters two and three.

21. A few brief titles illuminate this point. Consider, for instance, "The Serious Opinions of Charles Chaplin," in which reporter Jane Grant paraphrases Chaplin's claim "that he is a serious man, that he would like to play serious parts and that he would like to do many things – seriously" (*New York Times*, September 18 (1921): 41). The emphasis in this entry ties together the "serious" nature of the performer with his proper name, "Charles," an emphatic stress similarly trumpeted in Julian Johnson's three-page spread on the "real" Chaplin for *Photoplay* (May (1921): 81–83, 117), loudly titled "Charles, Not Charlie."

22. These phrases derive from Theodor Huff's 1951 biography of the comedian, *Charlie Chaplin* (Henry Schuman, Inc.) that John McCabe quotes in his later biography, also titled *Charlie Chaplin* (New York: Doubleday & Company, Inc., 1978), 55. For both writers the costume signifies a recognizable essence of the tramp character that Chaplin gradually refines in the 1920s. The full quote reads:

    > Chaplin's costume personifies shabby gentility – the fallen aristocrat at grips with poverty. The cane is a symbol of attempted dignity, the pert moustache a sign of vanity. Although Chaplin used the same costume (with a few exceptions) for almost his entire career, or for about twenty-five years, it is interesting to note a slight evolution: the trousers became less baggy, the coat a little neater, and the moustache a little trimmer through the years.

23. Quoted in Robinson, *Chaplin*, 164.

24. Carroll's "Notes on the Sight Gag" appears in Andrew S. Horton, ed., *Comedy/Cinema/Theory* (Berkeley: University of California Press, 1991), 25–42.

25. Ibid., 35.

26. See, respectively, Antony Anderson, "Shoulder Arms," *Los Angeles Times*, December 17 (1918): II.3; and "Chaplin as Soldier Drops Old Disguise," *New York Times*, October 21 (1918): 15.

27. Hillel Schwartz, *The Culture of the Copy: Striking Likenesses, Unreasonable Facsimiles* (New York: Zone Books, 1996).

28. Henri Bergson, "Laughter," in Wylie Sypher, ed., *Comedy* (Baltimore: Johns Hopkins University Press, 1956), 77.

29. See Gerald Mast, *The Comic Mind: Comedy and The Movies*, 2nd edn. (Chicago: University of Chicago Press, 1979), 89.

30. Andre Bazin, "Charlie Chaplin," in *What is Cinema?*, trans. Hugh Gray (Berkeley: University of California Press, 2005 [1967]), 151. See also Laleen Jayamanne, *Toward Cinema and its Double: Cross-Cultural Mimesis* (Bloomington and Indianapolis: Indiana University Press, 2001), 181–205 for a fascinating assessment of the peculiar "temporality" of Chaplin's performances.

31. Ibid., 149.

32. Walter Kerr, *The Silent Clowns* (New York: Alfred A. Knopf, 1975), 85.

33. These reports from the *Cleveland Plain Dealer*, June 9, 1915, and *New York World*, June 19, 1915 are quoted in Charles J. Maland, *Chaplin and American*

*Culture: The Evolution of a Star Image* (Princeton: Princeton University Press, 1989), 10–11. Chapter one of Maland's study offers a remarkably detailed account of "Chaplinitis" and provides a crucial prompt for my analysis here.

34. The two other titles, also made in the summer of 1915, are *Miss Minerva Courtney as Chaplin in Her Job in the Laundry*, and *Miss Minerva Courtney as Chaplin Putting It Over*. The extant print of *Miss Minerva Courtney in Her Impersonation of Charlie Chaplin* is housed at the Library of Congress.

35. I am referring most specifically to the third chapter of her book, *Female Spectacle: The Theatrical Roots of Modern Feminism*, titled "The Strong Personality: Female Mimics and the Play of the Self" (Cambridge, MA: Harvard University Press, 2000), 74–95.

36. Ruth Leys, "The Real Miss Beauchamp: Gender and the Subject of Imitation," in Judith Butler and Joan W. Scott, eds., *Feminists Theorize the Political* (New York, Routledge, 1992), 193; quoted in Susan Glenn, *Female Spectacle: The Theatrical Roots of Modern Feminism* (Cambridge, MA: Harvard University Press, 2000), 89

37. Gabriel Tarde, *The Laws of Imitation*, trans. Elsie Clews Parsons (New York: H. Holt and Company, 1903), 68.

38. Ruth Leys, "Mead's Voices: Imitation as Foundation, or, The Struggle Against Mimesis," *Critical Inquiry* 19 (1993): 278–279.

39. Baldwin's phrasing is quoted in Glenn, *Female Spectacle*, 91.

40. George Herbert Mead, *Mind, Self, and Society* (Chicago: University of Chicago Press, 1934), 138.

41. Tarde, *The Laws of Imitation*, xiv.

42. See Mead, "The Social Self," *Journal of Philosophy* 10 (1913): 377. Although Glenn does not consider Mead's language in this context, her argument foregrounds and develops the interrelationship of mechanical and artistic metaphors in the work of these social scientists beyond what I am capable of covering here.

43. Betty Fleet, "What Could Be Funnier, Minerva?" *Motion Picture Magazine*, April (1918): 37.

44. Charles Horton Cooley, *Human Nature and the Social Order* (New York: Scriber, 1922 [1902]), 302.

45. Maland, *Chaplin and American Culture*, 11.

46. "Mutual Introduces Vagabond Charlie," *Motography*, July 1 (1916): 20.

47. "New Chaplin Picture an April Release," *Motography*, April 6 (1918): 671.

48. These phrases from Chaplin's testimony were repeated often in the press at the time, neatly summarized in "Chaplin Tells How He Got His Waddle," *New York Times*, February 20 (1925): 19.

49. "Chaplin is Victor; New Foe Looms," *Los Angeles Times*, May 20 (1925): A1.

50. Dench, "Strange Effects of Photo-Plays," 788.

51. "Is Charlie Killing the Golden Goose?" *Chicago Daily Tribune*, July 13 (1915): 12.

52. Linda Williams, "Film Bodies: Gender, Genre, Excess," in Leo Braudy and Marshall Cohen, eds. *Film Theory and Criticism*, 7th edn. (New York: Oxford University Press, 2009), 605.

53. Henri Bergson, "Laughter," 77, 79.

54. Vincent Sherry, "An Anatomy of Folly: Wyndham Lewis, the Body Politic, and Comedy," *Modernism/Modernity* 4.2 (1997): 123.

55. MacKay summarizes this point as part of a brief introduction to his translation of Adorno's commentaries on Chaplin, which I will momentarily discuss. See Theodor W. Adorno, "Chaplin Times Two," 57

56. Theodor Adorno and Max Horkheimer, *Dialectic of Enlightenment*, trans. John Cummings (New York: Continuum, 1972), 141.

57. Adorno, "Chaplin Times Two," 60

58. Fredric Jameson, *Late Marxism* (London: Verso, 1990), 64.

59. Adorno, "Chaplin Times Two," 59.

60. Theodor Adorno, *Aesthetic Theory*, trans. Christian Lenhardt (Boston: Routledge, 1985), 455.

61. Miriam Hansen, "Benjamin and Cinema: Not a One-Way Street," *Critical Inquiry* 5.2 (1999): 138.

62. Hansen notes this genealogy in her essay, "Benjamin and Cinema," and refers us to Alma Law and Mel Gordon, *Meyerhold, Eisenstein, and Biomechanics: Actor Training in Revolutionary Russia* (Jefferson, McFarland, 1996), esp. 36–37, 207.

63. Sigmund Freud, *Jokes and Their Relation to the Unconscious*, trans. James Strachey (New York & London: W. W. Norton & Company, 1960), 237.

64. Ibid., 239.

65. Ibid., 240 (my emphasis).

66. Ibid., 240.

# contributors

**Muriel Andrin** teaches at the Université Libre de Bruxelles and the University of Antwerp, and organizes lectures and conferences at the Cinémathèque & ISELP (Institut Supérieur du Langage Plastique) in Brussels. She has published a book on American melodrama from her PhD thesis, entitled *Maléfiques: Le Mélodrame Filmique Américain et ses Héroïnes, 1940–1953* (Peter Lang Presses Interuniversitaires, 2005).

**Jennifer M. Bean** is Director of Cinema Studies and Associate Professor of Comparative Literature at the University of Washington. She is co-editor of *A Feminist Reader in Early Cinema* (Duke, 2002), and of a special issue of Camera Obscura on "Early Women Stars." Her book, *The Play in the Machine: Gender, Genre and the Cinema of Modernity*, is forthcoming from Duke University Press, and she is currently editing a volume on the origins of the American star system for Rutgers' "Star Decades" series.

**Eileen Bowser** is internationally known as a film archivist and as a film historian. She joined the staff of The Museum of Modern Art in 1953 and served as curator of the film archives in the Department of Film from

1976 to 1993. She has authored and edited a number of significant publications in the study of early film, including *The Transformation of Cinema: 1907–1915* (University of California Press, 1990), *The Slapstick Symposium* (FIAF, 1985), *The Movies* (co-author, Spring Books, 1972), *Biograph Bulletins, 1908–1912* (Octagon Books, 1973), *Film Notes* (MoMA, 1969), and *D. W. Griffith: American Film Master* (co-author, MoMA, 1965).

**Anke Brouwers** is a fellow of the Research Foundation at Flanders. She is currently preparing a PhD at the University of Antwerp on the films of Mary Pickford and Frances Marion. She has published in *Film International* and *Quarterly Review of Film & Video*.

**Hilde D'Haeyere** is a photographer working mainly for artists and architects. She is a part-time lecturer at the film department of the Royal Academy of Fine Arts (KASK) at University College, Ghent (Belgium), and contributes regularly to the annual lecture series organized by the Brussels Cinémathèque. Currently, she is working on a practice-based research project entitled "Stopping the Show" on the photographic aspects of silent slapstick comedy.

**Bryony Dixon** is a curator at the BFI National Archive with a specialism in silent film. She has researched and written on many aspects of early film, including the relationship between film and music hall. She co-directs the annual British Silent Film Festival, as well as programming for a variety of film festivals and events worldwide.

**Tom Gunning** is Edwin A. and Betty L. Bergman Distinguished Service Professor in the Department of Art History and the Cinema and Media Committee at the University of Chicago. Author of *D.W. Griffith and the Origins of American Narrative Film* (University of Illinois Press, 1991) and *The Films of Fritz Lang: Allegories of Modernity and Vision* (British Film Institute, 2000), he has written numerous essays on early and international silent cinema and on American cinema, including Hollywood genres and directors, as well as on the avant-garde film. He has lectured around the world, and his works have been published in a dozen different languages.

**Steven Jacobs** is an art historian (PhD) who specializes in the photographic and cinematic representations of architecture, cities, and landscapes. In 2007 he published *The Wrong House: The Architecture of Alfred Hitchcock* (010 Publishers). He has taught at various universities and art schools in Belgium and the Netherlands. He currently teaches film history at the Sint Lukas College of Art in Brussels, the Academy of Fine Arts in Ghent, and the University of Antwerp.

**Simon Joyce** is an Associate Professor of English at the College of William and Mary, where he teaches late nineteenth-century culture, silent film, and modernism. His most recent book is *The Victorians in the Rearview Mirror*

(Ohio University Press, 2007). He is currently at work, with Jennifer Putzi, on a study of Adam Kessel and the New York Motion Picture Corporation. Their essay, "'Greatest Combination in Motion Pictures': Film History and the Division of Labor in the New York Motion Picture Co." appeared in *Film History* 21.3 (2009).

**Rob King** is an Assistant Professor of Cinema Studies and History at the University of Toronto. His published work includes *The Fun Factory: The Keystone Film Company and the Emergence of Mass Culture* (University of California Press, 2009) and the edited collection, with Richard Abel and Giorgio Bertellini, *Early Cinema and the "National"* (John Libbey Press, 2009).

**Joanna E. Rapf** is a Professor of English and Film & Video Studies at the University of Oklahoma. The diverse subjects of her books include Buster Keaton, Sidney Lumet, and *On the Waterfront*. Her articles have appeared in numerous film journals and critical anthologies, including an essay on feminism and Jerry Lewis praised by the comedian himself in *Hollywood Comedians: The Film Reader* (Routledge, 2003).

**Barry Salt** has taught at the Slade School, University College and the Royal College of Art. He now teaches film history at London Film School. He is the author of *Film Style and Technology: History and Analysis* (1983, second edition 1992) and *Moving into Pictures: More on Film History, Style, and Analysis* (2006), both published by Starword, plus many published articles on film history.

**Amy Sargeant** teaches at the Department of Film and Television Studies at the University of Warwick. She has written on Russian Cinema (*Vsevolod Pudovkin*, 2000 and *Storm over Asia*, 2007, both I. B. Taurus) and British Cinema (*British Historical Cinema*, Routledge, 2002 and *A Critical History of British Cinema*, BFI, 2005). Having trained as an architect and worked as a production designer, she is especially interested in the relationship of cinema to the older arts, notably in avant-garde films of the 1920s. She is currently researching a history of screen advertising in Britain.

**Charles Wolfe** is Professor of Film and Media Studies at the University of California, Santa Barbara. He has published widely on various aspects of the history of commercial, independent, and documentary filmmaking in the United States, and is currently completing a book on Buster Keaton and American modernism for the University of California Press. With Edward Branigan, he is co-editor of the American Film Institute's Film Reader Series, published by Routledge.

# Index

Note: Figures in **bold** denote figures.